CUSTOMIZING
OS X

Fantastic Tricks, Tweaks, Hacks, Secret Commands, & Hidden Features to Customize Your OS X User Experience

EL CAPITAN EDITION

Tom Magrini

Created & Printed in the United States of America.

ISBN-13: 978-1517544188
ISBN-10: 1517544181

Terms & Conditions of Use

Some of the customizations contained in this book allow access to hidden preference settings not visible in the OS X System Preferences application. These customizations do not add to or change any part of the OS X operating system. The customization settings described in this book are additional preference settings defined by Apple and built into OS X. All of the customizations are reversable and can be reset to the OS X defaults. The customizations were tested in OS X El Capitan Beta versions and the Golden Master (OS X Version 10.11). There is always the possibility that future updates to OS X could cause some of the customizations to no longer work as expected.

While the author has taken every precaution in the preparation of this book, the author assumes no responsibility whatsoever for errors or omissions, or for damages resulting from the use of the information contained herein. The information contained in this book is used at your own risk. Any use of the information contained in this book constitutes your agreement to be bound by these terms and conditions.

Table of Contents

1

Customize OS X

OS X allows you to completely customize your user experience until your Mac has a look and feel different from everyone else's Mac. You can completely personalize your Mac, fine-tuning various aspects of the operating system to transform how you interact with it. Besides changing the look and feel, the customizations I'll show you will allow you to be more productive and efficient by making OS X more closely match your personal style and the way you work.

Why customize OS X? Because you can. It's that simple. The default OS X settings that come out of the box make your Mac incredibly easy and efficient to use. And for most people the defaults are all they'll ever need. But if you are reading this book, then you are not like most people. You want to tinker and tweak OS X to personalize it to the way you use your Mac. Besides, who wants their Mac to look, feel, and operate just like every one else's? And of course, its always cool to impress your friends when they notice your Mac does things theirs does not. This book will turn you into an OS X geek, showing you how to bend OS X to your every will.

You don't need to be a computer genius to customize your user experience. The customizations in this book fall into two categories – basic and advanced. Anyone with a little bit of familiarity with OS X can safely customize their user experience using the basic customizations. And don't let the word "advanced" scare you. Advanced customizations require only basic knowledge of how to use an application called Terminal. I'll teach you enough about Terminal in the next few pages to become truly dangerous (just kidding). My goal is not to turn you into a Terminal expert, but to give you a basic foundation so you can execute simple commands to customize your user experience. Once you have learned the basics of Terminal, you will be able to configure all of the OS X customizations, hacks, and tweaks in this book to unlock the OS X "hidden" features.

Each chapter focuses on customizing a particular aspect of OS X El Capitan. We'll start first with the basics of OS X customization in Chapter 1. I'll introduce you to the System Preferences application and the command line interface of Terminal.

Next up are Gestures in Chapter 2. Apple made a minor change to the trackpad gestures in El Capitan, so I added this new chapter covering the standard trackpad and mouse gestures. If you have upgraded to OS X El Captian from a previous version of OS X, this chapter will quickly familiarize you with the changes. If you are new to Macs and OS X, Chapter 2 will make you an expert on gestures. And once we have covered the basics, I'll show you how to go above and beyond the standard gestures by teaching you how to create your own personal, custom trackpad and mouse gestures. Your own custom gestures are guaranteed to increase your efficiency and productivity.

Once you've mastered these skills, we'll focus on the customization of each aspect of OS X starting first with the Desktop in Chapter 3. You'll learn how to customize the Desktop, personalize it, and make it more efficient.

In Chapter 4, we'll tweak Mission Control, which provides a view of everything on your Mac – application windows, apps in Full Screen and Split View mode, Desktops, and the Dashboard. You'll learn how to increase your desktop real estate workspace, unclutter your desktop, and efficiently manage window clutter.

We'll customize various options available in the Menu Bar, a component of the OS X Desktop in Chapter 5. I'll show you how to enable a cool new feature of El Capitan that lets you hide the Menu Bar when not in use. And I'll show you some Menu Bar apps available in the Mac App Store that will let you get more out of the Menu Bar.

Next up in Chapter 6 is the Dock, one of the most recognizable features of OS X, where I'll teach you how to fine-tune the default OS X Dock to make it your own personal, highly productive Dock.

Then we move on to Chapter 7 where you'll learn about Stacks, a cool feature of the Dock. You'll learn more than a dozen different tweaks guaranteed to increase your productivity.

Better searching is the topic of Chapter 8, where we'll customize Spotlight. I'll show you the new features Apple added to Spotlight in El Capitan and show you some tips and tricks for more accurate searches.

Next up is the Notification Center. In Chapter 9, I'll teach you how to fine tune this one-stop shop that consolidates alerts from a variety of sources. You'll learn how to completely customize your Today view with Apple's and third party widgets.

I'll show you a number of customizations for the Dashboard in Chapter 10 to make this feature a little more useful. I'll even show you how to completely disable the Dashboard.

In Chapter 11, we'll explore some tweaks to Launchpad, an OS X feature that blurs the line between OS X and iOS.

Chapter 12 focuses on Finder, the OS X file manager application, which provides a user interface to manage files, disk drives, network drives, and to launch applications. We'll customize Finder to make it more useful and more efficient.

Window snapping and management is the focus of Chapter 13. I'll help those former Microsoft Windows users who miss Windows' snapping feature. Everything is better on a Mac including window snapping. I'll show you how to get the same functionality with the addition of a low cost utility found in the Mac App Store that offers over 20 different window resizing and snapping options.

Next, we'll focus on customizing applications starting with Safari in Chapter 14 and will move on to Mail in Chapter 15. I'll show you how to customize Safari and Mail to make both perform more efficiently and add to your productivity.

The Internet is a dangerous place. Security & Privacy is the focus of Chapter 16, where I'll show you some tweaks to make your Mac more secure.

Chapter 17 is a giant grab bag containing a huge line up of tricks, tweaks, and hacks to customize OS X and a number of applications.

In Chapter 18 I'll introduce you to a slick little free tool that makes customization a breeze. You'll be able to accomplish some of my favorite tweaks without having to use Terminal.

We'll finish up with a chapter on boosting performance. Those of us with older Macs may have noticed El Capitan slowed things up a bit. I'll show you 23 tips to help you squeeze every drop of performance out of your older Mac when running OS X El Capitan.

System Preferences

Apple offers a number of basic customizations to tune OS X and its behavior. Most of these customizations can be accomplished using the OS X graphical user interface (GUI) through the **System Preferences** application. You can use the System Preferences application to modify many system-wide OS X settings.

Throughout this book I'll ask you to launch the **System Preferences** application in order to customize a specific OS X parameter. In OS X there are often multiple ways of doing the same thing and there are a number of different ways to launch Systems Preferences. You can launch the System Preferences application by any one of the following methods:

1. Click on the System Preferences icon in the **Dock**,
2. Launch System Preferences using Launchpad,
3. Select > **System Preferences...** from the Apple menu, or
4. Open **Spotlight**, search for System Preferences, and press the **return** key.

System Preferences will display a default set of 29 icons, called **Preference Panes**, organized into rows of four or five categories from top to bottom. The preference panes contain a tremendous amount of customization power to safely tweak your OS X user experience. In versions of OS X prior to OS X 10.10 Yosemite, Apple labeled the rows from top to bottom in this order: Personal, Hardware, Internet & Wireless, System, and Other. Even though the categories are no longer labeled, Apple still follows the same general categorization scheme of earlier versions of OS X.

The first row, the Personal category, contains a collection of eight system preference panes to customize the basic look and feel of OS X. Seven preference panes relating to hardware are located in the second row. The third row contains six preference panes that allow you to customize various Internet & Wireless preferences such as iCloud, Wi-Fi, and Bluetooth. Eight preference panes grouped into the fourth row are used to customize various system preferences such as Users & Groups, which disk to use for startup, Time

Machine backups, and the Date & Time preferences. A fifth category, called Other, is used for third party preference panes and is only visible if you have a third party application installed, like Adobe Flash Player. Clicking on any icon brings up the associated preference pane, which will allow you to modify various customization options.

Organize the Preference Panes Alphabetically

The organization of the preference panes in System Preferences is our very first customization. By default, the panes are organized by category. OS X allows you to change the display to alphabetical order. Select **View > Organize Alphabetically**.

There are a couple of advantages to organizing the preference panes alphabetically. The System Preferences window takes up less room on the desktop and you no longer have to know in which category a particular pane is located.

Select **View > Organize by Categories** to return to the default display.
The **View** menu also provides a drop down list of all the preference panes in alphabetical order, allowing you to make a quick selection.

A secondary click on the **System Preferences** icon in the Dock will also display the preference panes in alphabetical order. If you have a preference pane open, it is displayed at the very top of the list and a checkmark is shown next to its name in the alphabetical list.

At the very top of the System Preferences window is a toolbar with four controls: window controls, navigation buttons, a **Show All button**, and a Search field. The back button is grayed out until you navigate to a preference pane since is nothing to go back to until then. The forward button is grayed out until you click on a preference pane and then return to the main display. Essentially these navigation buttons serve the same purpose as they do in Safari, allowing you to navigate forward and backward through the panes.

Clicking and holding the **Show All button**, the button with a grid of 12 dots located to the right of the navigation buttons, displays an alphabetical list of the preference panes. If you know what preference pane you want, this option will get you there quickly. When viewing a preference pane, clicking the back button returns you to the main System Preferences display as does clicking the Show All button.

Search System Preferences

Sometimes finding the preference pane containing the specific setting you want to modify is not always intuitive. The **Search field** comes in handy when you know which particular setting you want to modify, but don't know where to find it.

As you type in the Search field, OS X highlights the panes related to your search and displays a list of suggested items in the Spotlight menu below the search field. Eventually, OS X will zero in on the applicable preference pane.

Even if you don't know exactly what the OS X setting is called, the Spotlight menu under the Search field offers suggestions to help you find the right preference pane. Click the highlighted preference pane or one of the items listed under the Search field to navigate to the appropriate preference pane. Any OS X setting controlled by the System Preferences application can be found using the search field.

Finding A Preference Pane Using Spotlight

Spotlight is the OS X search feature that allows you to search for items on your Mac and the Internet. To open **Spotlight**, click on the magnifying glass in the upper right corner of the Menu Bar or press **⌘space** (command+space).

If you don't know which Preference Pane contains the specific setting you want to modify, open **Spotlight** and start typing in the **Spotlight Search** field. As you type, Spotlight will offer results it thinks are likely matches, refining them as you type and organizing them into categories directly below the search field. Results are displayed in categories, with the **Top Hit**, the result Spotlight determined to be the most likely, highlighted at the top of the list. If you press **return**, OS X will launch the **Top Hit**. In the example above, when I searched for "Scrolling," Spotlight suggested two Preference Panes, Trackpad and Mouse. To open the desired Preference Pane, highlight it and click or press the **return** key.

Hide Preference Panes

Clicking and holding the **Show All** button reveals an alphabetical list of the preference panes and offers a **Customize...** option at the very bottom of the list. Selecting Customize... causes little checkboxes to appear at the lower right of each preference pane icon. Unchecking a checkbox hides the associated preference pane.

Why hide a preference pane? There are a few preference panes that you may never use or you've made changes in one or more and have no desire to make additional changes. Hiding preference panes removes superfluous clutter that distracts you from the panes you actually need.

When you are done unchecking or checking preference panes, click the **Done** button, which is located where the **Show All** button was. Note that unchecking a preference pane simply hides it from view. It does not delete the pane. We'll cover how to delete preference panes next. And don't worry, a hidden preference pane can always be unhidden by selecting **Show All > Customize...** and checking its checkbox.

Delete Preference Panes

As you use your Mac, you'll likely install and try software and uninstall it if it doesn't fit your needs. Often third party software comes with its own preference pane to modify various application preferences. Third party preference panes are shown in the bottom row of System Preferences. If you want to delete a third party preference pane for software you no longer use, secondary click on the preference pane to display the option to remove it.

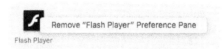

OS X will remove the preference pane icon from System Preferences and move the preference pane file to the trash.

Note that OS X only allows you to remove third party preference panes. OS X does not allow you to remove a system preference pane that is needed by OS X.

System Preferences is extremely powerful, giving you the power to customize a multitude of system-wide settings. In each of the basic customization sections of the coming chapters, we'll focus on a specific aspect of the OS X user experience, checking out options available to tweak. Even if you find System Preferences a little intimidating, I'll show you just how easy it is to customize your OS X user experience. It's your Mac, so feel free to customize, hack, and tweak it.

Advanced Customization

Apple offers a number of advanced customizations to change the behavior of OS X. Often these features are described as "hidden" or "secret" on various websites. There is nothing hidden or secret about these features other than the fact they are not directly accessible from the OS X GUI using System Preferences. These "hidden" features require you to enter commands in to an application called **Terminal**. Terminal provides a method for you to directly interact with the OS X operating system, allowing you to take your OS X customization to an entirely different level not achievable using System Preferences alone.

If entering commands into a command line interface sounds intimidating, it isn't. Don't let the word "advanced" scare you. First, I'll show you how to use the Terminal application. Once you have learned the basics of Terminal, you will be able to configure all of the OS X customizations, hacks, and tweaks in this book and unlock OS X's "hidden" or "secret" features. I have tested each of the commands shown in this book on my own MacBook Pro. Many represent my personal favorites.

Introduction to Terminal

 The average Mac user may never know the existence of the **Terminal** application. Everything the average Mac user needs to do can be accomplished through the OS X GUI. Those who know of Terminal's existence may avoid it because they find its archaic command line interface strange and intimidating. The modern computer user sees Terminal as a throwback to the old days of computing before GUIs became the norm. Terminal reminds us of a time when geeky computer scientists with thick glasses sat hunched over their keyboards, pounding away in a strange language more familiar to the computer than a human.

Why bother using Terminal in the first place? While Terminal appears at first glance to be a relic more appropriate for a museum then your modern, beautiful, and elegant OS X GUI, it is one of the most powerful, versatile, and useful applications in OS X. It has many uses beyond just customization of your OS X user experience. And as you'll see in the next few pages, Terminal may seem archaic, but it certainly isn't very intimidating.

Terminal can be used by users of all skill levels, even a novice Mac user who is learning about Terminal for the first time. We'll take some baby steps to build your confidence and learn the basics, enough so that you will be able to configure any of the OS X customizations, hacks, and tweaks in this book.

Before You Begin

Some of the customizations require you to use Terminal to change preference settings which are not visible in the OS X System Preferences. These preference settings do not add or change any part of the OS X operating system. The preference settings described in this book are defined by Apple as part of OS X. All of the customizations are reversible.

While the Terminal commands in this book are safe to use and I have tested them on my MacBook Pro in OS X El Capitan (OS X Version 10.11), you must enter the commands exactly as shown. I cannot be there to correct you if you fat finger a command, so make sure you have a current Time Machine backup in case you have to restore your Mac. To create a Time Machine backup, select **Back Up Now** from the **Time Machine** Menu Extra in the Menu Bar at the top of your desktop. Readers of the ebook edition are encouraged to copy and paste the commands into Terminal.

Terminal Basics

Let's open the **Terminal** application. Use Launchpad to open it. Terminal may be located in a folder called Other. You can also search for Terminal using Spotlight. It will show up as the Top Hit. You can open Terminal by navigating to the Applications folder, where it will be located in Utilities.

Terminal displays a text-based user interface showing the name of the computer and your location in the file system (normally your Home directory) followed by a $ sign. A gray rectangular cursor, called a **prompt**, waits patiently for your command. The default view is shown in the picture.

Basic Terminal Commands

The first thing you'll notice about Terminal is the **prompt**. The prompt is where we will enter all of the commands shown in this book. When you open Terminal, the first two lines will look something like this.

```
Last login: Mon Sep 7 07:58:17 on ttys000
Thomass-MacBook-Pro:~ thomasmagrini$ |
```

The first line tells you when you last logged in via the Terminal application. The second line contains the prompt. The beginning of the prompt tells you the machine you're logged into and your location in its file system. The cursor appears after the **$** sign. Depending on your selections in Terminal preferences the cursor may or may not be blinking and could appear as a block, an underline, or a vertical bar.

Commands are entered at the prompt. You do not have to use your mouse or trackpad as anything you type will appear at the prompt. Once a command has been completely entered, you will press the **return** key to execute it.

A behavior first time users often find odd is that Terminal will provide no feedback when a command is entered correctly. Feedback is only provided when an invalid command is entered. And don't worry, OS X will not make any changes if the command is not valid. If a command is entered correctly, a new prompt line will appear with the cursor awaiting your next command.

You will enter one command at a time into Terminal, pressing the return key after each command to execute it. Note that some commands shown in this book are case sensitive, therefore, you must enter each one exactly as shown.

If you purchased an e-book edition, I strongly recommend that you copy and paste the commands into the text editor. Once in text editor, check the command to make sure you copied the entire command, then copy and paste it over to Terminal. Why use the text editor and not paste the command directly into Terminal? Many ebook readers also copy the source – the title, author, and page number – none of which Terminal will understand.

So far it sounds pretty simple doesn't it? The advanced customizations in this book simply require you to type a couple of commands exactly as you see them into Terminal, pressing the return key after each command. All of the advanced customizations in this book are that simple to configure.

History Command

Before we finish our basic lesson on Terminal, I'll show you some commands that will come in handy as you configure the advanced customizations. The first command will provide a history of all the commands you have entered in your Terminal session. History comes in handy when you want to see what you did or you want to reuse a command.

```
history
```

Now is probably a good time to mention the typeface. All Terminal commands will be shown in the bold typeface shown above. When you see this typeface, it is your signal that these are commands you will enter into Terminal.

Next, try hitting the **up** arrow key. Terminal will display the **history** command at the prompt. When you have entered a number of commands, pressing the **up** arrow lists each command in reverse order, essentially going backwards through your history. Terminal will beep to let you know when you reach the end of your history. Conversely, the **down** arrow will move you forward through your history of commands. The up and down arrows come in handy when you need to enter a previous command again.

After entering a number of commands, the prompt will be at the bottom of the window and the Terminal window will be full of commands. If you want to clear the window, enter this command. Don't forget to hit the **return** key.

`clear`

Entering Long Commands

Some of the commands in this book are too long to fit on a single line in Terminal. A long command will simply flow onto the next line. A really long command can take two, three, or even four lines. Even though the command appears on multiple lines, it is still a single command and will not be executed until you press the **return** key. For example, note that the following command would appear on one line in the book as:

`defaults write com.apple.screencapture disable-shadow –bool TRUE`

However when typed into Terminal it appears on two lines as shown below. Remember, the command is not executed until you press the **return** key.

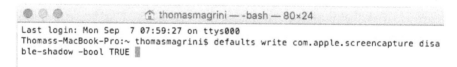

One Last Command

Occasionally I hear Mac users (usually the ones who recently switched from a Windows PC) pronounce OS X as OS "ex," like the letter "X." I hate to nitpick here, but the X is actually the Roman numeral ten. So unless you want to get a funny look from more seasoned Mac users, OS X should be pronounced as OS "ten."

If you don't believe me, just ask your Mac. First, make sure the sound is turned up so you can hear it. Enter the following command in the Terminal app. Don't forget to hit the **return** key.

`say "OS X El Capitan"`

2

Gestures

Hands down Apple has the best multitouch trackpad in the industry. No other computer manufacturer comes close. While I will cover both trackpad and mouse gestures, OS X El Capitan offers more gestures for the trackpad than it does for the mouse. Trackpad gestures allow precise, yet completely natural control over your Mac. I find that I am far more productive using a trackpad than a mouse. And once you have mastered trackpad gestures, it's hard to go back to a mouse.

If you're an experienced El Capitan user you may be thinking about skipping this chapter as you are already familiar with trackpad and mouse gestures. If that's the case, I suggest you skip directly to the Find a Lost Cursor section. In this section and the ones that follow I'll show you how to create your own custom trackpad and mouse gestures as well as a few other tips and tricks. If you upgraded to El Capitan from a previous version of OS X, you have probably noticed that Apple made some minor changes to gestures. In that case, I suggest you review the changes in this chapter.

A built-in trackpad is standard on the MacBook, MacBook Air, and MacBook Pro series of laptops. If you have an iMac, Mac Mini, or Mac Pro desktop computer and are using an Apple Magic Mouse, you only have access to a limited number of gestures. A Magic Mouse supports only six gestures while the Magic Trackpad supports fifteen. I highly recommend that you indulge yourself and spend $69 for an Apple Magic Trackpad so you can take advantage of the full set of gestures in OS X. It will look great next to your Apple Wireless Keyboard!

Users switching from a Windows PC typically find gestures to be very strange and foreign. Where is the right mouse button? Nevermind that, where is the left one?! However, with just a little practice, gestures become completely natural. In fact, gestures will become so natural that eventually you'll no longer need to think about which gesture does what. You'll rely completely on muscle memory, performing all fourteen trackpad gestures without any conscious effort. Once you have mastered the OS X gestures, you'll never want to go back to a Windows PC and mouse!

Let's first start with trackpad gestures then move onto mouse gestures.

Trackpad Gestures

 Apple enables eleven trackpad gestures by default, leaving four disabled. I suggest you turn on all of the trackpad gestures and spend about a half an hour in the Trackpad preference pane learning all the gestures. After a few days of practice, you'll find all of the gestures will become completely natural and you will no longer have to think which gesture accomplishes which task.

Besides enabling the gestures, the Trackpad preference pane also allows you to customize five of the gestures, allowing you to decide how many fingers you will use for certain gestures.

To configure tackpad gestures, open the **Trackpad** preference pane by launching the System Preferences application from the Dock or Launchpad and selecting the Trackpad preference pane. You can also launch from the Apple menu by selecting **> System Preferences... > Trackpad**.

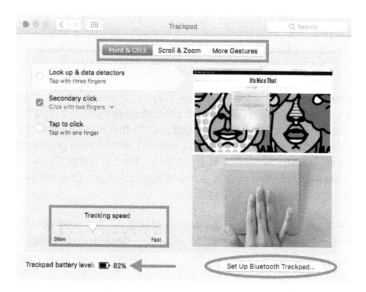

At the top of the trackpad preference pane are three tabs for each of the geture categories – **Point & Click**, **Scroll & Zoom**, and **More Gestures**. The current tab is highlighted in dark blue. In the picture above, the Point & Click tab is selected. The Tracking speed slider, which controls how quickly the cursor moves across the desktop is near the bottom of the pane. If you need to set up a new Apple Magic Trackpad, click the **Set Up Bluetooth Trackpad...** button at the lower right. At the lower left of the Trackpad preference pane, you can see how much power your Trackpad batteries have left.

The left side of the pane lists the available trackpad gestures with checkboxes next to each. To enable a gesture, check the checkbox. In the right hand pane, Apple included a video demonstrating what the highlighted gesture does and how to perform it. Slide your cursor and hover over any of the gestures and the video in the right pane will automatically change to demonstrate the highlighted gesture.

Look Up & Data Detectors

Selecting this gesture allows you to use a three finger tap on a word or phrase to look it up in the dictionary, thesaurus, and Wikipedia. In El Capitan, the **Look Up** feature will also show suggestions from iTunes, the App Store, movie showtimes, and nearby locations. The **Data Detector** feature recognizes certain types of data like dates and addresses, allowing you to add these to the Calendar or Contacts. This is an extremely handy feature.

For those of you with a newer Mac with a Trackpad that supports Force Touch, you can configure this gesture to use a **Force click with one finger**. Otherwise the default is a **Tap with three fingers**. This gesture is disabled by default. Check the checkbox to enable it.

Secondary Click

A secondary click is used to reveal context sensitive menus and is similar to a right button mouse click in the Windows world. Secondary click has three options – **Click or tap with two fingers**, **Click in the bottom right corner**, or **Click in the bottom left corner**. Personally, I prefer tapping with two fingers over using one of the corners. This allows me to execute a secondary click regardless of where my fingers are on the trackpad. I find the corner options to be a little restrictive.

Tap To Click

By default, this option is disabled which forces you to press down on the trackpad in order to click. Selecting this option will allow you to tap the trackpad with one finger to click. Enabling this gesture does not replace pressing down on the trackpad as both options are supported. Pressing down on the trackpad is still required to click and hold in order to drag, move, or lasso a bunch of files in Finder. Additionally, enabling **Tap to click** enables the two-finger tap for a secondary click.

What's Different from Yosemite?

If you upgraded from Yosemite, you may have noticed that a gesture is missing. The three finger drag is no longer in the Trackpad preference pane. Apple moved this gesture to the Accessibility preference pane. Check out the Configure Three finger Dragging section later in this chapter. This gesture is one of the most useful gestures, essentially accomplishing what a click, hold, and drag does in a single gesture.

Scroll Direction: Natural

Natural scrolling was much derided when it first appeared in OS X Lion. This is because the gesture is opposite how most of us learned how to scroll using scroll bars. Using a scrollbar, you scroll up to move your content down and scroll down to move your content up. OS X's natural scrolling works in the opposite direction. Your content moves in the same direction as your fingers, which is how scrolling works on an iPhone or iPad.

With natural scrolling, you swipe in the direction you want to move your content. If you want to move your content up, you swipe up with two fingers. Similarly, if you want to move your content down, you swipe down with two fingers. While I'll admit I was initially turned off, once I got my head around the fact that natural scrolling works exactly the same on my iPhone and iPad, it made perfect sense. Despite all the complaining in the media, OS X's natural scrolling is truly natural and makes far better sense than the odd way scrollbars work. The way scrollbars work is backwards, not OS X's natural scrolling.

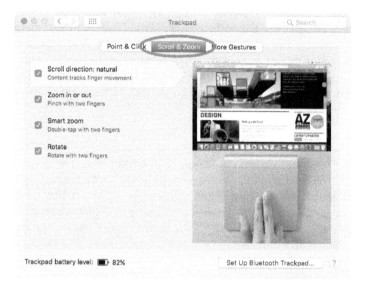

Scrollbars only appear along the right edge of a window when you are scrolling. This is configurable. I'll show you several scrollbar customizations in Chapter 12.

If you flick your fingers at the end of your swipe, you will generate momentum and scroll farther and faster than you would without flicking.

Rubberband scrolling lets you scroll a little further past the end of a file or webpage, and then bounces back to the end of the content. The rubberband animation lets you know you've reached the end. This is the same animation used by iOS on the iPhone and iPad.

Zoom In or Out

Similar to the two-finger pinch zoom of an iPhone or iPad, OS X allows you to spread two fingers to zoom in. Be sure to maintain continuous contact with the trackpad while spreading your fingers apart. To stop zooming, stop moving your fingers. A rubberband animation will let you know when you have reached the maximum limit of the zoom.

To zoom out, pinch your two fingers together and stop when you have reached the desired zoom. Rubberband animation will let you know when you have fully zoomed out.

When you have multiple tabs open in Safari, a two-finger pinch zoom on a webpage will execute the **Show All Tabs** command, displaying all of the webpage as a set of tabs. This is similar to entering ⇧⌘\ (shift+command+\). To take a tab back to full size, either click on it or zoom in by spreading two fingers apart.

Smart Zoom

Smart Zoom is another feature OS X adds from iOS on the iPhone and iPad. When you want to zoom in on an area of a webpage, double tap with two fingers and Safari will zoom in. Double tap again to zoom out.

Rotate

Rotate is another handy feature I use often in the Photos application and when working with PDF documents. Using two fingers you can rotate a picture or a page in a clockwise or counterclockwise direction.

Swipe Between Pages

Swiping between webpages is very much like thumbing through pages in a book. This gesture is used to move forward and backward through webpages in Safari by swiping right and left, respectively. The gesture is also used to scroll horizontally in documents. There are three options – two fingers, three fingers, or an option to use either two or three fingers.

Swipe Between Full Screen Apps

If you use Full Screen apps or Desktop Spaces, this gesture lets you swipe between them. The gesture can be set up to work with either three or four fingers. Swiping to the left moves the current desktop space left and reveals its neighboring space located to the right. Similarly, swiping to the right moves the current desktop right, revealing its neighboring space located to the left. A rubberband animation signifies that you have reached the last space or Full Screen app.

Notification Center

This gesture seems a little odd at first because you actually start off the trackpad. Starting at the right edge, swipe left with two fingers to reveal Notification Center. Swipe in the opposite direction to hide it. The customization of Notification Center is covered in detail in Chapter 9.

Mission Control

 Mission Control is a handy tool that provides a view of every application window running on every Desktop as well as applications in Full Screen or Split View mode. It allows you to quickly jump to another Desktop Space, Full Screen app, Split View apps, or an app window running in another space. Mission Control also allows you to move application windows from one Desktop Space to another by clicking and dragging or using the three finger drag gesture. Desktop Spaces can be created, deleted, or rearranged in Mission Control.

You can configure the Mission Control gesture to use either either three or four fingers when swiping up. The Mission Control gesture does the same thing as hitting the **F3** key, **^up** (control+up arrow), or clicking the Mission Control icon in Launchpad, the Dock, or in the Applications folder. Mission Control and Desktop Spaces are covered in detail in Chapter 4.

App Exposé

App Exposé is an OS X feature that allows you to see all the windows of an open application regardless in which space the window resides. It differs from Mission Control which allows you to see all windows of every open application active within a Desktop Space. The gesture to access App Exposé is to swipe down with the either three or four fingers.

Launchpad

 Launchpad is another feature OS X borrows from iOS. Launchpad allows you to review, launch, and organize the applications on your Mac in a very iOS-looking screen. The gesture to access Launchpad is to pinch with your thumb and three fingers. You can also access Launchpad by clicking the Launchpad icon in the Dock or launching it from the Applications folder. To exit Launchpad, press the **esc** key or use the **Show Desktop** gesture. Launchpad is covered in detail in Chapter 11.

Show Desktop

The Show Desktop gesture has two functions. It can be used to exit Launchpad or to completely clear all application windows from your desktop. This gesture is the opposite of the Launchpad gesture. Starting with your thumb and fingers close together on the trackpad, spread them apart to show the desktop or exit Launchpad.

Enable Three Finger Dragging

The three finger drag gesture is one of the most useful trackpad gestures accomplishing what a click, hold, and drag does in a single gesture. If you upgraded from Yosemite, you may have noticed that this gesture is missing from the Trackpad preference pane. The gesture is still available in El Capitan. Apple moved it to the Accessibility preference pane.

To enable three finger dragging, open the **Accessibility** preference pane in the System Preferences application by selecting > **System Preferences...** or by launching System Preferences from the Dock, Launchpad, or from the Applications folder.

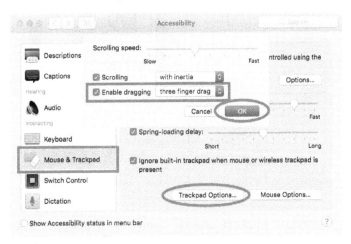

Select **Mouse & Trackpad** from the column on the left side of the Accessibility preference pane. Next, Click the **Trackpad Options...** button to open a drop-down configuration sheet. Check **Enable dragging** if not already checked and select **three finger drag** from the drop-down menu at the right. Click **OK** to finish.

To use the three finger drag gesture, position your cursor over the title bar of a window, place three fingers on your trackpad, and move the window anywhere on the desktop or to another Desktop Space. Lift your fingers off the trackpad when done. This gesture can also be used to copy or move files in Finder. Position the cursor over a file or folder and use the three finger drag to copy it or move it to a new location. You can also use it to drag a file to the Trash.

If you happen to see an image on a webpage that you want to download, position your cursor over the picture and use a three finger drag to copy it to a Finder window or to the Desktop. The three finger drag is also handy for selecting text. Position the cursor in a sentence and use the three finger drag gesture either forward or backward to select the text. You can also use the gesture to select files in Finder or a group of emails in Mail.

Place the cursor on a window title bar and use the three finger drag to move it a little. Leaving two fingers on the trackpad, flick your third finger left or right. The window will coast for a little while and slowly come to a stop. Coasting can also be used to select files, text, or any items in a list, and window snapping, although it does require some practice.

Adjust the Trackpad Tracking Speed

If you are using your trackpad for the first time, you may notice that the cursor moves pretty slowly across the screen. If you want the cursor to move more or less quickly, you can adjust the tracking speed.

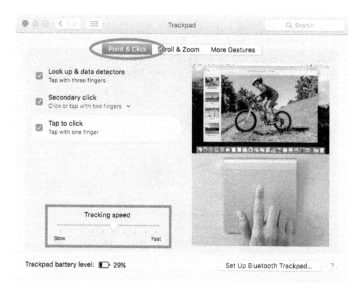

To adjust your trackpad's tracking speed, open the **Trackpad** preference pane by launching the System Preferences application from the Dock or Launchpad and selecting the Trackpad preference pane. You can also launch from the Apple menu by selecting > **System Preferences... > Trackpad**. Click on the **Point & Click** tab if not already highlighted. Move the Tracking speed slider to change the trackpad tracking speed. Changes take effect immediately so you can try out your new tracking speed and adjust if necessary.

Enable Trackpad Drag Lock

By default, when dragging an item from one location to another the drag ends when you remove your finger (or fingers if you configured three finger drag) from the trackpad. If you were dragging a file from one folder to another, the drag ends the moment you remove your fingers from the trackpad and the file will then be moved to its new location.

The **Drag Lock** feature changes this behavior so that the drag ends when you tap the trackpad once upon reaching the destination. This means that if you accidentally lift your fingers off the trackpad, the drag will not end nor will the item be copied by mistake into the wrong folder. Drag Lock comes in handy when you're dragging an item from one side of the screen to another as you often run out of trackpad before completing the drag.

To enable Drag Lock, open the **Accessibility** preference pane in the System Preferences application. Next, scroll down and select **Mouse & Trackpad** in the left-hand pane. Click the **Trackpad Options...** button.

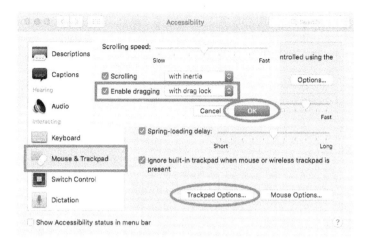

Next, check the checkbox next to **Enable dragging** and select **with Drag Lock** from the pull-down menu. Click the **OK** button to enable.

An added benefit of enabling Drag Lock is that it makes using the spring-loaded folders feature easier. For more information on spring-loaded folders, see the chapter on Finder.

Unfortunately, unlike previous versions of OS X, you cannot configure both three finger dragging and drag lock in El Capitan.

Ignore the Built-in Trackpad

I often use my external Bluetooth trackpad when I'm using my MacBook Pro. However, I find it annoying when I accidentally brush against my MacBook Pro's built-in trackpad and the cursor flies off into left field. OS X has a solution for this annoyance.

To ignore the built-in trackpad, open the **Accessibility** preference pane in the System Preferences application. Next, scroll down and select **Mouse & Trackpad** in the left-hand column. Check the checkbox next to **Ignore built-in trackpad when mouse or wireless trackpad is present**.

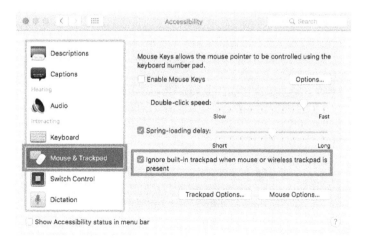

When this checkbox is checked, OS X will ignore the built-in trackpad on your MacBook Pro, MacBook Air, or MacBook when it is connected to an external Bluetooth mouse or trackpad. To disable this feature, uncheck the checkbox.

Another option is to simply turn off Bluetooth in the menu bar. Turn Bluetooth back on to utilize your external mouse or trackpad and ignore your built-in trackpad.

Mouse Gestures

 The Magic Mouse supports six gestures and due to its limited surface space, only supports one or two finger gestures. Similar to the trackpad gestures, it takes only a short amount of time before the mouse gestures become completely natural.

To configure mouse gestures, open the **Mouse** preference pane by launching the System Preferences application from the Dock or Launchpad and selecting the **Mouse** icon. You can also launch from the Apple menu by selecting > **System Preferences... > Mouse**.

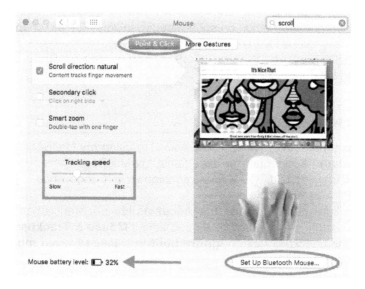

At the top of the mouse preference pane are two tabs for the each category of gestures – **Point & Click** and **More Gestures**. The current tab is highlighted in dark blue. In the picture above, the Point & Click tab is selected. The Tracking speed slider, which controls how quickly the cursor moves across the desktop is near the bottom of the pane. If you need to set up a new Apple Magic Mouse, click the **Set Up Bluetooth Mouse...** button at the lower right. At the lower left of the Mouse preference pane, you can see how much power your Mouse batteries have left.

The left side of the pane lists the available mouse gestures with checkboxes next to each. To enable a gesture, check the checkbox. In the right hand pane, Apple included a video demonstrating what the highlighted gesture does and how to perform it. Slide your cursor and hover over any of the gestures and the video in the right pane will automatically change to demonstrate the gesture.

The best way to learn the gestures in OS X is to watch the video in the Mouse preference pane and try it for yourself. In no time at all, you'll learn all of the gestures and will wonder how you could have used a computer without them.

Scroll Direction: Natural

Natural scrolling was much derided when it first appeared in OS X Lion. This is because the gesture is opposite how most of us learned how to scroll using scroll bars. Using a scrollbar, you scroll up to move your content down and scroll down to move your content up. OS X's natural scrolling works in the opposite direction. Your content moves in the same direction as your fingers, which is how scrolling works on an iPhone or iPad.

With natural scrolling, you swipe in the direction you want to move your content. If you want to move your content up, you swipe up with one finger. Similarly, if you want to move your content down, you swipe down with one finger. While I'll admit I was turned off initially, once I got my head around the fact that natural scrolling works exactly the same on my iPhone and iPad, it made perfect sense. Despite all the complaining in the news media. OS X's natural scrolling is natural and makes far better sense than how scrollbars work. The way scrollbars work is backwards, not OS X's natural scrolling.

Scrollbars only appear along the right edge of a window when you are scrolling. This is configurable. I'll show you several scrollbar customizations in Chapter 12.

If you flick your fingers at the end of your swipe, you will generate momentum and scroll farther and faster than you would without flicking.

Rubberband scrolling lets you scroll a little further past the end of a file or webpage and then bounces back to the end of the content. The rubberband animation lets you know you've reached the end. This is the same animation used by iOS on the iPhone and iPad.

Secondary Click

A secondary click is used to reveal context sensitive menus and is similar to a right button mouse click in the Windows PC world. On the Magic Mouse, secondary click has two options – **Click on right side** or **Click on left side**.

Smart Zoom

Smart Zoom is another feature OS X borrows from iOS on the iPhone and iPad. When you want to zoom in on a webpage double tap your Magic Mouse with one finger and Safari will zoom in. Double tap again to zoom out.

Swipe Between Pages

Swipe between pages in Safari is very much like thumbing through pages in a book. This gesture can be used to move forward and backward through webpages by swiping right or left, respectively. The gesture is also used to scroll horizontally in documents. There are three options – swipe with one finger, swipe with two fingers, or an option to use either one or two fingers.

Note that if you configure swiping between pages to use two fingers, the swipe between Full Screen apps checkbox will uncheck itself and become disabled. So if you want to use both gestures, using one finger to swipe between pages is the only option that will allow you to turn on swiping between Full Screen apps.

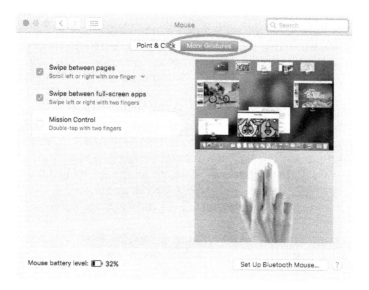

Swipe Between Full Screen Apps

If you use fullscreen apps or Desktop Spaces, this gesture will allow you to swipe between them. Swiping to the left with two fingers moves the current Desktop Space left and reveals its neighboring space located to the right. Similarly, swiping to the right reveals the neighboring Desktop Space located to the left. A rubberband animation signifies that you have reached the last Desktop Space or Full Screen app.

Note that if you want to use both swipe between pages and swipe between Full Screen apps gestures, you must configure swipe between pages to use one finger.

Mission Control

Mission Control is a handy tool that provides a view of every application window running on every Desktop as well as all applications running in Full Screen and Split View modes. It allows you to quickly jump to another Desktop Space, Full Screen app, or an app window running in another Desktop. Mission Control also allows you to move application windows from one Desktop Space to another by clicking and dragging. Desktops can be created, deleted, or rearranged using Mission Control.

The Mission Control mouse gesture is a double-tap with two fingers. The Mission Control gesture does the same thing as hitting the **F3** key, **^up** (control+up arrow), or clicking the

Mission Control icon in Launchpad, the Dock, or in the Applications folder. Mission Control and Desktop Spaces are covered in detail in Chapter 4.

Adjust the Mouse Tracking Speed

If you are using your mouse for the first time, you may notice that the cursor moves pretty slowly across the screen. If you want the cursor to move more or less quickly, you can adjust the tracking speed.

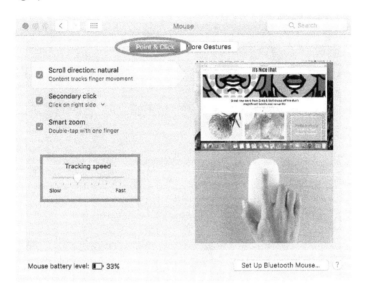

To adjust your trackpad's tracking speed, open the **Mouse** preference pane by launching the System Preferences application from the Dock or Launchpad and selecting the Mouse preference pane. You can also launch from the Apple menu by selecting **🍎 > System Preferences... > Mouse**. Click on the **Point & Click** tab if not already highlighted. Move the Tracking speed slider to change the mouse tracking speed. Changes take effect immediately so you can try out your new tracking speed and adjust if necessary.

Find a Lost Cursor

Have you ever lost the cursor? Sometimes it's difficult to find the cursor on the desktop, particularly when it's hidden in the desktop background. How do you find it? Most people either shake the mouse or shake a finger back and forth rapidly hoping they will be able to see the moving cursor. El Capitan added a neat little feature that capitalizes on this behavior by making the cursor grow progressively larger as you move your finger back and forth on the trackpad or shake your mouse. Your cursor will grow from it's normal size to gigantic. Check out the gigantic cursor next to El Capitan in the picture.

This feature, called shake to locate, is disabled by default. To enable shake to locate, open the **Accessibility** preference pane in the System Preferences application by selecting **🍎 > System Preferences...** or by launching System Preferences from the Dock, Launchpad, or from the Applications folder.

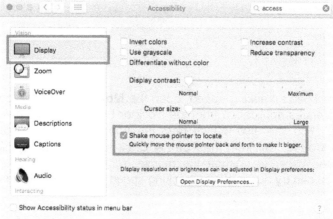

Next, select **Display** from the column on the left side of the Accessibility preference pane. Check the checkbox next to **Shake mouse cursor to locate** to enable this feature. Now if you lose track of the cursor, you can quickly find it by rapidly shaking your mouse back and forth or by placing a finger on the trackpad and moving it back and forth rapidly.

Adjust the Double-Click Speed

If you find the default double-click speed either too slow or too fast for your liking, OS X allows you to adjust it. To change the double-click speed, open the **Accessibility** preference pane by launching the System Preferences application and selecting the **Accessibility** icon or from the Apple menu by selecting **> System Preferences... > Accessibility**.

Next, select **Mouse & Trackpad** in the left-hand pane. Use the slider in the right-hand pane to adjust the **Double-click speed**. The slider adjusts the double-click speed for both the mouse and trackpad.

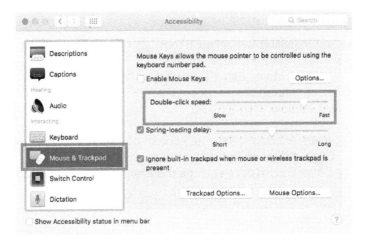

Create Custom Gestures

Now that you are familiar with the standard out-of-the-box El Capitan gestures, let's learn how to create your own custom gestures. OS X provides a set of fifteen standard trackpad gestures and another six for your Magic Mouse. But what if you want to squeeze every drop of productivity from your trackpad or mouse? Creating your own custom gestures for common tasks will increase your productivity, efficiency, and truly personalize your OS X user experience. Several utilities exist that allow you to create custom gestures, but my favorite application is **BetterTouchTool** by Andreas Hegenberg.

BetterTouchTool lets you assign various actions to trackpad and mouse gestures that you create. You can create custom gestures using one, two, three, four, or five fingers combined with a tap, double-tap, tip-tap, swipe, or in combination with one or more modifier keys: ⇧ **fn** ^ ⌥ ⌘ (shift, function, control, option, and command). For those with a new MacBook Pro with a trackpad that supports Force Touch, BetterTouchTool offers eleven different Force Touch gestures. You can assign your own gesture to any keyboard shortcut or to one of over 125 predefined actions. Gestures can be created that are specific to an application or can be used system-wide.

BetterTouchTool also includes some window snapping capabilities available in another app from Andreas Hegenberg that I highly recommend, BetterSnapTool. Since I cover window snapping with BetterSnapTool in detail in Chapter 13, I won't discuss the basic window snapping capability of BetterTouchTool here.

Note there is one word of caution. Unlike BetterSnapTool, BetterTouchTool is not available in the Mac App Store. At the time of this writing BetterTouchTool was still in alpha. Essentially that means you might run into a bug (there is a bug reporting function), some features might not work as expected, and you are using it at your own risk. Despite this warning, I have not run into any issues and I consider BetterTouchTool to be the best application available to create customized gestures. BetterTouchTool is available for free, although a donation is requested, at: http://www.boastr.de.

Getting Started

After downloading and installing BetterTouchTool, you'll notice a new Menu Extra in the Menu Bar. Click the BetterTouchTool Menu Extra to reveal the menu and select **Preferences** to open the BetterTouchTool main window.

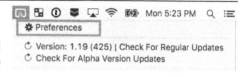

BetterTouchTool's main window offers a choice of **Simple** or **Advanced** tabs with additional tools. Click **Advanced** if not already highlighted. Next, click **Advanced Settings** to display BetterTouchTool's settings preference pane as shown below.

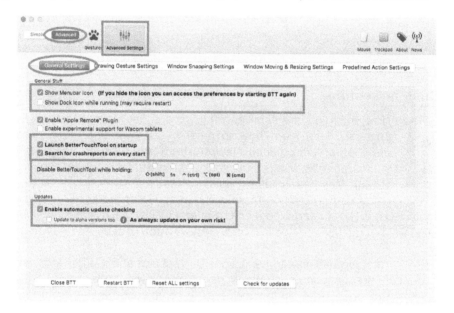

Click **General Settings**. On this page, you can enable or disable BetterTouchTool's Menu Extra. It is enabled by default and it allows you quick access to configure or modify any gestures you created. By default, the BetterTouchTool icon does not appear in the Dock. If you want it in the Dock, check the checkbox next to **Show Dock Icon while running** and restart your Mac to take effect.

You can choose to launch BetterTouchTool on startup, which I recommend to ensure BetterTouchTool runs each time your restart your Mac. This checkbox is checked by default as well as the checkbox next to **Search for crashreports on every start**. I also recommend you leave this checkbox checked.

You can configure one or a combination of the following modifier keys to temporarily disable BetterTouchTool: ⇧ fn ^ ⌥ ⌘ (shift, function, control, option, and command). Check the desired modifier keys if you wish to enable this functionality.

The checkbox next to **Enable automatic update checking**, is checked by default. This allows BetterTouchTool to automatically check for updates and ensures that you always have the latest version. You can decide whether you want to update alpha versions, which warns you that you are updating at your own risk. I suggest sticking with the default, which is to not update alpha versions.

Two additional options allow you to enable the Apple Remote plug-in (enabled by default) and to enable experimental support for Wacom tablets, which is disabled by default.

Create a Custom Trackpad Gesture

To create a custom trackpad gesture, first click **Gestures** in the BetterTouchTool toolbar at the top of the main preference window. Next, click **Trackpads**, if not already highlighted, to display the trackpad gesture palette where you will create, modify, and delete your custom gestures.

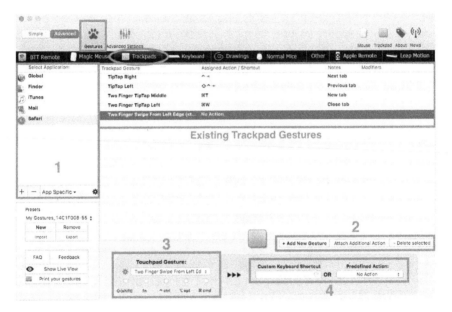

The main window displays any existing gestures. In the example above, you can see I have created 4 custom trackpad gestures for Safari, which is highlighted in the column at (1). My first custom gesture is a TipTap Right, which, if I have multiple tabs open, will move to the next Safari tab to the right. A tip-tap is accomplished by placing two fingers on the trackpad and tapping with either the left or right finger while keeping the other finger on the trackpad. A TipTap Left gesture moves to the previous Safari tab. I can create a new Safari tab with a Two Finger TipTap Middle. While a Two Finger TipTap Left closes the current active Safari tab. A two finger tip-tap is accomplished by placing three fingers on the trackpad and tapping with the left, middle, or right finger while keeping the other two fingers on the trackpad. The final gesture in the list, a Two Finger Swipe From Left Edge, is being created as it currently has no action associated with it.

Creating a new trackpad gesture is simple. First, determine if your new gesture will be **Global** or specific to an application. Global gestures work regardless of which application is currently active. Application specific gestures work only in the application for which they were created. You can also see that I have created application specific gestures for Finder, iTunes, Mail, and Safari in the example above.

If your new gesture will be global, click on **Global** at the top of the column at (1). If your gesture will be application specific, click the **+** button at the bottom left of (1) to open your Applications folder and select the desired application.

Next, click **+ Add New Gesture** from (2) and select your trackpad gesture from the drop-down menu under **Touchpad Gesture** at (3). BetterTouchTool supports 1-, 2-, 3-, 4-, and 5-finger gestures, custom gestures you create, and Force Touch gestures in combination with single or double taps, tip-taps, swipes up, down, left, or right, click swipes up, down, left or right, and trackpad location with 1-, 2-, and 3-finger gestures. Add one or more modifier keys to your gesture, if desired. Modifier keys serve two purposes. First, to ensure that you will not accidentally execute a gesture. And second, they allow you to use the same gesture for different actions.

Next, assign a keyboard shortcut by typing it in the field below **Custom Keyboard Shortcut** at (4). Or select from one of over 125 pre-defined actions from the drop-down menu under **Pre-Defined Action** at (4). You can add notes to your gesture, if you wish, by entering them in the **Notes** field in the list of existing gestures. Close the BetterTouchTool window when finished and try out your new custom trackpad gesture.

That's how simple it is to create a custom trackpad gesture in BetterTouchTool. The only limit to the number of gestures is your imagination and the amount of time you have to create them. Have fun creating your own gestures!

To modify an existing gesture, highlight it and make the desired changes in (3) and (4). To delete an existing gesture, first highlight it and click **- Delete selected** in (2).

Create a Custom Magic Mouse Gesture

Creating a custom gesture for your Magic Mouse is very similar to creating a trackpad gesture. To create a custom Mouse gesture, first click **Gestures** in the BetterTouchTool toolbar. Next, click **Magic Mouse**, if not already highlighted, to display the Magic Mouse gesture palette where you will create, modify, and delete your custom gestures.

The main window displays any existing gestures. In the example above, you can see I have created 2 custom mouse gestures for iTunes, which is highlighted in the column in (1). My first custom gesture is a TipTap Right, which, will advance to the next song in iTunes. A tip-tap is accomplished by placing two fingers on the mouse and tapping with either the left or right finger while keeping the other finger on the mouse. A TipTap Left gesture plays the previous song.

Creating a new mouse gesture is simple. First, determine if your new gesture will be **Global** or specific to an application. Global gestures work regardless of which application is currently active. Application specific gestures work only in the application for which they were created. You can also see that I have created application specific gestures for Finder, iTunes, Mail, Microsoft Word, and Safari.

If your new gesture will be global, click on **Global** at the top of the column at (1). If your gesture will be application specific, click the **+** button at the bottom left of (1) to open your Applications folder and select the desired application.

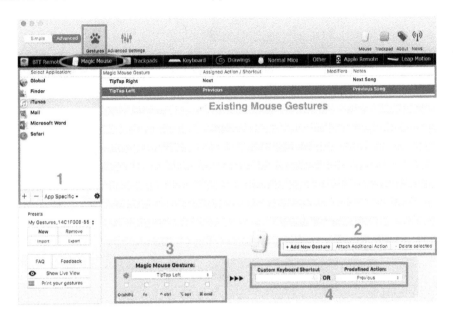

Next, click **+ Add New Gesture** from (2) and select your mouse gesture from the drop-down menu under **Magic Mouse Gesture** at (3). BetterTouchTool supports 1-, 2-, 3-, and 4-finger gestures in combination with single or double taps, tip-taps, and swipes up, down, left, or right. Add one or more modifier keys to your gesture, if desired. Modifier keys serve two purposes. First, to ensure that you will not accidentally execute a gesture. And second, they allow you to use the same gesture for different actions.

Next, assign a keyboard shortcut by typing it in the field below **Custom Keyboard Shortcut** at (4). Or select from one of over 125 pre-defined actions from the drop-down menu under **Pre-Defined Action** at (4). You can add notes to your gesture, if you wish, by entering them in the **Notes** field in the list of existing gestures. Close the BetterTouchTool window when finished and try out your new custom mouse gesture.

That's how simple it is to create a custom mouse gesture in BetterTouchTool. The only limit to the number of gestures is your imagination and the amount of time you have to create them. Have fun creating your own gestures!

To modify an existing gesture, highlight it and make the desired changes in (3) and (4). To delete an existing gesture, first highlight it and click **- Delete selected** in (2).

Create a Multiple Action Gesture

BetterTouchTool doesn't limit your gestures to a single action. In the example below, I have two application specific gestures for Microsoft Word. The first is a Four Finger Tap combined with the ^ ⌥ ⌘ (control, option, and command) modifier keys. This gesture will save and then close my currently active Word document.

The second is a Four Finger Double Tap combined with the ^ ⌥ ⌘ (control, option, and command) modifier keys. This gesture will save my currently active Word document and then quit the Word application.

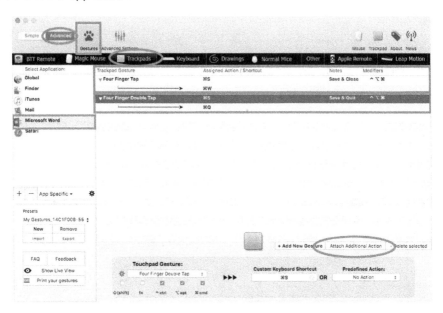

To create a multiple action gesture, create your gesture as described in the last two sections. To attach a second action, click to highlight the gesture as shown in the picture. Next, click **Attach Additional Action** and then enter a **Custom Keyboard Shortcut** or select a **Predefined Action** from the drop-down menu. Lather, rinse, and repeat if you want to add more actions. Close BetterToolTouch and give your new multiple action gestures a try!

Multiple action gestures are denoted by the small triangle to their left. Click the triangle to expand the gesture and see the other actions.

Sharing Gestures

If you want to share gestures with friends and family or want to create a backup file, BetterTouchTool lets you export them.

First, click **Gestures**, then **Magic Mouse** or **Trackpads**, as appropriate. Click **Export** under **Presets** at the lower left. A save dialog will open. Name your file, choose the save location, select a tag if desired, and press **Save**.

To import a gesture file, click **Import** under **Presets** at the lower left. Browse to the file, select it, and click **Open**.

3

Desktop

The **Desktop** is the main component of OS X through which you interface with your Mac. It provides the majority of your user experience. All folder, file, and application windows appear on the Desktop. Although you work within an application, the application is delivered to you on the OS X Desktop. The Desktop has three major components – the **Menu Bar**, the **Dock**, and the **Desktop** itself – as shown in the picture below. Additional items highlighted are the **Apple Menu**, **Application Menu**, **Status Menu**, **Spotlight**, **Notification Center**, and the **Finder** and **Trash** icons in the Dock. The picture of El Capitan in Yosemite National Park is the default wallpaper.

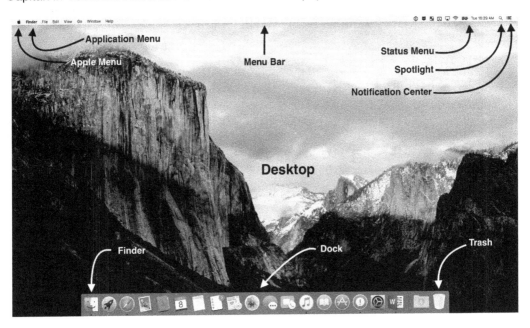

A horizontal translucent bar, called the **Menu Bar**, anchored across the top of the Desktop. There are two halves to the Menu Bar. The left half, shown below, is comprised of two elements, the **Apple Menu** and the **Application Menu**.

🍎 **Safari**   File   Edit   View   History   Bookmarks   Window   Help

The **Apple Menu**, denoted by the , is a drop-down menu where you can access system-wide commands that allow you to update OS X, purchase application software from the Mac App Store, see hardware information, configure System Preferences, open recent applications and documents, force quit misbehaving apps, and put your Mac to sleep, restart, shutdown, or log out.

To the right of the menu is the **Application Menu**, which provides drop-down menus filled with commands and tools common to all applications as well as any menus specific to the currently active application. The name of the currently active application is shown to the right of the menu, in this case Safari, therefore the first drop-down menu is called the **Safari Menu**. The Application Menu will change as you open other applications and make them active, however, the drop-down menus for **File**, **Edit**, **View**, **Window**, and **Help** are common from application to application.

There are three elements on the right side of the Menu Bar, the **Status Menu**, the **Spotlight** icon, and the **Notification Center** icon, from left to right. Note that if you upgraded from a previous version of OS X or customized your Status Menu (as I did), it will look different than what is shown below.

Tue 3:56 PM

The **Status Menu** displays the status of and allows quick access to various OS X features via small icons called **Menu Extras**. In the picture above, the **Menu Extras** are, from left to right, 1Password, Unclutter, BetterSnapTool, BetterTouchTool, AirPlay, AirPort, Battery, and Date & Time.

Next to the Menu Extras are icons for **Spotlight** and **Notification Center**, respectively. Clicking the **Spotlight** icon launches Spotlight, where you can search for files, folders, applications, events, reminders, music, movie showtimes, nearby locations, iTunes, the App Store, messages, essentially anything on your Mac. Spotlight is also a universal search engine that can search the Internet without having to launch Safari. Spotlight searches the Internet, returns Wikipedia pages, searches your bookmarks and web browsing history, Maps, and iTunes including movies, music, and podcasts.

In addition to searching your Mac, Spotlight now shows suggestions from the Internet, iTunes, the App Store, movie showtimes, locations nearby, and more. To make suggestions more relevant to you, Spotlight includes your approximate location with search requests to Apple.
You can change this in Preferences. Learn more...

In the upper right hand corner of the Menu Bar is the icon for **Notification Center**, a one-stop shop that consolidates notifications from any application that supports notifications including Mail, Messages, Reminders, iTunes, and Calender, third party applications like Evernote, Facebook, Twitter and LinkedIn. You can even configure Notification Center to provide notifications from any website that supports Apple's push notification service.

First, I'll show you how to customize your Desktop. You'll learn techniques and customizations to manage desktop clutter that inevitably comes with using any computer. Then, you'll learn how to customize the Menu Bar in the next chapter. After that, I'll show you techniques to manage application windows and learn how to increase your desktop space. The Dock is so customizable, I wrote a chapter specifically focusing on its customization. Because Stacks, which are a component of the Dock, are also extremely customizable, they deserved their own chapter too. After the chapters on the Dock and Stacks, you'll learn about Spotlight and how to customize it and search more efficiently and accurately. Then we'll explore Notification Center's features and customize it too. First, let's start with your first desktop customization, changing the desktop wallpaper.

Change the Desktop Wallpaper

The most noticeable item on your Desktop is the wallpaper, also called the background. In OS X El Capitan, the default wallpaper is a beautiful picture of El Capitan at sunset in wintery Yosemite National Park, California. Apple chose to name its OS X 10.11 release after El Capitan, a granite rock formation rising more than 3,000 feet above the Yosemite Valley floor. El Capitan is the largest granite monolith in the world and is a favorite of rock climbers. Apple included a second desktop background, called El Capitan 2, which is actually a picture of Half Dome against a starry night sky. Half Dome is granite rock formation at the eastern end of Yosemite Valley and it rises 4,737 feet above the valley.

While the pictures of El Capitan and Half Dome are stunning, you don't have to live with the desktop wallpaper Apple chose for you. Apple included a number of other images from which you can select including backgrounds from previous releases of OS X. Or if you wish, you can change your wallpaper to any picture or set of pictures you want.

There are often numerous ways to do the same thing in OS X. It is up to you to decide which method works best for you. To change your desktop wallpaper, secondary click anywhere on the Desktop to display the Desktop context menu. Select **Change Desktop Background...** to open the **Desktop & Screen Saver** preference pane.

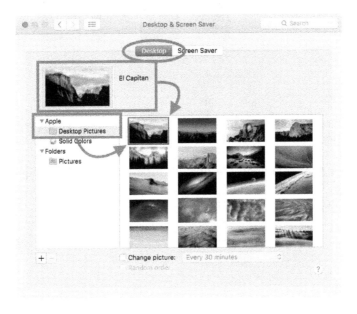

Or another option is to open the **Desktop & Screen Saver** preference pane in the System Preferences application. Once the **Desktop & Screen Saver** preference pane appears, ensure the **Desktop** tab is selected. The current desktop wallpaper is shown in the upper left portion of the pane. The left hand pane allows you to select from a number of images from Apple, solid colors, or a picture in a folder on your Mac. Thumbnails of the images are previewed in the right pane. If the thumbnail previews are too small for you, use the pinch zoom gesture to make them bigger.

Apple provides a number of standard wallpaper images under **Apple > Desktop Pictures**. If you like one of the standard images, click to select it. Apple also offers a set of solid color wallpaper images under **Apple > Solid Colors**.

You don't have to settle for one image, you can select them all and OS X will change your desktop wallpaper at an interval chosen by you. Check the checkbox next to **Change picture** and select how frequently you want OS X to change your desktop wallpaper. You have a choice of getting a new desktop wallpaper image when logging in, when waking from sleep, every 5 seconds, 1 minute, 5 minutes, 15, minutes, 30 minutes, every hour, or every day. When you check **Change picture**, the picture in the upper left of the **Desktop & Screen Saver** preference pane will change to show a set of circular arrows.

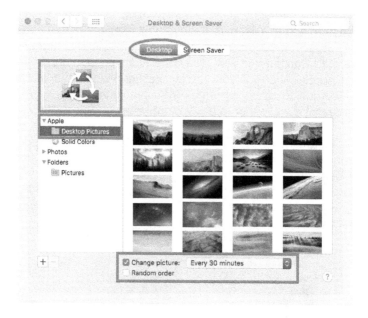

By default, OS X will cycle through the wallpaper sequentially from the first picture to the last. Check the checkbox next to **Random order** and OS X will select images randomly.

Now that we know how to change the default desktop wallpaper using the set of images provided by Apple, let's leverage this knowledge to really personalize your desktop using your own images from the Photos application.

Use a Picture from Photos as your Desktop Wallpaper

 You can use an image of your choice as your desktop wallpaper, sharing it directly from the **Photos** application. Open the Photos application, find your desired picture, and click on it. A blue border will appear around the photo. Click the **Share** button located on the upper right of the Photos toolbar and select on **Set Desktop Picture** from the drop-down menu. You can also secondary click on your chosen picture to reveal a contextual menu. Select **Share > Set Desktop Picture** from the contextual menu. Alternatively, you can select **File > Share > Set Desktop Picture**.

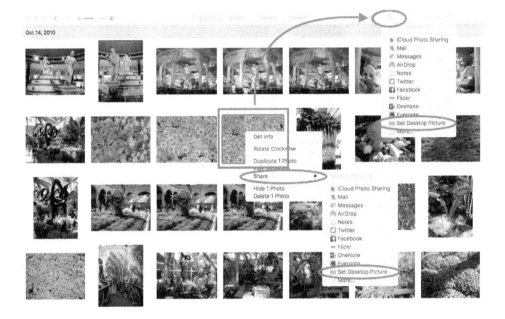

If the size of your photo doesn't match the screen size of your Mac, open the **Desktop & Screen Saver** preference pane in the System Preferences application. Ensure the **Desktop** tab is selected. Use the drop-down menu to the right of the photo you selected. Choose the display option that works best – **Fill Screen**, **Fit to Screen**, **Stretch to Fill Screen**, **Center**, or **Tile**.

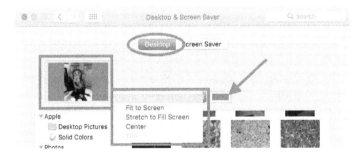

Note that the size of your photo my not match the screen size of your Mac. A photo in portrait mode doesn't fit well since your Mac's screen is in landscape. In that case, you can change how the photo will display using the drop-down menu to the right of the photo you selected. You have five choices: **Fill Screen**, **Fit to Screen**, **Stretch to Fill Screen**,

Center, or **Tile**. I never use Stretch to Fill Screen as this selection changes the aspect ratio of the photo and distorts the image.

For photos in portrait mode, **Fit to Screen** typically works best because the entire photo will be displayed. For photos in landscape mode, **Fill Screen**, **Fit to Screen** or **Center** generally works best. For both the **Fit to Screen** or **Center** options, you'll notice a colored rectangle to the right of the drop-down menu. Clicking on the colored rectangle reveals a color wheel that lets you choose the color of the bars that appear on the left and right of your photo when it doesn't fill the entire desktop.

Configure Multiple Pictures from Photos as your Desktop Wallpaper

You can choose multiple pictures in Photos for your Desktop Wallpaper and have OS X rotate through them. Open the **Desktop & Screen Saver** preference pane in System Preferences. Click on the gray triangle next to Photos in the left column to open a list of moments, collections, years, places, shared photos, albums, faces, and your photo stream. Click on one of the items in the list and select the photos you want as your wallpaper. Choose to display the photos sequentially or in random order. And don't forget to select how often you want OS X to change your picture.

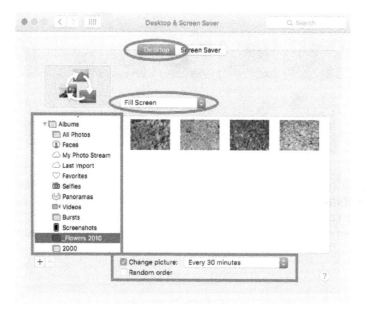

If your pictures are not in the same moment, collection, year, place, or album, create a new album in Photos and add your pictures to it. You can create a new album in Photos by selecting **File > New Album...** or by entering ⌘N (control+N). Once you have finished, launch the System Preferences application and open the **Desktop & Screen Saver** preference pane. In the left column, expand Photos using the triangle, scroll to your new album, select it, and choose the display options. Be sure to configure how frequently your pictures change and whether OS X should display them sequentially or randomly.

Configure Wallpaper from your Photo Stream

Photos saved to your iCloud Photo Stream can be configured as your desktop wallpaper. Open the **Desktop & Screen Saver** preference pane from System Preferences. Next, click the **Desktop** tab. In the left hand column, expand **Photos** using the small triangle and scroll down until you see **My Photo Stream**. You can select an individual photo from the right pane or select your entire Photo Stream.

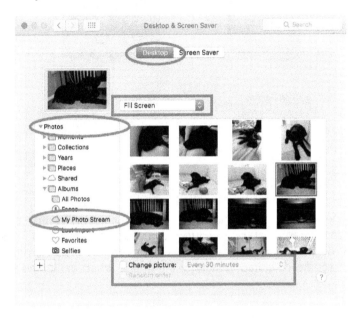

If the size of your photo doesn't match the screen size of your Mac, use the drop-down menu to the right of the photos you selected and select the option that works best – **Fill Screen**, **Fit to Screen**, **Stretch to Fill Screen**, **Center**, or **Tile**. For photos in portrait mode, **Fit to Screen** typically works best because the entire photo will be displayed. For photos in landscape mode, **Fill Screen**, **Fit to Screen** or **Center** generally works best. For both the **Fit to Screen** or **Center** options, you'll notice a colored rectangle to the right of the drop-down menu. Clicking on the color reveals a color wheel that lets you choose the color of the bars that will appear on the left and right of your photo when it doesn't fill the entire desktop. Be sure to configure how frequently the pictures change and whether you want your pictures displayed sequentially or randomly.

Use Images in a Folder as Desktop Wallpaper

Another option for your desktop wallpaper is to utilize a folder containing images. I like to collect desktop wallpaper from the Internet, usually landscape scenes. I have hundreds of pictures in a folder called **Wallpaper** located in the **Pictures** folder of my **Home** directory. If you want to download wallpaper from the Internet, the first thing you need to do is to understand the resolution of your monitor.

To find the resolution of your monitor, select > **About This Mac**. Click on the **Displays** tab to see your displays. The resolution of your monitor is listed under the name of the display. For example, the resolution of my 15-inch MacBook Pro's built-in monitor is 1680 x 1050. The numbers represent the width and height of the screen in pixels with the first number representing the width and the second, the height. The larger the numbers, the higher the resolution. I have an external monitor with a resolution of 1920 x 1080 pixels.

So when searching Google images (http://images.google.com) or any site with desktop wallpaper, you don't want just any picture, you want pictures that match the native resolution of your display. A picture with a resolution smaller than the native resolution of your display will become pixelated, distorting the image when expanded to fit your higher resolution display.

Another important number is the aspect ratio, which is the proportional relationship between a display's width and its height. For my MacBook Pro's built-in display, the aspect ratio is calculated by dividing 1680 (its width) by 1050 (its height). The result is 1.6 which equates to an aspect ratio of 16:10. An image with an incorrect aspect ratio will not fit properly on the desktop. When looking for wallpaper to fit my MacBook Pro, I look for images with a 16:10 aspect ratio and a minimum resolution of 1680 x 1050 pixels.

Another common aspect ratio is 16:9. If you have an external monitor that you purchased within the past year or so, its aspect ratio is most likely 16:9. For example, I also have an external 27-inch display. Its native resolution is 1920 x 1080 pixels. Dividing 1920 by 1080 yields 1.77, which equates to a 16:9 aspect ratio. When looking for wallpaper to fit my external monitor, I look for images with a 16:9 aspect ratio and a minimum resolution of 1920 x 1080 pixels.

To add a folder of images, open the **Desktop & Screen Saver** preference pane in the System Preferences application. Click the + (plus) sign at the lower left of the preference pane to open a **Finder** window so you can navigate to and select the folder containing your pictures. You can also drag a folder into the left column of the preference pane from Finder. To make the folder active, click on it and then choose display, frequency, and randomization options. If the thumbnail previews are too small for you, use the pinch zoom gesture to make them bigger.

To remove a folder, highlight it and click the – (minus) button.

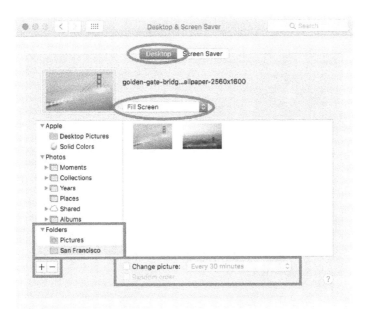

One of the advantages of using a single folder as the source for your desktop wallpaper is that OS X will automatically use any new photos added to your folder without any further configuration. Remember to configure the frequency and order (sequential or random) that OS X will use to change the wallpaper.

Access Hidden Wallpaper Collections

Apple bundled 43 beautiful high resolution images in OS X El Capitan that you can use as desktop wallpaper. There are 17 gorgeous images from *National Geographic* along with 9 **Aerial** images, 9 images of the **Cosmos**, and 8 **Nature Patterns**. Apple intended for you to use these images as screensavers, but it only takes a couple of steps to add them to your wallpaper collection.

To use these hidden screensaver images as wallpaper, open **Finder** and enter ⇧⌘**G** (shift+command+G) to open the **Go to the folder** dialog box. Enter the following path and click **Go**.

`/Library/Screen Savers/Default Collections/`

Finder will display four folders, numbered from 1 to 4 and labeled *National Geographic*, **Aerial**, **Cosmos**, and **Nature Patterns**, respectively. Each one contains high resolution images you can use as wallpaper.

To use any of these collections as your wallpaper, open the **Desktop & Screen Saver** preference pane in the System Preferences application. Click on the **Desktop** tab at the top of the pane. Drag each of the folders or just the ones you want to the bottom of the left-hand column under **Folders**. You can now select your desktop wallpaper from any of these folders.

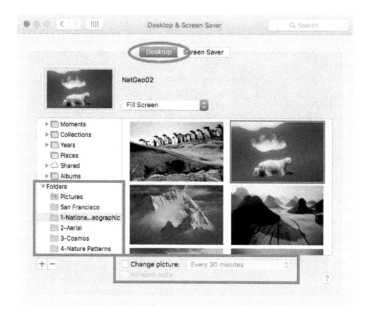

If you already have a folder configured as the source for your desktop wallpaper, another option is to copy the individual picture files into your wallpaper folder. Just open each of the collections by double-clicking its folder. Select the images you like and drag them into the source folder for your wallpaper.

Configure the Screensaver

Screensavers are a throwback to the days of ancient cathode ray tube (CRT) monitors. If an image was displayed for too long on a CRT monitor, it would eventually burn a ghost image onto the screen. This phenomenon is called phosphor burn in. Screensavers were designed to prevent phosphor burn in by filling the screen with moving images or patterns when the screen was not in use. Modern computers use Liquid Crystal Display (LCD) or Light Emitting Diode (LED) technology which is not susceptible to phosphor burn-in. Today screensavers are primarily used for entertainment purposes.

If you would like to configure a screensaver, open the **Desktop & Screen Saver** preference pane in the System Preferences application. Click on the **Screen Saver** tab at the top of the pane.

OS X El Capitan offers 19 different screensaver options, which are shown in the list of screensavers on the left side of the **Desktop & Screen Saver** preference pane. Any screensaver chosen in the left-hand side of the pane is previewed in the right pane. Apple includes four default collections: **National Geographic**, **Aerial**, **Cosmos**, and **Nature Patterns**, accessible under the drop-down list next to **Source** on the right side of the preference pane. You also have the option of choosing **Recent Photos Events** or a library from the Photos app or a folder containing images. Select **Photo Library...** or **Choose Folder...**, respectively.

Checking the checkbox next to **Shuffle slide order** displays the images randomly.

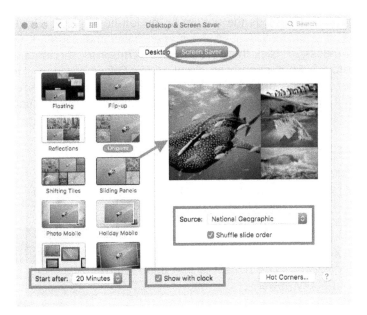

Select an inactivity time from the drop-down menu next to **Start After**. You can start your screen saver after 1, 2, 5, 10, 20, 30, or 60 minutes of inactivity.   You also can select **Never**, which effectively disables the screen saver. If you want the screen saver to display the time, check the checkbox next to **Show with clock**.

Display a Message as the Screen Saver

OS X lets you display a message on your computer as your screensaver. To configure a message, first open the **Desktop & Screen Saver** preference pane in the System Preferences application. Click on the **Screen Saver** tab at the top of the pane.

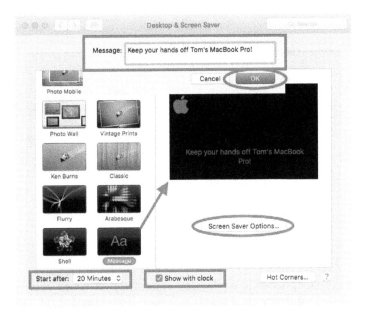

Choose **Message**, found towards the bottom of the left-hand pane. By default, OS X will display the name of your computer as the screen saver message. If you would like to display your own message, click the **Screen Saver Options...** button and configure your message in the drop-down configuration sheet. Click **OK** when done. Don't forget to set the inactivity timer from the drop-down menu under **Start after**. Check the box next to **Show with clock** if you would like to show the time along with your message.

Permanently Disable the Screen Saver

Screen savers are a throwback to the early days of computing where external monitors were gigantic CRTs. Modern monitors are not susceptible to phosphor burn in, therefore screensavers serve no purpose other than their entertainment value.   If you don't want to use a screensaver, OS X offers an option to turn off the display after a period of inactivity. The benefit is that this feature saves electricity or battery power.

To permanently turn off the screen saver, choose the **Never** option from the **Start After** drop-down menu on the **Desktop & Screen Saver** preference pane. To learn how to put the display to sleep after a period of inactivity, see the next section.

Put the Display to Sleep

If you don't want to use a screensaver, another option is to simply put your display to sleep after a period of inactivity. To configure the display sleep timer, open the **Energy Saver** preference pane in the System Preferences application.

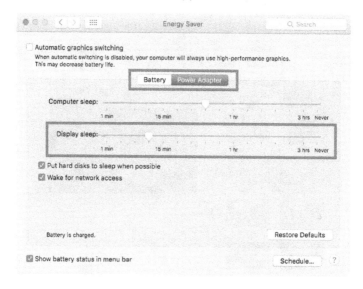

Note that the display sleep timer is configured separately for when your Mac is on battery or AC power. Select **Battery** or **Power Adapter** from the top of the **Energy Saver** preference pane. Next, configure the inactivity timer under **Display sleep** by dragging the slider to the left or right until the desired inactivity time has been selected. Be sure to configure inactivity timers for both **Battery** and **Power Adapter** if you own a MacBook, MacBook Air, or MacBook Pro. When the inactivity timer expires, your computer's display will go to sleep (go dark).

Set Up Hot Corners

The **Hot Corners** feature allows you to assign a specific action to each of the four corners of your desktop. The associated command is executed by moving your cursor to one of the corners of your desktop. The supported commands include starting or disabling the screen saver, opening Mission Control, application windows (App Exposé), showing the Desktop, Dashboard, Notification Center, Launchpad, or putting the display to sleep. To assign commands to Hot Corners, first open the **Desktop & Screen Saver** preference pane in the System Preferences application.

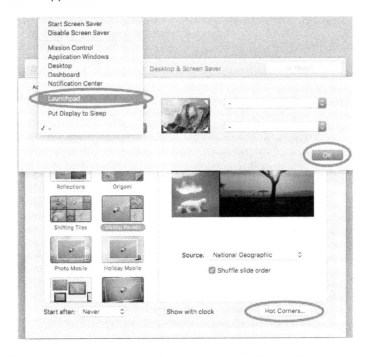

Next, click the **Hot Corners...** button at the lower right of the preference pane to reveal the drop-down dialog box shown below. Assign an action to each of the four **Hot Corners** using the drop-down menu for each of the corners. Click **OK** when finished, then close the **Desktop & Screen Saver** preference pane.

To execute the command assigned to a **Hot Corner**, simply move your cursor to the appropriate corner. Moving your cursor back to the corner reverses the command.

To turn off **Hot Corners**, open the **Desktop & Screen Saver** preference pane and select the **Screen Saver** tab. Next, click the **Hot Corners...** button in the lower right corner of the pane. Select the – from the drop-down menu for each corner that you want to turn off.

Hot corners can also be configured from the **Mission Control** preference pane. To set up Hot Corners, first open the **Mission Control** preference pane in the System Preferences application.

Next, click the **Hot Corners...** button at the lower left of the pane to reveal the drop-down dialog box. You can assign a command to each corner. The supported commands are the same as those in the Desktop & Screensaver preference pane and include starting or disabling the screen saver, opening Mission Control, application windows (App Exposé), showing the Desktop, Dashboard, Notification Center, Launchpad, or putting the display to sleep. Moving your cursor to a Hot Corner executes the assigned command. Moving your cursor back to the corner reverses the command.

To turn off Hot Corners, open the **Mission Control** preference pane and click the **Hot Corners...** button in the lower left corner. Select the – from the drop-down menu for each corner that you want to turn off.

Hot corners can be configured from either the **Desktop & Screen Saver** or the **Mission Control** preference panes.

Avoid Accidentally Triggering a Hot Corner

The **Hot Corners** feature is very handy, but one problem is that simply moving the cursor near a **Hot Corner** can accidentally trigger the associated command. For example, moving the cursor to the menu often accidentally triggers the command associated with the upper left corner.

To avoid accidentally triggering a Hot Corner, configure the Hot Corners feature to utilize a modifier key. For example, you can configure Hot Corners so that the ⌥ (option) key must be held down to execute the command when the cursor is moved to a Hot Corner. Using a modifier key will eliminate the possibility of accidentally triggering a Hot Corner.

To configure Hot Corners to require a modifier key, open the **Desktop & Screen Saver** preference pane in the System Preferences application. Click on the **Screen Saver** tab at the top of the pane. Next click the **Hot Corners...** button at the lower right to display the Hot Corners configuration drop down menu.

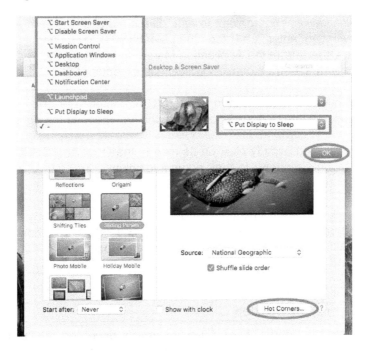

To add a modifier key, hold down the desired modifier key when selecting an action from the drop-down menu. For example, I am holding down the ⌥ (option) key while selecting the **Launchpad** command in the picture shown above. Note that the **Put Display to Sleep** command is configured to require the ⌥ key. Any of the following modifier keys are supported: ⇧ ⌘ ^ ⌥ (shift, command, control, or option). OS X will even allow you to use any combination of two, three, or even all four of the modifier keys.

Once you have configured a modifier key, Hot Corners will only work when you're holding down the modifier key(s) you specified, thereby eliminating the possibility of accidentally triggering a Hot Corner.

Hide Applications to Clean Up Desktop Clutter

Too many windows open on the desktop can be a distraction especially if you are trying to concentrate on one particular window. Of course you could always minimize or close all the windows or quit the applications entirely to clean up the clutter. But that takes time and you may not want to quit all applications because you want to leave them open for later use. In that case, quitting or closing windows are not viable options. You could minimize each window, however that could take a lot of time if you have lots of windows open. And minimized windows clutter the right side of the Dock, making each icon smaller and more difficult to differentiate as the Dock expands across the desktop.

A handy feature is to hide all the other applications except for the one you are working in. Hiding an application causes all of its windows to instantly disappear without crowding the Dock. Because OS X will remember where the windows were located before you hid them, the windows will return to their original positions when unhidden. If you have lots of applications open and want to hide all but the application in which you are working, enter ⌥⌘H (command+option+H). You can also choose **Hide Others** from the Application Menu. In the example, selecting **Safari > Hide Others** hides all applications except for Safari.

To hide the currently active application, enter ⌘H (command+H) or select the **Hide** option from the Application Menu, the first menu to the right of the menu.

To unhide any application, simply click on its icon in the Dock and OS X will immediately restore the application's windows to their original locations. You can use **App Exposé** to see the windows of any application, whether hidden or not.

How do you know which applications are hidden and which are not? By default, the OS X Dock does not differentiate between applications that are hidden and those that are not. A tweak I will show you in the chapter on customizing the Dock will allow you to differentiate between hidden and unhidden applications.

Remove Devices from the Desktop

OS X displays icons of external hard drives or optical drives on the desktop when you connect them to your computer. These icons represent yet more desktop clutter. There is no need to display external devices on the desktop as they are available in the **Devices** list in the Finder sidebar. OS X allows you to stop external devices from appearing on the desktop. Additionally, turning off the display of external devices is particularly useful when you are using a Volumes Stack, which will display all of your internal and external drives and optical drives as a single stack in the Dock. See the chapter on Stacks to see how to create a Volumes Stack.

To turn off the display of external devices on your desktop open **Finder** and select **Preferences...** from the Finder menu in the menu bar or enter ⌘, (command+comma). By default, OS X will display icons for external hard drives, CDs, DVDs, and iPods. To disable this feature, uncheck the checkboxes next to each of these items in the Finder preference pane. Changes take effect immediately and any device icons on your desktop will disappear. Don't worry. Your devices have not been removed. They have been hidden and can still be accessed from the Device list in Finder or through a Volumes Stack.

To return to the OS X default, open Finder and enter ⌘, (command+comma) to open the Finder Preferences. Then check the checkboxes next to **External disks** and **CDs, DVDs, and iPods**.

Create a Pristine Desktop

Unfortunately for most users, the desktop quickly turns out to be the catch-all location for documents and other stuff they're working on. Screenshots are saved to the desktop by default and many downloaded applications save items there too. Desktop clutter can become overwhelming and detract from your ability to get work done. Not only does the mess make the desktop look unsightly, it steals CPU and memory resources because each icon must be rendered and its contents previewed. If your desktop has more icons than wallpaper, you have inadvertently made your Mac slower by forcing OS X to dedicate resources to render the clutter.

Items saved to the desktop aren't really saved to the desktop. They are actually saved to the **Desktop** folder located in your **Home** directory. The Desktop folder is easily accessible from your Home directory, the Finder Sidebar, or from a document stack in the Dock. See the chapter on customizing Stacks to learn how to create a Desktop Stack.

If you want a really clean desktop and a faster Mac, this OS X tweak will give you a pristine desktop, free of clutter. Essentially this tweak turns off desktop icons, completely preventing them from being displayed in the first place. This tweak will also prevent you from dragging icons onto the desktop. It will also turn off your ability to secondary click on the desktop to create new folders, Get Info, or change the desktop background. However, all of these features are accessible via other means.

Launch **Terminal** and enter the following commands.

```
defaults write com.apple.finder CreateDesktop -bool FALSE

killall Finder
```

Any icons that normally would have appeared on your desktop are safely tucked away in the Desktop folder in your Home directory, where they belong. This is a handy tweak if you are about to give an important presentation and you are embarrassed by your lack of desktop cleanliness.

To return to the default and risk a messy desktop and slow Mac, enter the following commands in Terminal.

```
defaults write com.apple.finder CreateDesktop -bool TRUE

killall Finder
```

Unclutter Your Desktop

Despite the unsightly clutter, it is often very convenient to store files on the desktop. Say if you are writing a book on how to customize OS X and take a large number of screenshots, which are saved to the desktop by default. Having these files instantly available on the desktop is not only convenient, it helps with productivity. Too bad it is so unsightly. Wouldn't it be great if there was an app that could provide you the convenience of storing files on the desktop without the unsightly clutter?

This is where an app, appropriately named **Unclutter**, comes to the rescue. Written by Eugene Krupnov, Unclutter creates a handy place on your desktop to store files, notes, and the clipboard history. Configuring the Pristine Desktop tweak on the last page and tweaking Unclutter to use the Desktop folder gives you a completely clean desktop while making all files in the Desktop folder instantly available from the Unclutter app.

Unclutter is available from the Mac App Store for $5.99 at the time of this writing at: https://itunes.apple.com/us/app/unclutter/id577085396?mt=12.

To use Unclutter, move your cursor to the very top of your screen and scroll down with two fingers on your trackpad or Magic Mouse. The Unclutter window will drop from below the Menu Bar. The default configuration of Unclutter is shown below. Your clipboard history is shown at the left, files in the center, and notes on the right. Click anywhere outside Unclutter, on the desktop or an application window, and the Unclutter window will disappear under the Menu Bar.

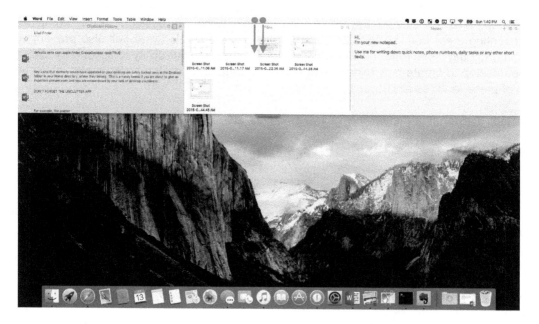

The clipboard history can store the last 10, 25, or 50 items that were copied or cut. You can scroll through them, selecting the one you need, and pasting it again. While I initially purchased Unclutter for quick access to files that would normally be on my Desktop, I find the clipboard history to be one of its most useful features.

Files can be easily dragged into Unclutter's "drop-zone" located at the very top of your screen above the Menu Bar. Dragging a file into the drop-zone causes the Unclutter window to slide down from under the Menu Bar. Simply drop your file in the files area.

Let's customize Unclutter. Unclutter places a Menu Extra in the Menu Bar. Click on the Unclutter menu extra and select **Preferences...** or enter ⌘, (command+comma) while the Unclutter window is displayed.

First, let's configure Unclutter's **General** preferences. Click the **General** tab, if not already highlighted By default, Unclutter does not run when you start your Mac. I suggest checking the checkbox next to **Launch Unclutter at startup** to ensure Unclutter is always available when you restart your Mac.

The Unclutter window appears when you move your cursor to the very top of your screen and scroll down with two fingers. If you would like to add a modifier key, check the checkbox next to **hold** and select your modifier. You have a choice of ⌘, ⌥, or ⇧ (command, option, or shift).

You do not have to use the two-finger scroll to activate Unclutter and display the Unclutter window. By checking the checkbox next to **wait**, you can configure Unclutter to reveal its window when you move your cursor to the very top of your screen and wait. You can configure the wait time to a half second, 1 second, or 2 seconds.

To configure a keyboard shortcut to reveal the Unclutter window, enter your desired shortcut in the box next to **or just press**. I've configured Unclutter to display its window when I enter ⌥U (option+U).

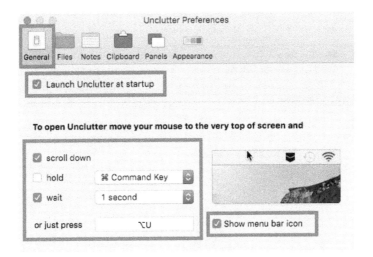

To disable the two-finger scroll to reveal the Unclutter window, uncheck the checkbox next to **scroll down**. If you leave this checkbox checked, as I did, the two-finger scroll will work with both the wait and keyboard shortcut options enabled. This allows you multiple methods to access the Unclutter window.

Unclutter puts a menu extra in the Menu Bar. If you do not want Unclutter's menu extra on your Menu Bar, uncheck the checkbox next to **Show menu bar icon**.

By default, Unclutter saves files to its own location. I find it very convenient to change the default location to the **Desktop** folder in my Home directory. This allows me to use the Pristine Desktop tweak for a completely clean desktop, yet still have quick access to files saved in my Desktop folder. Additionally, Unclutter warns you that to enable Spotlight search for the files it has saved requires you to move files to a different location.

To change the default save location for files in Unclutter, click on the Unclutter menu extra and select **Preferences...** or enter ⌘, (command+comma) while the Unclutter window is displayed. Click the **Files** tab. Select **Open...** from the drop-down menu next to **Store files in**. Navigate to your desired location (I use my Desktop folder) and click **Open**.

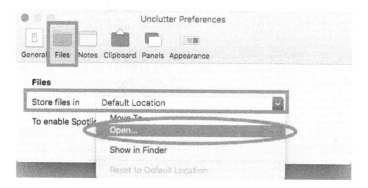

Similarly, clicking on **Notes** in the Unclutter preference pane allows you to change the location in which notes are saved.

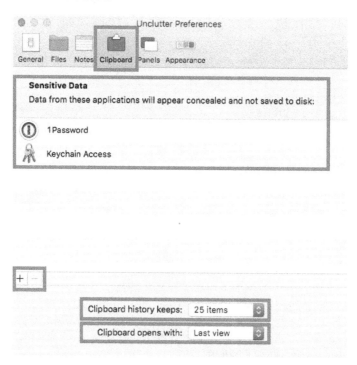

Sometimes you do not want certain data saved to Unclutter's clipboard history. For example, if you use Keychain or another password manager like 1Password, you probably don't want your passwords saved to the clipboard history. To exempt data from certain applications, first click on the **Clipboard** tab in the Unclutter preference pane. Next, click the **+** at the lower left and browse to the application you wish to exempt. Click on it and then click the **Open** button. Unclutter will not show data from any application in its **Sensitive Data** list.

From the **Clipboard** tab, you can configure the number of items Unclutter will save in the clipboard history. Use the drop-down menu next to **Clipboard history keeps** to select 10, 25, or 50 items.

By default, **Clipboard opens with:** is set to **Last view**. Last view displays the last clipboard item viewed. I have found it more convenient to configure this to **History**, which displays the clipboard history. You have a choice of **Item content**, **History, or Last view**.

The **Panels** tab in the Unclutter preference pane lets you disable any panels you do not want to use. By default, the checkboxes next to **Clipboard**, **Files**, and **Notes** are checked. If you do not wish to use a feature, uncheck the checkbox next to it. In the picture, you can see that I only use Clipboard and Files and have disabled Notes.

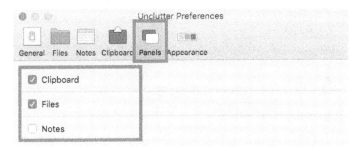

The last customizable item is under the **Appearance** tab. By default, Unclutter matches its theme to how you have configured the Menu Bar. If you are using the default Menu Bar, Unclutter will use its **Light** theme. If you have configured the dark Menu Bar, Unclutter will automatically select its **Dark** theme. If you prefer one theme over the other, you can select it using the drop-down menu next to **Theme:**. Unclutter will use your desired theme regardless of the configuration of the Menu Bar.

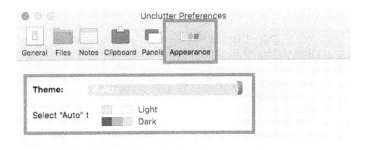

Change the Cursor Size

Have you ever lost your cursor? While you can use the **Shake mouse cursor to locate** feature to find a lost cursor, maybe the default OS X cursor is a little bit too small, especially if you're using a larger monitor. For example, the cursor is sized perfectly for my 15-inch MacBook Pro. But when I connect my MacBook to my 27-inch monitor, it is so small I often have trouble finding it. OS X allows you to change the size of the cursor from the default size to a gigantic one.

To change the cursor size, open the **Accessibility** preference pane in the System Preferences application. Select **Display** in the left-hand column if it is not already highlighted. Slide the **Cursor Size** slider until your cursor is at a comfortable size.

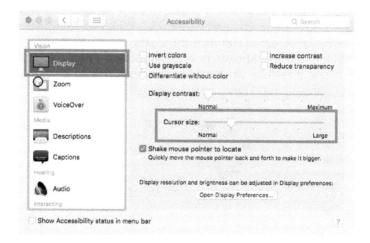

Even a small change makes a big difference when using a large monitor. Note that changing the cursor size also changes the size of the text input cursor in word processing applications and the crosshairs used to take screenshots.

Change the Desktop Icon Size

If you still want to see icons for devices and files on your desktop, OS X gives you the option of changing the icon size. To change the desktop icon size, click anywhere on the Desktop and enter ⌘J (command+J). This will launch the **Desktop** view options panel. Note that the Pristine Desktop hack must be disabled for ⌘J to work.

Use the **Icon size** slider to make the desktop icons appear smaller by dragging the slider to the left. Or, if you want to make the icons appear bigger, drag the slider to the right. The OS X default size is 64 x 64. Changes take effect immediately so you can use the slider to find the size that is right for you.

The next slider controls the tightness of the grid separating the desktop icons. For tighter spacing, drag the slider to the left. For more open spacing, drag the slider to the right.

The next section controls the size and location of the text label. OS X places the text label underneath the icon using a 12-point font. OS X lets you choose any text size between 10- and 16-points in 1-point increments. The text label can be located at the bottom, which is the default, or to the right of the icon by selecting the appropriate radio button.

By default, **Show item info** is off. Checking this option adds the file size or, in the case of a hard drive, the free space, to a second line of the text label.

By default, the **Show icon preview** checkbox is checked. Unchecking this box disables the OS X preview function. Only default icons indicating the application in which the file was created will be displayed instead of previewing the file contents.

The last option available, **Sort by** allows you to choose a default sort option. By default, the sort is set to **None**. The available sort options include sorting by **Name**, **Kind**, **Date Modified**, **Date Created**, **Date Last Opened**, **Date Added**, **Size**, or **Tags**. The **Snap to Grid** option will organize your desktop icons into a grid. Once you have finished configuring your options, close the Desktop view panel to save.

Reduce Transparency

One of the most striking features of OS X El Capitan is the transparent effect of windows, toolbars, title bars, the Menu Bar, and the Dock. If you own a newer Mac, particularly one with a retina display, this eye candy looks amazing. If your Mac is older, you may notice a considerable drop in responsiveness and speed when opening windows. The one single change you can make to OS X to increase performance on an older Mac is to reduce transparency. Reducing transparency also improves contrast and readability.

If you don't like transparency or if you feel it is slowing down your older Mac, you can reduce it in the Accessibility preference pane in the System Preferences application.

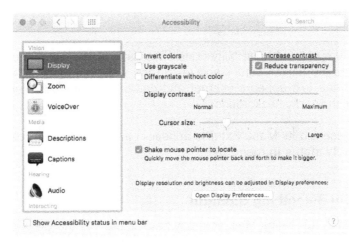

Select **Display** from the left-hand column if it is not already highlighted. Check the box next to **Reduce transparency**. To enable, simply uncheck the checkbox. This change takes effect immediately.

Increase Contrast

El Capitan replaced Yosemite's Helvetica Neue system font with the slightly more readable San Francisco font. Characters in the San Francisco font are a little taller and less wide than Helvetica Nueu. However, paired with El Capitan's transparency feature, you may find San Francisco challenging to read if you have an older, non-retina Mac. The thinness of the font combined with the lack of contrast can make menu items appear a little blurry.

You can significantly improve the readability of the OS X system font by reducing transparency and increasing contrast. An additional benefit of increasing contrast is that it makes El Capitan's user interface appear less flat by darkening the borders and text of buttons and other interface elements.

To increase contrast, open the **Accessibility** preference pane in the System Preferences application. Select **Display** from the left-hand pane if it is not selected already. Check the checkbox next to **Increase contrast**. Note that checking **Increase contrast** also checks the box next to **Reduce transparency**. To revert back to the OS X default, uncheck both boxes, starting with **Increase contrast**. Changes take effect immediately.

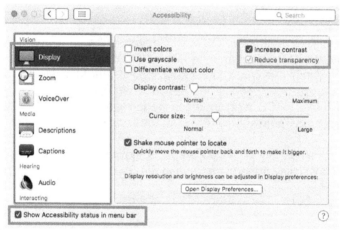

Compare the picture of the Accessibility preference pane above with the one shown in the last section. Note the darker border and text in the window's menu bar. With increase contrast enabled, the text appears sharper and darker and interface elements stand out more clearly from their gray backgrounds.

If you want the Accessibility Menu Extra to appear in the Menu Bar, check the box next to **Show Accessibility status in menu bar**.

Change the Font Smoothing Strength

If you have an older, non-retina Mac, you may have found that the OS X system font, San Francisco, appears blurry and is harder to read compared to older versions of OS X, which used Lucida Grande. Turning off LCD font smoothing in the **General** preference pane in System Preferences is not a good option as doing so makes the system font appear jagged and thinner. However, manually tweaking font smoothing can make subtle improvements in the appearance of San Francisco on your non-retina Mac.

To change the strength of font smoothing, launch the Terminal application and enter the following commands. Log out and log in for this change to take effect.

```
defaults -currentHost write -globalDomain AppleFontSmoothing -int 2
```

When you use the command above to change the font smoothing value, a – will appear next to **Use LCD font smoothing when available** in the **General** preference pane in the System Preferences app as shown below.

To revert back to the OS X default font smoothing strength, enter the following commands. Log out and log in for this change to take effect.

```
defaults -currentHost write -globalDomain AppleFontSmoothing -int 3
```

Changing the integer to 0 has the same effect as disabling LCD font smoothing in the General preference pane. Another valid entry is the integer 1, however, the difference between 1 and 2 is so subtle that it is almost impossible to discern.

Show the Desktop

Have you ever wanted to look at a pretty desktop picture only to find your desktop is cluttered with windows? OS X offers a number of methods to quickly clear the clutter to view your desktop wallpaper and put the clutter back when done.

If you configured the **Show Desktop** trackpad gesture, the quickest method to show the desktop is by spreading your thumb and three fingers on your trackpad. All open windows will be pushed off screen. Reverse the gesture to return the windows to their original locations. Pressing **fn F11** also clears the desktop. Note that you will have to hold down the **fn** (function) key while pressing **F11** as this key is normally used to lower the volume. Press **fn F11** to return the clutter.

A couple of other options are to hold down the ⌘ (command) key while pressing **F3,** which is normally used to launch Mission Control. Enter **⌘F3** again to return the windows to their original locations on the desktop.

Precisely Adjust the Display Brightness

Sometimes it seems you never can get the display brightness adjusted to your liking. One segment more is too much. One less is too little. Wouldn't it be awesome if you could adjust the display brightness in smaller increments? OS X El Capitan has a solution!

Holding down the ⇧ ⌥ keys (shift+option) while adjusting the display brightness allows you to precisely adjust the volume in quarter-segment increments. This trick also works when adjusting the volume and the brightness of the keyboard backlight.

Remove the Sleep, Restart, & Shutdown Buttons from the Login Screen

At the bottom of the login screen are three buttons – **Sleep**, **Restart**, and **Shut Down**. OS X lets you remove these buttons if you do not want them on your login screen. Removing these buttons leaves you with one and only one option on the login screen – to log in.

To remove the Sleep, Restart, and Shut Down buttons from the login screen, open the **Users & Groups** preference pane in the System Preferences application. Next, unlock the preference pane by clicking on the padlock in the lower left corner, if locked. Enter your password when challenged. Select **Login Options** at the bottom left.

Uncheck the checkbox next to **Show the Sleep, Restart, and Shut Down buttons**. To put the buttons back on your Mac's login screen, check this checkbox.

4

Mission Control

 Mission Control is the OS X feature that provides a view of everything on your Mac – application windows, Full Screen apps, Split View apps, Desktop Spaces, and the Dashboard. It allows you to quickly jump to another Desktop, Full Screen app, apps running in Split View mode, an app running in another space, or to the Dashboard. Mission Control also allows you to move windows to other Desktops and create, rearrange, and delete Desktops.

To open **Mission Control** use the trackpad gesture (swipe up with either 3 or 4 fingers), launch it from **Launchpad**, launch it from **Spotlight**, press the **F3** key, or enter **^up** (control+up arrow).

Mission Control and its elements are shown in the picture. For the El Capitan release, Apple made a slight cosmetic change to Mission Control. Instead of displaying a ribbon of desktop thumbnails as in Yosemite, the ribbon at the top of the Mission Control screen simply lists the active Desktops by name. Only when you move your cursor into the ribbon do the Desktops and Full Screen apps expand into thumbnails as shown on the next page.

The ribbon lists four Desktop Spaces, numbered Desktop 1 to 4 from left to right, and iTunes, which I have expanded to a Full Screen application. Each Desktop Space is a virtual desktop, created using the **Spaces** feature, and each one can have one or more application windows assigned to it. The Spaces feature is a nifty way of increasing desktop real estate to accommodate more windows. Spaces are covered in the next section.

You can rearrange the order of the Desktops by clicking, dragging, and dropping them. Any Desktop, Full Screen application, Split view apps, or the Dashboard can be rearranged. El Capitan will renumber the desktops accordingly as you rearrange them. Desktops will always be numbered from left to right starting from Desktop 1 at the left.

Navigating between the desktops, Full Screen apps, Split View apps, and the Dashboard in Mission Control is done by swiping either three or four fingers to the left or right on the trackpad. If you are using a Magic Mouse, swiping left or right with either one or two fingers will navigate between the Desktops. You can also hold down the ^ (control) key and press the left or right arrow to navigate. Clicking on any thumbnail in the ribbon makes it active, bringing it, and the applications which are assigned to it, to the front.

The Dock appears at the bottom of Mission Control, letting you launch applications into the active Desktop, which is highlighted by a blue border in the ribbon at the top of your screen. If you try to launch an application while viewing a Full Screen app in Mission Control, the app will open in Desktop 1.

Add More Desktop Space

Desktop clutter can be a real productivity killer. If you have ever opened lots of applications on your Mac, you know how hard it is to sift through all of the windows looking for a particular one. If you only had more Desktop space, your Desktop would not be so cluttered and life would be so much easier. OS X granted your wish. You can add more desktop space with an OS X feature called **Spaces**.

Spaces is a feature of **Mission Control** that allows you to create virtual desktops. These virtual desktops add more desktop real estate for application windows. Using Spaces, you can create additional Desktops, each containing a unique application or set of applications. Multiple Desktops remove clutter by allowing you to assign windows to separate Desktops instead of piling all the windows onto your main desktop. For example, let's say you were writing a book on customizing OS X using Microsoft Word, you can run Word on Desktop 1, and create separate Desktop Spaces for iTunes, Mail, and Safari – effectively quadrupling your desktop real estate! Spaces is so flexible that windows from the same application can even be split between different Desktops.

Mission Control is the command center for Spaces, allowing you to create new Desktops, see and manage your Desktops, and see which application windows are assigned to each one. To create a new Desktop Space, first open Mission Control by using the trackpad gesture, launching it from Launchpad or Spotlight, pressing the **F3** key, or by entering ^**up** (control+up arrow).

If you have never created a Desktop Space, the ribbon at the top of Mission Control will show only your main desktop, called **Desktop 1**. Creating a new Desktop Space is as simple as moving your cursor to the + (plus) sign at the far right edge of the Mission Control ribbon. When your cursor reaches the + sign, it will expand to reveal a partial Desktop containing a gray +. Clicking this partial desktop or the + creates a new virtual desktop.

OS X El Capitan will allow you to create up to 16 Desktop Spaces, numbered sequentially from left to right starting with **Desktop 1**.

The picture above shows 4 Desktops, numbered 1 through 4, in the Mission Control ribbon. iTunes is running in Full Screen mode between Desktops 3 and 4. Microsoft Word and Safari are running in Split View mode between Desktops 1 and 2. The Dashboard is disabled by default, and is therefore not shown. Did you notice anything about the spaces in the picture? Each Desktop can have its own desktop wallpaper.

Remove a Desktop Space

Removing a desktop space is done in **Mission Control**. Hover your cursor over the desktop you want to remove in the top ribbon. An **X** will appear in the upper left corner of the Desktop thumbnail. Click the **X** and OS X will remove the space. Any application windows located in the deleted Desktop will be reassigned to the desktop in the foreground.

Any Desktop Space with the exception of the Dashboard, Full Screen applications and Split View apps can be deleted in Mission Control. Full Screen and Split View apps are not deleted, but you can use Mission Control to take an app out of Full Screen or Split View mode. Hover your cursor over a Full Screen app or Split View apps in the Mission Control ribbon and a two arrows will appear in the upper left corner. Click on the arrows and the app will exit Full Screen mode and move to the next available Desktop to the left. The Dashboard cannot be deleted, but you can disable it in System Preferences.

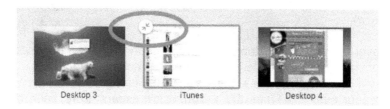

Another method to remove a desktop is to move your cursor into the Mission Control ribbon and hold down the ⌥ (option) key. An **X** will appear in the upper left hand corner of every Desktop. Remove Desktop Spaces by clicking on the **X** while keeping the ⌥ (option) key depressed. Full Screen and Split View apps will display two arrows, allowing you to exit Full Screen or Split View mode. Release the ⌥ key when finished.

Take an App to Full Screen Mode in Mission Control

Apple introduced Full Screen mode in OS X Lion and has tweaked this feature in every release since then. You can take any window to Full Screen mode by clicking the green button in the window's Title Bar. Or you can take an app to Full Screen in Mission Control.

Activate Mission Control and navigate to the Desktop with the app you want to make Full Screen. Drag the window onto the Mission Control ribbon either between two Desktops or to the end of the Desktop ribbon. A new Desktop Space will appear with a **+** (plus) sign as shown below. Drop the app onto this new Space to enter Full Screen mode.

Exit Full Screen Mode

You have several options to exit Full Screen mode. You can hover your cursor over a Full Screen app in the Mission Control ribbon and two arrows will appear in the upper left corner. Click on the arrows and the app will exit Full Screen mode and its window will move to the next available Desktop.

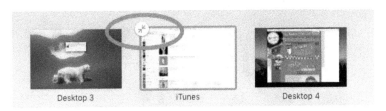

Desktop 3   iTunes   Desktop 4

A second method is make the app active and move your cursor to the top of your screen to reveal the Menu Bar and Title Bar controls. Click on the green button on the Title Bar to exit Full Screen mode and restore the window to its original size. If you click on the red button in the Title Bar, you will close the window. You can also press the **esc** (escape) key or enter **^⌘F** (control+command+F) to restore the window to its original size.

Use Split View to View 2 Apps Side by Side

A brand new feature in OS X El Capitan is the ability to quickly place two applications side by side on the same Desktop. While you could have done this with an add on application like BetterSnapTool in previous versions of OS X, El Capitan is the first release to provide this feature natively in the OS X operating system. Split View is a great feature when you need to compare two documents side by side or need to move information from one document to the other. There are two different methods to put two apps into Split View.

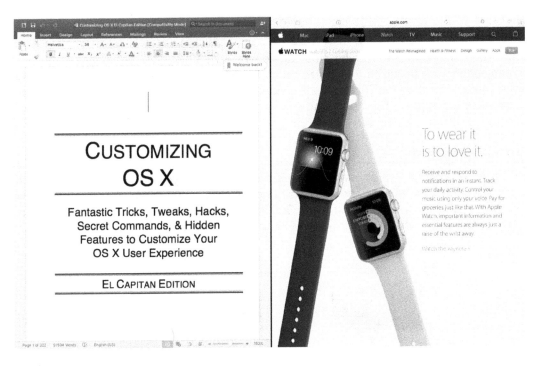

First, ensure that both application windows are in the same Desktop. Next, click and hold the green button in the first application's Title Bar. Release your hold and the window will snap to the left side of your desktop. If you want the window on the right half of the screen, drag it to the right side of the desktop before releasing your hold on the green button. Finally, click on the thumnail of the second application that you want to occupy the other half of your desktop. It will immediately snap into place.

The second method is to use Mission Control. The advantage of using Mission Control is that the application windows do not have to start out on the same Desktop. They can be in different Desktops or you can create an entirely new Desktop Space for your Split View.

If neither application window is running in Full Screen or Split View mode, open Mission Control and navigate to the desktop with the first application window by swiping left or right with three or four fingers. Drag the first window to an existing Desktop or create a new Desktop by dragging the window between two Desktops or to the the end of the Mission Control ribbon. Next, navigate to the Desktop with the second application window and drag and drop it onto the Desktop where you placed the first window. The occupied half of this Desktop will blur and the other half will have a **+** sign in it. Drop the app on the **+** sign.

If the first application is already running in Full Screen mode, simply drag and drop the second application window onto the **+** sign in the thumbnail containing the first app.

Resize Windows in Split View

Once your two apps are running side by side in Split View, you can adjust how much screen space each occupies. To resize an application window running in Split View mode, place your cursor in on the vertical black divider separating the two apps. A double headed black arrow will appear. Click and drag this arrow to resize the windows.

Exit Split View Mode

Similar to exiting Full Screen mode, there are several ways you can exit Split View mode and restore the application windows to their original sizes. You can hover your cursor over the Split View thumbnail in the Mission Control ribbon and two arrows will appear in the upper left corner. Click on the arrows and the apps will exit Split View mode.

Perhaps you don't want to restore both apps to their original sizes. You can restore the application window you no longer want in Split View mode to its original size while keeping the other window in Full Screen mode. Move your cursor to the top of your screen to reveal the Menu Bar and Title Bar controls. Click on the green button on the Title Bar of the app you no longer want in Split View. The other app window will restore to Full Screen mode.

Another option is to make the app you no longer want in Split View mode active and press the **esc** (escape) key or enter **^⌘F** (control+command+F). The other app window will restore to Full Screen mode.

View Desktop Spaces without Activating Them

If you want to see which windows are assigned to a particular Desktop without making it active, hold down the ⌥ (option) key and click on the desired Desktop on the Mission Control ribbon. OS X will switch to that Desktop without making it active, letting you see its application windows. When you want to make the Desktop active, simply release the ⌥ (option) key and click on the Desktop.

Turn Off Automatic Space Rearrangement

After working with Desktop Spaces for a while you may notice something odd. Your Desktops seem to automatically rearrange themselves. No, your Mac is not haunted by gremlins and you're not losing your mind. OS X rearranges desktops based on their most recent use. Therefore, Desktop 4 can work its way up to become Desktop 2 if the applications on Desktop 4 are used more recently than the applications on Desktops 2 and 3. If you find this behavior confusing or disturbing, OS X allows you to disable it.

To disable automatic Desktop Space rearrangement, open the **Mission Control** preference pane in the System Preferences application. Uncheck the box next to **Automatically rearrange Spaces based on most recent use**.

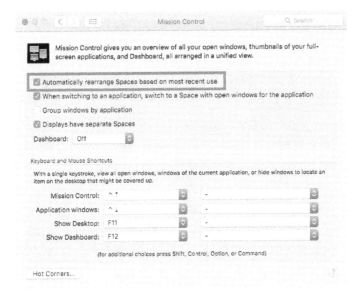

Disable Separate Spaces on other Displays

OS X El Capitan allows you to have a separate, independent set of Desktop Spaces for each monitor in your system. In a dual-monitor set up, you can have up to 32 Desktops! If your Mac has multiple displays, this feature is enabled by default.

An added benefit to this feature is that each display has its own Menu Bar and Dock. Since the Menu Bar is available on all displays, you do not have to move your cursor back to the main display to access the Menu Bar or the Dock. This provides a more independent treatment of each display rather than other displays being merely extensions of the main display as they were in versions of OS X prior to 10.9 Mavericks.

If you wish to disable this feature and revert back to the behavior of earlier versions of OS X, open the **Mission Control** preference pane in the System Preferences application. Uncheck the box next to **Displays have separate spaces**. You will have to log out and log back in for the change to take effect.

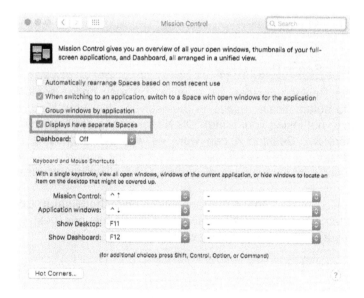

Note that if you disable Displays have separate spaces, you will no longer enjoy the benefit of each display having its own Menu Bar and Dock. They will only appear on the main display. To learn how to move the Menu Bar to another display, see Chapter 5.

To turn this feature back on, open the **Mission Control** preference pane and check the box next to **Displays have separate Spaces**. You will need to logout and log back in for the change to take effect.

Create Keyboard Shortcuts for Spaces

A handy method to quickly navigate between desktops is to set up keyboard shortcuts. Creating a keyboard shortcut for each Desktop Space allows you to jump between Desktops without swiping or using Mission Control. Keyboard shortcuts are by far the quickest way to jump between Desktop Spaces because you can move directly from Desktop 1 to Desktop 4 using a single keyboard shortcut.

To set up keyboard shortcuts, open the **Keyboard** preference pane in the System Preferences application. Next, select the **Shortcuts** tab if not already selected. Click on **Mission Control** in the left-hand column.

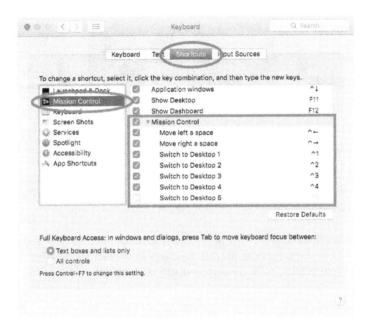

Scroll to the bottom of the right-hand column to see all of the **Switch to Desktop #** shortcuts. Two shortcuts are enabled by default, **^left** (control+left arrow) and **^right** (control+right arrow), which will move left or right, respectively. However, the **Switch to Desktop #** shortcuts are disabled. Check the checkboxes next to each of your desktops to enable the shortcuts. Once enabled, simply type the number of the desktop space you want to go to while holding down the **^** (control) key. OS X will immediately jump to that space.

Note that if you add more desktops, you will have to go back to the Keyboard preference pane to turn on the shortcuts for any newly created Desktops. Notice that **Switch to Desktop 5** is not checked in the picture above. I created Desktop 5 after checking the 4 other Switch to Desktop options and closing the Keyboard preference pane, therefore, its keyboard shortcut is disabled.

Move a Window to Another Desktop

An application window can be moved from one desktop space to another in **Mission Control** by dragging the window from the active Desktop dropping it onto its new destination desktop. In Mission Control, hover your cursor over an application window and it will become highlighted by a blue border. Next, drag and drop the window to your desired destination desktop space in the ribbon at the top of Mission Control.

You can move an application window to any desktop. Multiple application windows can be assigned to the same desktop space. Windows from the same application can be split across multiple desktop spaces. This is quite handy when working with two or more documents from the same application. The only restriction is that you cannot assign an application window to the Dashboard or to a Full Screen application. If you do drag and drop another application onto an application in Full Screen Mode, both apps will enter Split View mode.

Move All Windows of an Application to Another Desktop

Mission Control allows you to move individual application windows to another desktop space. But what if you have multiple windows open in a particular application and want to move all of them to another desktop? OS X has a solution for you.

If you wish to move all windows of an application to another Desktop space, first open the **Mission Control** preference pane in the System Preferences application. Ensure the checkbox next to **Group windows by application** is checked.

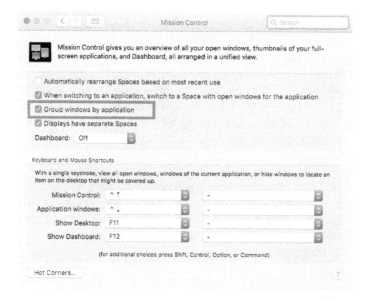

To move all of the windows of an application, open **Mission Control** using the trackpad gesture (swipe up with either 3 or 4 fingers), launch it from Launchpad or Spotlight, press the **F3** key, enter **^up** (control+up arrow), or launch it using the Mission Control icon in the Dock. Click, drag and drop the application's icon (shown below the application's windows) to the desired destination Desktop. All the windows will move as a group to your desired destination.

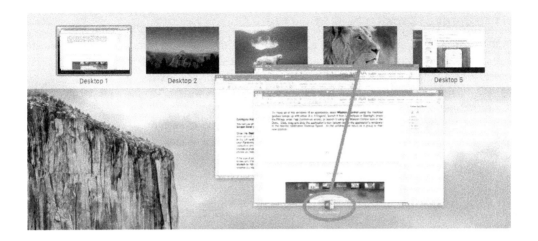

Move a Window & Create a New Desktop Space

You can move an application window and create a new Desktop for it at the same time. To move an application window and simultaneously create a new Desktop, open **Mission Control**. Hover your cursor over the application window you intend to move. The window will become highlighted by a blue border. Drag the window to the upper right corner of Mission Control onto the **Add Desktop Button** to simultaneously create a new desktop and assign the application window to it.

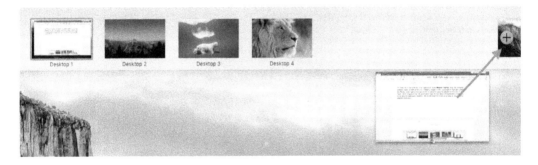

This particular move is sometimes difficult to do as OS X will often assume that you want to take the application to Full Screen Mode instead of simply moving it to a new Desktop without resizing. You'll often see the behavior shown in the picture below, which will take the application to Full Screen mode when you drop it. So this takes a little practice to get right. Otherwise, you can always create a new Desktop first and then drag and drop the application onto it. Using this method avoids inadvertently resizing the app to Full Screen.

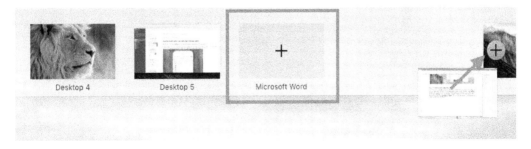

Navigate Between Desktop Spaces

Let's quit **Mission Control** so I can show you how to navigate between desktops without launching Mission Control. Navigating between desktops outside Mission Control is the same as navigating between them inside Mission Control. Swipe left or right with either three or four fingers on the trackpad. If you are using a Magic Mouse, swiping left or right with either one or two fingers will navigate between your desktops. You can also hold down the ^ (control) key and press the left or right arrow to move left or right through your Desktops, respectively. Switching to an application automatically switches your Desktop to the Desktop Space in which the app resides.

Drag an Application Window To Another Desktop

There are several methods to move an application window to another Desktop. You could use the methods described earlier to move a window via **Mission Control**. Another method is to drag the window over to the left or right edge of the desktop until the cursor reaches the edge of the screen and can no longer move any further. After a delay of a couple of seconds, OS X will move the window to the neighboring desktop.

Note that if you have multiple monitors, moving a window to the right or left edge of your desktop will move the application window to the other monitor. Depending on how you configured your displays in the **Display** preference pane determines the arrangement of the two monitors and whether your second monitor is to the left or right.

To configure the arrangement of your monitors, open the **Displays** preference pane in the System Preferences application.

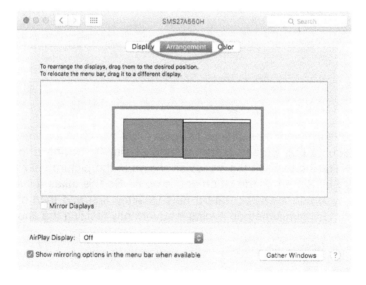

From the **Displays** preference pane, select **Arrangement**. Drag the displays shown in the center of the preference pane to your desired position. The Menu Bar can be relocated from one display to another by dragging and dropping it.

Remove the Drag Delay When Moving Windows between Spaces

If you move an application window between desktops by dragging it to the left or right edge of the desktop, you will notice a slight delay before OS X moves the window to the neighboring desktop. You can completely remove this delay by entering the following commands in Terminal.

```
defaults write com.apple.dock workspaces-edge-delay -float 0

killall Dock
```

Now you can move a window to the neighboring desktop space without the delay. However, I've found that without a delay, a window will fly across all the Desktops before I have a chance to drop it. So the delay we just eliminated was actually somewhat useful, albeit longer than necessary. The following commands will configure a ½ second delay, just long enough to prevent a window from flying out of control but shorter than the default.

```
defaults write com.apple.dock workspaces-edge-delay -float 0.5

killall Dock
```

Feel free to play with the decimal number after **-float** to adjust the delay to your personal preference.

To revert to the default OS X behavior, enter the following commands in **Terminal**.

```
defaults delete com.apple.dock workspaces-edge-delay

killall Dock
```

Assign an Application to a Desktop

If you really value organization, OS X El Capitan lets you assign an application to a specific Desktop and ensure it will always open in that Desktop. By assigning applications to desktops, you will insure certain applications appear on the desktop(s) of your choice. Another option is to create themed Desktop. For example, you can have one desktop for all of your social media applications, another for your productivity apps, another for browsers, etc. How you organize your apps is up to you.

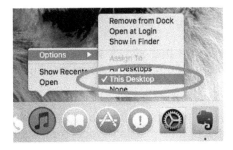

To assign an application to a specific desktop, first navigate to the desktop to which you want to assign the application. If you need to create a new desktop space, first launch

Mission Control and click the **Add Desktop Button**. Find the application in the **Dock**. If the application is not in the Dock, launch the application using **Launchpad** to make it appear in the Dock. Secondary click on the application icon in the Dock to reveal the **Options** submenu as shown above. By default, the **None** option is checked, which allows the application to be run on any desktop. To assign the app to the current desktop, select **This Desktop** from the submenu.

If your Mac has multiple displays, you can assign an app to a Desktop on a specific display. With two displays, the **Options** submenu will offer options for each display.

Assigning an application to a desktop does not prevent you from later moving that application to another desktop. Also, the application does not have to be added to the Dock. Once an application has been assigned to a Desktop, it will always appear on its assigned Desktop regardless of how it was launched.

Assign an Application to Every Desktop

OS X offers an option to assign an application to every desktop. This is a handy feature if you have an application you use frequently and desire quick access to it.

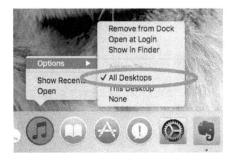

Find the application in the Dock. If the app is not in the Dock, launch it using Launchpad to make it appear in the Dock. Secondary click on the application icon in the Dock to reveal the **Options** submenu. To assign the app to every desktop, select **All Desktops**.

Toggle Mission Control On & Off

 There are many ways to launch **Mission Control**. You can launch it using a trackpad gesture, open it from Launchpad or Spotlight, press the **F3** key, or enter **^up** (control+up arrow).

OS X offers one more alternative that allows you to toggle Mission Control on and off. Press and hold the **F3** key to toggle Mission Control on. The moment you release the **F3** key, Mission Control will toggle off.

By the way, this trick also works with the **F4** key to toggle Dashboard or Launchpad on and off, depending on the age of your Mac and its keyboard configuration.

Speed Up Mission Control Animation

When opening **Mission Control**, OS X runs an animation that gradually shrinks your active desktop to about 66% of its normal size. When closing Mission Control, the animation runs in reverse. If you want this animation to run a little quicker, OS X offers a tweak to speed up the animation.

To speed up Mission Control's opening and closing animations, enter the following commands in Terminal. Be sure to press the **return** key after entering each line. This change takes effect immediately and will also change the **App Exposé** animation.

```
defaults write com.apple.dock expose-animation-duration -float 0.15

killall Dock
```

The number after **–float** is the amount of time in seconds the animation will run, so you can test various settings until the animation runs as quickly (or slowly) as you want it.

To revert back to the OS X default animation for Mission Control and App Exposé, enter the following commands. This change takes effect immediately.

```
defaults delete com.apple.dock expose-animation-duration

killall Dock
```

Disable Mission Control Animation

If you prefer to open and close Mission Control immediately without the animation, OS X provides a tweak to turn it off.

To disable Mission Control's opening and closing animations, enter the following commands in Terminal. Be sure to press the **return** key after entering each line. The change will take effect immediately and will also disable the **App Exposé** animation.

```
defaults write com.apple.dock expose-animation-duration -int 0

killall Dock
```

The number after **–int** is the amount of time in seconds the animation will run, so you can test various settings until the animation runs as quickly (or slowly) as you want it.

To revert back to the OS X default animation for Mission Control and App Exposé, enter the following commands. This change takes effect immediately.

```
defaults delete com.apple.dock expose-animation-duration

killall Dock
```

Assign a Hot Corner to Mission Control

The Hot Corners feature allows you to assign a specific action to each of the four corners of your desktop. The associated command is executed by moving your cursor to one of the corners. The supported commands include starting or disabling the screen saver, opening Mission Control, application windows (App Exposé), showing the Desktop, Dashboard, Notification Center, Launchpad, or putting the display to sleep.

To assign commands to Hot Corners, first open the **Mission Control** preference pane in the System Preferences application.

Next, click the **Hot Corners...** button at the lower left to reveal the **Active Screen Corners** drop-down sheet. Choose which corner you want to use to launch Mission Control. Click **OK** when finished, then close the Mission Control preference pane.

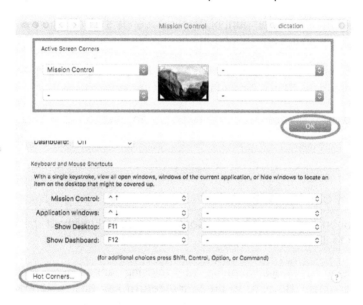

It may be advantageous to consider selecting the upper left or upper right screen corner to activate Mission Control. The reason for this is when using either of these corners, the ribbon will open immediately when Mission Control activates.

Once Mission Control has been assigned a Hot Corner, you can toggle Mission Control on and off by moving your cursor to the assigned corner of the desktop. Mission Control can also be closed by pressing the **esc** key or the **F3** key.

To turn off Hot Corners, open the **Mission Control** preference pane and click the **Hot Corners...** button in the lower left corner. Select the – from the **Active Screen Corners** drop-down sheet for each corner that you want to turn off.

To learn how to avoid accidentally triggering the Mission Control Hot Corner, see "Avoid Accidentally Triggering a Hot Corner" in Chapter 3. Hot corners can also be configured from the **Desktop & Screen Saver** preference pane.

Quick Look

When application windows are grouped in **Mission Control**, it is sometimes difficult to differentiate between them because they are grouped one on top of the other. This is especially true if you have a lot of windows open on the same desktop and are using a computer with a small screen like an 11-inch MacBook Air. The solution is **Quick Look**.

To see the contents of any window in Mission Control, hover over it with the cursor and when a blue border appears around the window, press the **spacebar**. Mission Control will zoom the highlighted window. To toggle the zoom off, press the spacebar again and the window will shrink back to its original size.

An alternative method to activate Quick Look is to scroll up with two fingers on the trackpad. First, hover your cursor over the window you are interested in seeing. When the window is highlighted with a blue border, scroll up using two fingers to activate Quick Look. Scroll down with two fingers to toggle Quick Look off.

Change the Quick Look Size

Notice the difference between the **Quick Look** sizes when using the spacebar versus scrolling up with two fingers. The two-finger scroll method yields a much smaller Quick Look size compared to the spacebar method. This tweak will allow you to increase the size of the two-finger scroll Quick Look preview. To make the windows expand to the same size as the spacebar method, launch Terminal and enter the following commands.

```
defaults write com.apple.dock expose-cluster-scale -float 1

killall Dock
```

If this is too big, you can change the numeric value after **-float** For example, using 0.5 makes the window expand larger than the default but not as large as the previous command. Try changing the numeric value after **-float** to find the size that works best.

```
defaults write com.apple.dock expose-cluster-scale -float 0.5

killall Dock
```

To revert to the default, enter the following commands.

```
defaults delete com.apple.dock expose-cluster-scale

killall Dock
```

Ungroup Application Windows in Mission Control

Mission Control will group windows from the same application for a cleaner display. However when windows are grouped together, the contents of the windows below the top window are difficult to see without using Quick Look. OS X offers an option to ungroup windows of the same application to make it easier to discern their contents without having to use Quick Look.

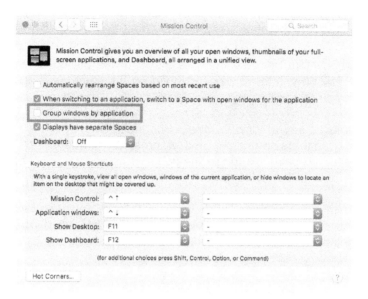

To ungroup application windows in **Mission Control**, open the **Mission Control** preference pane in the System Preferences application. Uncheck the checkbox next to **Group windows by application**. With this option unchecked, windows from the same application are displayed separately, making it easier to distinguish their contents without resorting to Quick Look.

Change the Keyboard Shortcut to Mission Control

The default keyboard shortcut to launch **Mission Control** is ^**up** (control+up arrow). If you want to create your own keyboard or mouse shortcut, the lower half of the **Mission Control** preference pane allows you to do so.

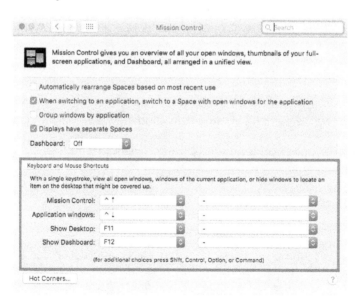

To change the keyboard shortcut or to create a mouse shortcut, open the **Mission Control** preference pane in the System Preferences application. Use the drop-down menu next to Mission Control under **Keyboard and Mouse Shortcuts** located in the lower half of the pane to select your desired keyboard shortcut. The right-hand column allows you to create a mouse shortcut. You can use the ⇧ ⌘ ^ ⌥ (shift, command, control, or option) keys alone or in combination as modifiers for both the keyboard and mouse shortcuts. OS X will even allow you to use any combination of two, three, or even all four of the modifier keys. Hold down the modifier key when selecting the shortcut from either drop-down list.

The bottom half of the preference pane also allows you to create or change keyboard and mouse shortcuts for **Application windows** (App Exposé), **Show Desktop**, or **Show Dashboard**.

App Exposé removes desktop clutter to reveal all the windows of a chosen application. To launch App Exposé, select an application with multiple open windows and enter ^**down** (control+down arrow). You can than select the desired window by pointing and clicking to make it active. App Exposé can also be executed with a trackpad gesture of swiping three or four fingers down.

Pressing **fn F11** clears the desktop of all open windows by pushing them off the edge of the screen. You have to hold down the **fn** (function) key while pressing **F11** since this key is used to lower the volume. Press **fn F11** again to restore the windows.

Pressing the **fn F12** key launches the Dashboard. You have to hold down the **fn** (function) key while pressing **F12** as this key is used to raise the volume. Note that on older keyboards the **F4** key launches the Dashboard, so you may find **fn F12** to be redundant. On newer keyboards, the **F4** key is used to open Launchpad.

To turn off any of the shortcuts, select the – option from the drop-down list.

Open Mission Control by Dragging a Window to the Top of the Screen

A new feature in OS X El Capitan is a handy shortcut that lets you simultaneously open Mission Control and drag a window to another desktop. Simply drag a window to the very top of your screen and continue dragging as if you were trying to push the window off the screen. Mission Control will launch almost immediately and its ribbon will open, allowing you to move the window to another Desktop or to take it to Full Screen or Split View mode.

5

Menu Bar

OS X El Capitan offers a number of customizations for the **Menu Bar** including changing its color and rearranging or deleting the Menu Extras in the **Status Menu**. There are two halves to the Menu Bar. The left half displays the **Apple** and **Application** menus while the right half, shown below, displays the **Status Menu**. Note that if you upgraded from a previous version of OS X or customized your Status Menu (as I did), it will look different than what is shown below.

The **Status Menu** displays the status of and provides quick access to various OS X features via small icons called **Menu Extras**. Menu Extras are also called menulets, menu items, or status items. **Menu Extras** are used to show the status of and to configure various OS X features and third party applications.

At the far right of the Menu Extras are icons for **Spotlight** and **Notification Center**. We will cover Spotlight and Notification Center in later chapters.

Enable Dark Mode

The **Menu Bar** is translucent by default, using white as its base color. This allows the colors of the desktop wallpaper to show through. In OS X Yosemite, Apple answered the call of many longtime Mac users who longed for a dark Menu Bar. Apple kept this feature in El Capitan. **Dark Mode** changes the base color of the Menu Bar, drop-down menus, Spotlight, and the Dock to black while still maintaining some translucency and the OS X layered 3D appearance. With Dark Mode enabled, the text changes to a higher contrast white against a dark background.

To enable Dark Mode, open the **General** preference pane in the System Preferences application. Next, check the checkbox next to **Use dark menu bar and Dock.**

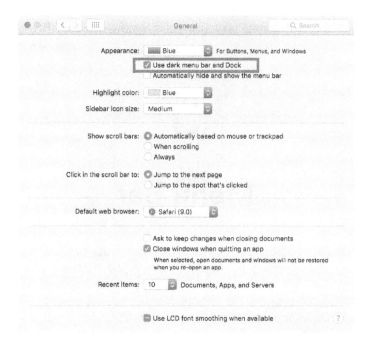

To keep with the general motif of El Capitan's Dark Mode, you may wish to also change the **Appearance** of buttons, menus, and windows as well as the **Highlight Color** from the default **Blue** to **Graphite**. These changes take effect immediately.

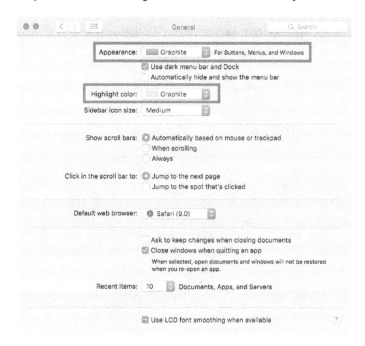

To return to the system default, uncheck **Use dark menu bar and Dock** in the **General** preference pane.

Enable the Hidden Keyboard Shortcut for Dark Mode

You can toggle **Dark Mode** on and off using a keyboard shortcut, which is disabled by default. To enable this hidden keyboard shortcut, launch the Terminal application and enter the following command. Do not press the **return** key until you have entered both lines.

```
sudo defaults write /Library/Preferences/.GlobalPreferences.plist
_HIEnableThemeSwitchHotKey -bool TRUE
```

Enter your administrator password when challenged. You will need to logout and log in to enable this keyboard shortcut.

The hidden keyboard shortcut is **^⌥ ⌘T** (control+option+command+T).

To return OS X to the default and disable this keyboard shortcut, enter the following command into Terminal. Do not press the return key until you have entered both lines.

```
sudo defaults write /Library/Preferences/.GlobalPreferences.plist
_HIEnableThemeSwitchHotKey -bool FALSE
```

Enter your administrator password when challenged. You will need to logout and log in for this change to take effect.

Add a Menu Bar to Each Display

In a multiple monitor setup, you have three options to configure the behavior of your displays. The first option is to treat each display independently, each with its own **Menu Bar**. Since the Menu Bar is available on all displays, you do not have to move the cursor back to the main display to access Menu Bar features. An added benefit of enabling this feature is that you can have a separate, independent set of Desktops for each monitor in your system. In a dual-monitor set up, you can have up to 32 Desktops!

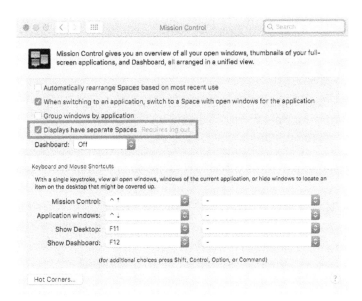

To add a Menu Bar to each display, open the **Mission Control** preference pane in the System Preferences application. Check the checkbox next to **Displays have separate Spaces**. You will need to logout and log in for the change to take effect. When you launch Mission Control you will now see an independent ribbon on each display showing the Desktops available for each display.

Relocate the Menu Bar to Another Display

Your second option is to treat your second monitor as an extension of your main display. First, ensure that the checkbox next to **Displays have separate Spaces** in the **Mission Control** preference pane is unchecked. If you need to uncheck the box, you will need to logout and log in for this change to take effect.

Next, you need to configure on which display the Menu Bar will appear. To relocate the Menu Bar to another display, open the **Displays** preference pane in the System Preferences application. Select the **Arrangement** tab if not already highlighted. Drag the Menu Bar, which is represented by a white bar at the top of one of the displays, to the desired display.

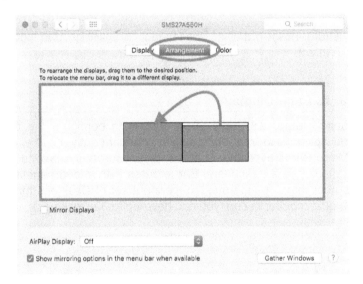

Mirror Displays

Your final option for a multiple monitor setup is to mirror the displays. Mirroring displays your Mac's video output on both monitors. This feature comes in handy when you need to project your display during a presentation. You will be able to see what the audience is seeing without having to turn around and look at the external monitor or projected image.

To mirror your displays, open the **Displays** preference pane in the System Preferences application. Select the **Arrangement** tab if not already highlighted. Check the checkbox next to **Mirror Displays**. Note how the representation of the displays at the center of the preference pane changes when mirroring is enabled. This change takes effect immediately.

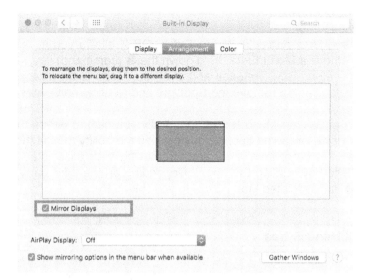

Your Mac will attempt to match the closest resolution between the primary and secondary displays when mirroring.

If you ever need to quickly mirror your Mac's display, you can toggle mirroring on and off with the keyboard shortcut ⌘**F1** (command+F1). This keyboard shortcut works with any external monitor, projector, or display connected through AirPlay.

Rearrange the Menu Extras

The **Menu Extras** in the **Status Menu** are displayed generally in the order in which they started. If you launch a new third party application that provides a Menu Extra, it will appear at the far left of the Status Menu. Not all applications have an associated Menu Extra. Native OS X Menu Extras will display on the right half of the Status Menu, while third party Menu Extras appear on the left.

Third Party Menu Extras   Native OS X Menu Extras

If you don't like the order of the Menu Extras, OS X allows you to move them by holding down the ⌘ (command) key while dragging them to a new location on the Status Bar. The selected Menu Extra will turn gray while you are dragging it. Move it left or right to your desired location. Other Menu Extras will politely move out of the way to make room. Note that you can only reorder the Menu Extras within the Status Bar. You cannot relocate a Menu Extra to the left side of the Menu Bar as it is reserved for the Apple and Application Menus.

With the exception of the Spotlight and Notification Center Menu Extras, you can rearrange any of the native OS X Menu Extras. Unfortunately, many third party applications stubbornly refuse to let you rearrange their associated Menu Extra.

Take care not to drag a Menu Extra off the Menu Bar as you will accidentally remove it.

Remove a Menu Extra

If you have no need for a particular **Menu Extra**, OS X allows you to remove it from the **Status Bar**. To remove a Menu Extra, hold down the ⌘ (command) key while dragging the Menu Extra off the Menu Bar. Release and poof, the Menu Extra disappears in a puff of smoke! Note that you cannot remove the Spotlight and Notification Center Menu Extras.

As for third party application Menu Extras, generally you cannot delete them using the ⌘ (command) key. However, some applications provide the ability to hide their Menu Extra in their preferences. For other third party apps, removing their associated Menu Extra can only be accomplished by quitting the app. Depending on the third party application, you may be stuck with its associated Menu Extra in your Menu Bar.

Add Native OS X Menu Extras

You can add Native OS X **Menu Extras** to the Menu Bar by checking the checkbox in the associated preference pane in System Preferences. Another option is to open the Menu Extras folder and select the Menu Extra you want to add.

Launch **Finder** and press ⇧⌘G (shift+command+G) to display the **Go to the folder** dialog box. Enter the following into the field and click **Go**. All Native OS X Menu Extras supplied by Apple are located in this folder:

`/System/Library/CoreServices/Menu Extras`

Find the Menu Extra you wish to add and double-click to add it. Note that third party application Menu Extras are added when the application is installed, launched, or by checking an option in the application specific preferences. These Menu Extras will appear in your Menu Bar while the third party application in running.

Hide the Menu Bar

A new feature in OS X El Capitan allows you to automatically hide the Menu Bar when it is not in use. Hiding the Menu Bar off screen provides more desktop real estate and less distractions. And when combined with the Dock auto hide feature I'll show you in the next chapter, you'll be simply amazed at the amount of clean, uncluttered desktop real estate these two features provide. See the section "Hide the Dock" in the next chapter to learn how to automatically hide the Dock.

Menu Bar auto hiding is disabled by default. To enable Menu Bar auto hiding, open the **General** preference pane in the System Preferences application. Check the checkbox next to **Automatically hide and show the menu bar**.

With this feature enabled all you need to do to unhide the Menu Bar is to move your cursor to the top of the screen and leave it there for a moment. The Menu Bar bar will automatically appear and then disappear when no longer needed.

To return to the OS X default and disable Menu Bar auto hiding, open the **General** preference pane and uncheck the checkbox next to **Automatically hide and show the menu bar**.

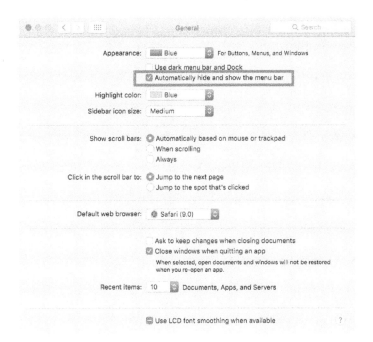

Customize the Date and Time

By default, the **Date & Time Menu Extra** displays the the day of the week and current time. Its drop-down menu lets you switch between an analog or digital clock. When the clock is configured as analog, a tiny clock is displayed in the Menu Bar. Clicking it reveals the drop-down menu which displays the day of the week, date, and time in hours, minutes, and seconds. When the clock is configured as digital, the drop-down shows the day of the week and the date.

The Menu Extra also provides direct access to the **Date & Time** preference pane in System Preferences where the remaining configuration options are located. Selecting **Open Date and Time Preferences...** takes you directly to the **Clock** pane of the **Date & Time** preference pane.

If you don't want to see the date and time in your Menu Bar, you can remove them entirely by unchecking the checkbox next to **Show date and time in the menu bar**.

If you decide to keep the date and time, it does not have to look like the OS X El Capitan standard clock. You have the option of separately configuring how the time and date are displayed. The time can be shown in either analog or digital format. If you select digital, you have 3 additional configuration options. The time can be displayed with or without seconds. The colons separating hours, minutes, and seconds can be set to flash on and off. And you have the option of displaying a 12-hour or 24-hour clock. If you select the 12-hour option, you can choose whether to show AM and PM. Check the checkboxes next to the options you wish to configure. If you select the analog clock you are prevented from configuring any additional options as they are all grayed out.

For the date, you have the option of showing the day of the week in addition to displaying the date.

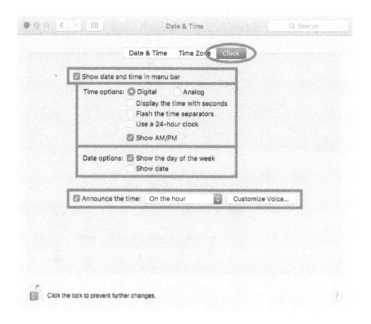

You can also configure OS X to announce the time on the quarter, half, or hour by checking the checkbox next to **Announce the time**. Choose how often you want the time announced from the drop-down menu and then click **Customize Voice...** to access the voice sheet to select the voice you wish to use.

Connect to WiFi with the AirPort Menu Extra

The **AirPort Menu Extra** allows you to turn Wi-Fi connectivity on and off, connect to a Wi-Fi network, create Wi-Fi networks, or open the Network preference pane. From the AirPort Menu Extra you can connect to any of the Wi-Fi networks listed, which are shown with their relative signal strengths. The more dark lines radiating outward, the stronger the Wi-Fi signal is. If your smartphone supports a Wi-Fi hotspot, you'll see it listed here.

A small padlock next to the network name indicates a password is needed to join this Wi-Fi network. Public Wi-Fi networks which are open for anyone to connect to are denoted by the lack of this padlock. Note that public Wi-Fi networks transmit data without any encryption. Therefore, the data you transmit and receive can be seen by others running packet analyzer software.

The bottom section of the drop-down menu allows you to join other Wi-Fi networks that are not listed as available networks. You can use the **Join Other Network...** option to connect to a network which is hidden (i.e., not broadcasting its network name). A dialog box will appear where you can enter the network name and choose from 6 security options. Once you have selected the security, the dialog box asks you to enter the network password. Checking the **Remember this network** checkbox tells OS X to remember this Wi-Fi network, allowing you to connect again without entering the password. Clicking the **Show Networks** button displays the available Wi-Fi networks to which you can connect. Click **Join** when finished.

You can open the **Network** preference pane in the System Preferences application by choosing **Open Network Preferences...** from the AirPort Menu Extra drop-down menu. This preference pane allows you to turn Wi-Fi off and on and connect to a network. Clicking the **Advanced** button allows you to see, reorder, and remove the Wi-Fi networks your Mac has previously joined. Drag and drop the Network Name to rearrange your preferred networks. It is best to have the networks you join most frequently at the top of the list. To remove a Wi-Fi network, highlight it and click the – button.

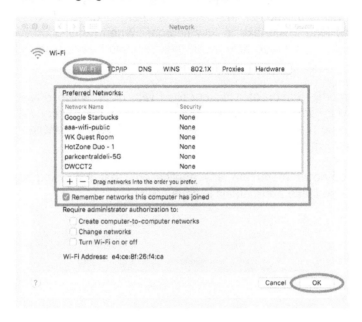

OS X will remember the Wi-Fi networks your Mac has joined and will add them to the Preferred Networks list. Unchecking the checkbox next to **Remember networks this computer has joined** will disable this feature.

Hold Down the Option Key with the AirPort Menu Extra

Holding down the ⌥ (option) key while clicking on the **AirPort Menu Extra** provides additional Wi-Fi information that can be used to troubleshoot any connectivity issues.

Two diagnostic options are available which are helpful when you are trying to troubleshoot Wi-Fi connectivity problems. **Create Diagnostics Report On Desktop...** will do just that, create a diagnostics report in your Desktop folder for use by Apple technicians to troubleshoot Wi-Fi problems. **Open Wireless Diagnostics...** launches an application that will detect common Wi-Fi problems.

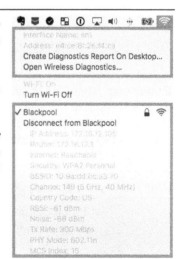

Change How Battery Power is Displayed

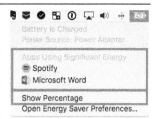

If you're working on a MacBook, MacBook Air, or MacBook Pro, you will want to keep the **Battery Menu Extra** in your Menu Bar so you can keep an eye on how much power your battery has left. The information displayed by the Battery Menu Extra depends on whether your laptop is plugged into AC power or is running on battery. When plugged into AC power, the Battery Menu Extra will tell you whether the battery is charged or is charging and how long it will take to fully charge. When running on battery power, the Battery Menu Extra will tell you how much time remains before your battery runs out of power.

OS X shows a representation of a battery filled with black which drains as your battery power drains. When your battery is almost out of power, the battery will turn red. If you want a more precise reading a battery power, select **Show Percentage** from the Battery Menu Extra drop-down menu.

Listed in the drop-down menu are any applications that are using significant energy, allowing you to close these applications to save power.

If you're not interested in seeing how much power your battery has left you can remove the Battery Menu Extra. Select **Open Energy Saver Preferences...** from the drop-down menu to open the **Energy Saver** preference pane in System Preferences. Uncheck the checkbox next to **Show battery status in menu bar**.

Pair Bluetooth Devices with the Bluetooth Menu Extra

Bluetooth is a short range wireless technology that lets you pair headsets, smartphones, printers, cameras, tablets, keyboards, a mouse, and a trackpad to your Mac. The **Bluetooth Menu Extra**, lets you turn Bluetooth on and off, pair your Mac with a Bluetooth device, send or browse files on a paired device, and open the **Bluetooth** preference pane.

The Bluetooth Menu Extra lists devices paired with your Mac. If the name of the device is bold, it indicates the device is currently connected. Hovering over any of the connected devices with your cursor allows you to disconnect the device, see its battery level, or open its associated preference pane in System Preferences.

To send files or browse files on paired Bluetooth devices which support file storage, launch the OS X **Bluetooth File Exchange** application from the Launchpad.

Selecting **Open Bluetooth Preferences...** opens the **Bluetooth** preference pane in System Preferences. From here you can turn Bluetooth off and on, pair Bluetooth devices, and connect and disconnect paired devices. When the checkbox at the bottom of the pane is checked, the Bluetooth Menu Extra will appear in the Menu Bar.

Holding down the ^ (control) key while clicking any device listed will display a submenu allowing you to disconnect, rename, or remove the device. The submenu also displays the address of the Bluetooth device.

Clicking the **Advanced...** button at the lower right of the preference pane displays a drop-down sheet with options to run the **Bluetooth Setup Assistant** if a keyboard, mouse, or trackpad is not detected. You can also configure Bluetooth devices to wake your Mac from sleep.

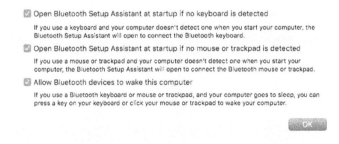

Hold Down the Option Key with the Bluetooth Menu Extra

Holding down the ⌥ (option) key while clicking on the **Bluetooth Menu Extra** provides an option to **Create Diagnostic Report on the Desktop...** which helps Apple troubleshoot any Bluetooth issues on your Mac.

Highlighting any of the paired devices will display a secondary menu allowing you to connect or disconnect it, remove it, see its signal strength, address, battery level, or open its associated preference pane in System Preferences.

Switch Users Fast with the Fast User Switching Menu Extra

The **Fast User Switching Menu Extra** appears immediately to the left of Spotlight. It lets you "fast switch" between users on your Mac. It also provides access to two other features – the **Login Window...** and the **Users & Groups** preference pane. If you have multiple users configured in the User & Groups preference pane, the users are listed in the drop-down menu with the current user grayed out. The Fast User Switching feature allows you to quickly switch to one of the other users.

Selecting **Login Window...** will lock your Mac without logging you out. Selecting **Users & Groups Preferences...** will take you to the **Users & Groups** preference pane where you can add or remove users, change your password and profile picture, enable parental controls, and choose login items.

This Menu Extra can be enabled and disabled from the User & Groups preference pane. Select **Users & Groups Preferences...** or launch System Preferences and choose the **Users & Groups** preference pane. Next, unlock the preference pane by clicking on the padlock in the lower left corner, if locked. Enter your password when challenged. Select **Login Options** at the bottom left.

To enable the Fast User Switching Menu Extra, check the checkbox next to **Show fast user switching menu as**. OS X offers 3 display choices for this Menu Extra: **Full Name**, **Account Name**, or **Icon**.

To disable the Fast User Switching Menu Extra and remove it from the Menu Bar, uncheck the checkbox next to **Show fast user switching menu as**.

Volume Menu Extra

The **Volume Menu Extra** is rather simple. It provides only one control, allowing you to change the volume. Use the slider to adjust the volume up or down.

Only when you hold down the ⌥ (option) key does the Volume Menu Extra become interesting. Clicking on the Volume Menu Extra while holding the ⌥ (option) key displays all of your audio input and output devices including any AirPlay devices. This allows you to quickly switch between any input or output device.

To add the Volume Menu Extra to the Menu Bar, open the **Sound** preference pane in the System Preferences application. Check the checkbox next to **Show volume in menu bar** at the bottom of the Sound preference pane.

Mirror your Display to an AppleTV with the AirPlay Menu Extra

If you own an Apple TV, the **AirPlay Mirroring Menu Extra** lets you send video from your Mac to your Apple TV. **AirPlay** only works on Macs manufactured beginning in 2011. If your Mac does not support AirPlay, you will not see the AirPlay Mirroring Menu Extra.

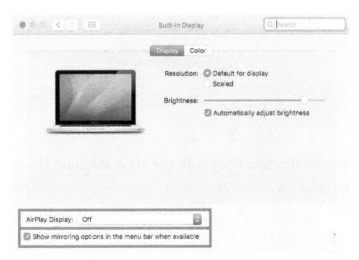

If you select **Open Displays Preferences…**, you will open the **Displays** preference pane in System Preferences. Unchecking the checkbox next to **Show mirroring options in the**

menu bar when available in the lower left corner of the pane removes the Airplay Menu Extra from the Status Bar.

Send an iMessage with the Messages Menu Extra

The **Messages Menu Extra** allows you to send a new message and to change your current status. The Messages Menu Extra is added to the Menu Bar using the Messages preference pane.

To add the Messages Menu Extra to the Menu Bar, launch the **Messages** application. Next, open the Messages preferences from the **Messages** menu by selecting **Messages > Preferences...** or by entering ⌘, (command+comma). Click the **General** tab if not already selected. Check the checkbox next to **Show status in menu bar** under **Account status** to add the Menu Extra to the Menu Bar. Unchecking this checkbox removes the Menu Extra from the Menu Bar.

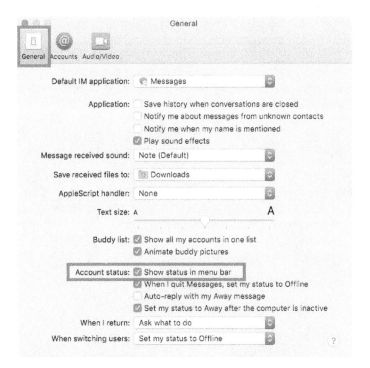

Backup your Data or Restore Files with the Time Machine Menu Extra

 Time Machine is the OS X backup utility which automatically backs up your entire Mac, including all system files, applications, accounts, preferences, email messages, music, photos, movies, and documents to an external drive or AirPort Time Capsule. Not only does Time Machine back up everything, it also remembers how your Mac looked on any given day in the past.

The **Time Machine Menu Extra** tells you when and to where Time Machine last backed up your Mac. By selecting **Back Up Now** you can immediately initiate a backup. To restore any lost

files, select **Enter Time Machine**, find the file(s), and restore them.

Selecting **Open Time Machine Preferences...** will open the **Time Machine** preference pane in System Preferences. This preference pane lets you turn **Time Machine** off and on, see the day and time of the last back up, and add or remove back up destinations.

At the bottom of the Time Machine preference pane is a checkbox next to **Show Time Machine in menu bar**. Checking this box will place the Time Machine Menu Extra on your Menu Bar.

Manage your Clipboard History

 The OS X clipboard saves only one item at a time, so when you copy a new item, the clipboard wipes the previously copied entry. A clipboard history manager is a must have third party utility. Instead of copying and pasting one item at a time, a clipboard manager saves your clipboard history, allowing you to find, copy, and paste a previously copied item.

Clipboard Guru is a simple and efficient clipboard manager that keeps your clipboard history in a handy Menu Extra on the Menu Bar. Simply pick the desired item from Clipboard Guru's drop-down menu and paste it. Clipboard Guru lets you choose from one of three pre-defined shortcuts – ^⌘V, ⇧⌘V, or ⌥⌘V, which pop the Clipboard Guru menu onto the currently active application. This allows you to access your clipboard history without having to use the Menu Bar.

Clipboard Guru is available from the Mac App Store for 99¢ at the time of this writing at: https://itunes.apple.com/us/app/clipboard-guru-history-snippet/id804607288?mt=12.

Change the Display Resolution from the Menu Bar

 Prior to the Mountain Lion release of OS X, you could change your display's resolution directly from the Menu Bar. If you need to change your resolution in El Capitan, you have to open the **Displays** preference pane in System Preferences. A nifty little app called **Display Menu** lets you change the resolution on any display connected to your Mac including the built-in display of a MacBook, MacBook Air, or MacBook Pro.

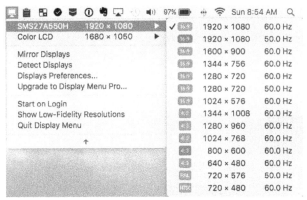

For most users, you'll want to keep your Mac's display at its optimal resolution. However, the ability to quickly and easily change the display resolution is important to parents who have young children or people who are visually impaired.

Display Menu also lets you quickly enable or disable display mirroring and access the **Displays** preference pane in the System Preferences application.

Display Menu is available from the Mac App Store for free at the time of this writing at: https://itunes.apple.com/us/app/display-menu/id549083868?mt=12.

Access Finder from the Menu Bar

 If you want super quick and easy access to your Home folder, XMenu is a free app that will put a drop-down Finder menu on your Menu Bar. XMenu offers numerous configuration options that allow you access to your Application, Home, Documents, and Developer folders directly from the Menu Bar.

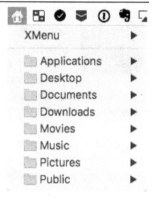

When run for the first time, XMenu places only your Application folder in the Menu Bar. To add additional folders, you'll need to open XMenu's preference pane by selecting **XMenu > Preferences...** from the XMenu's Menu Extra. From the preference pane you can configure which folders you want in your Menu Bar by checking the checkbox next to each.

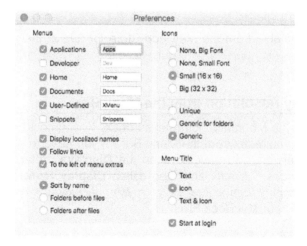

XMenu features a user-defined option so you can add specific folders, apps, or documents to the Menu Bar. Check the checkbox next to **User-Defined**. Next, launch Finder and open your Home directory. While holding down the ⌥ (option) key, select **Go > Library** from the Finder menu. Browse to the following directory:

```
/Library/Application Support/XMenu/Custom
```

Drag and drop aliases of your files, folders, and apps that you want to quickly access into this directory and they will appear in XMenu on your Menu Bar.

Xmenu places itself next to Notification Center, but you can choose to move it to the left so it can join your other third party Menu Extras. XMenu features numerous configuration options in its preferences that allow you to select the font and icon sizes, the display order, and its Menu title. If you want XMenu to be available when you start your Mac, check the checkbox next to **Start at login**.

XMenu is available from the Mac App Store for free at the time of this writing at: https://itunes.apple.com/us/app/xmenu/id419332741?mt=12.

Control iTunes from the Menu Bar

BarTunes lets you control iTunes from the Menu Bar. It has the usual features you would expect, it displays the song currently playing and allows you to play/pause, skip to the next song, go back to the previous song, and rate songs. BarTunes can display album artwork in the Menu Bar, but I found this too tiny.

A nice feature is the ability to add back, play/pause, and skip controls directly on the Menu Bar. Select **Open at login** from the BarTunes drop-down menu if you want BarTunes available each time you start your Mac.

BarTunes is available from the Mac App Store for free at the time of this writing at: https://itunes.apple.com/us/app/bartunes-menu-bar-controller/id444425546?mt=12.

Manage your Screenshots

If you take tons of screenshots, you need Quickshot, a screenshot manager that helps you keep track of your screenshots. All of your screenshots are accessible from the Menu Bar via Quickshot's Menu Extra. Screenshots can be dragged from Quickshot and dropped into a document.

Quickshot is available from the Mac App Store for $1.99, but was on sale for 99¢ at the time of this writing at: https://itunes.apple.com/us/app/quickshot-menubar-screenshot/id965442961?mt=12&ign-mpt=uo%3D4.

Monitor Battery Status

Battery Monitor does just what its name implies, letting you access and monitor information about your MacBook's, MacBook Air's, or MacBook Pro's battery from the Menu Bar. Battery Monitor also includes a widget for the Notification Center and is the same app I recommend in Chapter 9. Battery Monitor displays the current charge level, time remaining, the cycle count, and battery capacity and current charge in mAh. Battery Monitor was available for free in the Mac App Store at the time of this writing at: https://itunes.apple.com/us/app/battery-monitor-health-status/id836505650?mt=12.

Take Control of Spotify

Amplify is an application that lets you take better control of Spotify. It features a Menu Extra that displays the current song being played, lets you skip, go back, play/pause, shuffle, and control the volume. You can see the album artwork for the current song and can enable desktop notifications in the form of Banners. Amplify lets you customize your own keyboard shortcuts to control playback. Amplify works with both free and premium Spotify accounts and is available for free at the Mac App Store at the time of this writing at: https://itunes.apple.com/us/app/amplify-for-spotify/id1025490895?mt=12.

6

Dock

Whether you are starting your Mac for the first or the thousandth time, the most iconic and recognizable feature of the OS X desktop is the **Dock**. The Dock is one of the most customizable features of OS X. By default, the Dock appears as a strip of application and folder icons at the bottom of the desktop. The Dock serves a twofold purpose, combining the functions of an application launcher and a taskbar to switch between running applications. The Dock is an ingenious feature of OS X that provides a convenient and speedy method to launch applications, open documents and folders, or switch between running applications with a single click of your trackpad or mouse.

Since the Dock operates as both an application launcher and switcher, applications that are running are denoted by a tiny black circle beneath their icon. Apps that are not permanently kept in the Dock will appear at the end of the strip of application icons when they are launched.

The **divider** is the vertical black line separating applications from Stacks, minimized windows, documents, and the trash can. Apps go to the left of the divider. Everything else goes on the right. Clicking the yellow button in the Title Bar of a window will minimize it to the right side of the Dock. Clicking on a minimized window on the right side of the Dock maximizes it, restoring it to its normal size before it was minimized.

Put Apps in Order

The first order of business in customizing the **Dock** is to put the application icons in the order in which you want to see them. This is easily accomplished by moving your cursor to the application icon you wish to move, clicking and holding, and immediately dragging it horizontally along the Dock to its new location. If you click and hold too long without moving the icon, a menu will appear and you won't be able to move the icon. In this case, click anywhere on the Desktop and try again. While you are moving the icon other icons will politely move out of its way. Once in its desired location, simply release your hold.

Remove Apps from the Dock

Once you have your application icons in the right order, the next step is to remove apps that you don't want to see in the **Dock**. Note that when you remove an application from the Dock, you are not removing it from your Mac. You only remove its alias from the Dock. The application remains safely in the **Applications** folder.

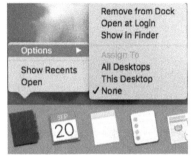

There are always multiple ways of doing things in OS X. It is your personal choice which method you prefer. You can always click and hold the icon you wish to remove until a contextual menu appears. You can also make this menu appear by using a secondary click, holding the control key down while clicking or by using the two-finger tap gesture. If two-finger tap doesn't work, it means you haven't yet customized the trackpad. Select **Options > Remove from Dock**.

An application that is running behaves differently. You can click and hold the icon or use a secondary click to make a contextual menu appear. Select **Options** and a submenu appears. Note the checkmark next to **Keep in Dock**. Select Keep in Dock to remove the checkmark. The menu will disappear along with the checkmark. Since the application is running, its icon will not disappear from the Dock until you quit it.

The fastest and easiest way to remove an app icon from the Dock is to drag it up past the middle of the desktop. About half way up the screen **Remove** will appear above the icon. Release the icon to remove it. If the app icon jumps back to the Dock, it means one of two things. Perhaps you didn't move it far enough away from the Dock. Be sure to move it far enough from the Dock until **Remove** appears above the application's icon. The other possibility is the app is running. If the app is running, it won't disappear until you quit it.

Oops! Everyone panics the first time they accidentally remove the wrong application icon from the Dock and see it disappear in a puff of smoke. Don't worry. This is an easy fix. Simply add the application back to the Dock. We'll cover how to do that next.

Add Apps to the Dock

Adding an application to the **Dock** is even easier than removing one. Of course, there are multiple ways to do so. The simplest method is to launch the application. Its icon will appear at the end of the strip of apps just to the left of the divider. Drag it to the left to its desired location. The simple act of moving an app icon to the left along the Dock is a signal to OS X that you want to keep the app in the Dock. Another method to add a running application's icon to the Dock is to use the secondary click to reveal a contextual menu. Select **Options > Keep in Dock** to put a checkmark next to **Keep in Dock**.

Another method is to open the **Applications** folder in Finder, select the application icon, and drag it to the Dock. Note that you are not moving the app. You are creating an alias on the Dock. Finally, you can add an application to the Dock using a keyboard shortcut. Select the desired application's icon from the **Applications** folder and enter the keyboard shortcut ⇧^⌘T (shift+control+command+T).

Control Application Behavior

The **Options** menu contains several options to control how an application behaves. Checking **Open at Login** opens the app immediately upon logging in to your Mac. This is handy if you have an application or set of applications you open every time you start your Mac. For example, if you always open Safari, Mail, and iTunes as soon as you login, setting these apps to open at login will save you from having to launch each one. Use the secondary click to make the **Options** menu appear and select **Open at Login**. A checkmark indicates the application will open when you login or start your Mac. If you no longer want an application to open when you log in, select **Options > Open at Login** to remove the checkmark.

If you want to see the folder where the application is located in Finder, choose **Show in Finder**. Normally this will immediately open the Applications folder with the application highlighted. However, occassionally applications are mistakenly installed in other folders. This is handy if you need to navigate to the application's location to move or uninstall it.

The **Assign To > This Desktop** feature allows you to assign an application to appear on a specific Desktop. This feature is handy if you prefer certain applications to always appear on specific desktops.

It is quite common to have more than one window open for the same application. As your desktop becomes crowded with open windows from multiple applications, it becomes increasingly difficult to find a specific window. This is especially true if you moved a window or two to another Desktop. The **Show All Windows** command executes a feature called **App Exposé**, which removes the desktop clutter to reveal all the windows of the chosen application regardless on which Desktop they reside. You can than select the desired window by pointing and clicking on it, making it active and placing it on top of all other windows. The App Exposé feature can also be executed with a trackpad gesture by swiping down with three or four fingers.

Finally, OS X will display the recent items in a list above the **Options** menu. This is a handy feature if you need to reopen a document you recently closed.

The Other Side of the Divider

The Dock's vertical black divider separates applications from Stacks, minimized windows, documents, and the trash can. The icon at the end of the Dock that looks like a translucent white trash can is the **Trash**, a temporary holding area for files you want to delete. You can move files to the Trash by dragging them onto its icon. Another option is to utilize a secondary click on a file in Finder to display a contextual menu and select **Move to Trash**.

Once items are in the Trash, the icon changes to display a full trash can. If you secondary click on the Trash when there are items in it, you have the option to **Empty Trash** or to display its contents in Finder with the **Open** command. The latter feature is handy if you accidentally drag a file into the trash and want to pull it back out. To restore a file you accidentally placed in the trash, secondary click on the file and select **Put Back** to return the file to its original location. Select **Empty Trash** to empty the trash can. A warning appears to confirm that you really want to empty the trash.

Delete a File Immediately from the Trash

A new feature Apple added to the El Capitan release of OS X is the ability to delete files immediately when they are in the Trash without deleting any of the other files located there.

To delete a file immediately from the Trash, first open the Trash by secondary clicking on its icon in the Dock and selecting **Open** from the contextual menu. The **Trash** Finder window will open. Highlight the file you want to delete and secondary click on it to reveal another contextual menu and select **Delete Immediately...**. You also can hold down the ⌥ (option) key while selecting **File > Delete Immediately...** or enter the keyboard shortcut ⌥⌘delete (option+command+delete). A dialog box will appear to confirm the deletion and warn you that this action cannot be undone. Click the **Delete** button to delete the file immediately or **Cancel**.

Note that the Delete Immediately option will only appear in the **File** menu when you are holding down the ⌥ (option) key. When the ⌥ (option) key is held down, **Put Back** will change to **Delete Immediately**.

Hide the Dock

Although the Dock is a very useful feature of OS X, it takes up a significant amount of real estate at the bottom of the desktop. This can sometimes be problematic when moving your cursor to the bottom of a window as the cursor will sometimes inadvertently interact with the Dock. OS X gives you the option of hiding the Dock when not in use. And when combined with the Menu Bar auto hide feature I showed you in the last chapter, you'll be simply amazed at the amount of clean, uncluttered desktop real estate these two features provide. See the section "Hide the Menu Bar" in the last chapter to learn how to automatically hide the Menu Bar.

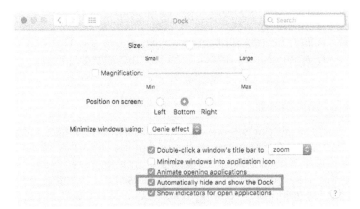

To turn Dock hiding on, open the Dock preference pane from System Preferences. Check the box next to **Automatically hide and show the Dock**. The change will take effect immediately.

The Dock will now slip beneath the bottom of your desktop when not in use. To make the Dock reappear, simply position your cursor at the bottom edge of the desktop or enter ⌥⌘D (option+command+D).

Hiding can also be enabled from the Dock itself. Position your cursor over the Dock divider. When the cursor turns into a two-headed vertical white arrow, use a secondary click to open the Dock contextual menu. Select **Turn Hiding On**. To turn hiding off, secondary click the divider to open the Dock contextual menu and select **Turn Hiding Off**.

You can also use a keyboard shortcut to make the Dock disappear and reappear on demand by entering ⌥⌘D (option+command+D).

Magnify the Dock Icons

Magnification is a handy feature that allows you to conserve desktop real estate by keeping your Dock small and magnifying icons as you move the mouse cursor over them. Magnification is particularly useful if you prefer a small Dock or your Dock is crowded with a large number of icons. As you add more icons to the Dock, it will become smaller, adjusting its size to fit horizontally across the bottom of the Desktop. If you have lots of icons in your Dock or prefer a small Dock, it may be difficult to distinguish application icons from each other. With magnification enabled, the icons in the Dock will magnify as you move the cursor over them.

Magnification is enabled from the **Dock** preference pane in System Preferences. Check the box next to **Magnification**. Use the slider to select your desired level of magnification from "Min," which is no magnification, to "Max," which is 128 pixels. This change will take effect immediately.

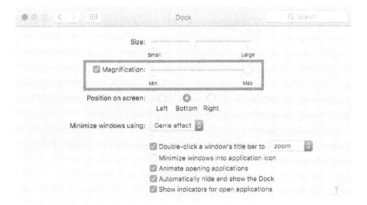

You can also enable magnification from the Dock itself. To **Turn Magnification On**, position your cursor over the Dock divider. When the cursor turns into a two-headed vertical white arrow, use a secondary click to open the Dock contextual menu. Select **Turn Magnification On**. To turn magnification off, secondary click the divider to open the Dock contextual menu and select **Turn Magnification Off**.

Add More Magnification

If you want more magnification, you can set magnification levels up to a ridiculously large 512 pixels. Open Terminal and enter the following commands. The 256 at the end of the first command doubles the default maximum magnification level.

```
defaults write com.apple.dock largesize -float 256
```

```
killall Dock
```

Why not go all the way and double the magnification level again?

```
defaults write com.apple.dock largesize -float 512
```

```
killall Dock
```

Now that's ridiculously large! You can enter any integer between 1 and 512 to set the magnification level to your desired level.

Enter the following commands to revert to the default maximum magnification level.

```
defaults write com.apple.dock largesize -float 128
```

```
killall Dock
```

Toggle Dock Magnification On or Off

Holding down the ⇧^ keys (shift+control) while moving your cursor across the Dock will toggle magnification on or off. If you have Dock magnification disabled, holding the ⇧^ keys while moving your cursor across the Dock will temporarily turn magnification on. Conversely, if you have Dock magnification enabled, holding the ⇧^ keys while moving your cursor across the Dock will temporarily turn magnification off.

Relocate the Dock

The default position of the Dock is at the bottom of the Desktop. OS X allows you to relocate the Dock to either the left or right edges of the Desktop.

To relocate the Dock, open the **Dock** preference pane in System Preferences. Select the **Left**, **Bottom**, or **Right** radio button next to **Position on screen**.

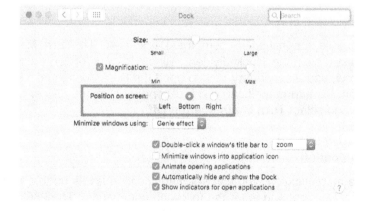

You can also relocate the Dock from the Dock itself. Position your cursor over the Dock divider. When the cursor turns into a two-headed vertical white arrow, use a secondary click to open the Dock contextual menu. Select **Position on Screen** and select **Left**, **Bottom**, or **Right**. Your selection will take effect immediately.

The picture below shows what the Dock looks like when configured at the left, bottom, or right edge of the desktop. You can see that the Dock icons are smaller when the Dock is configured for the left and right edges of the desktop.

Change How Windows Minimize

OS X features two animation effects when windows are minimized or maximized. The default is **Genie Effect**, in which windows minimize or maximize like a genie entering or exiting a magic lamp. The second option is the **Scale Effect**, where a window scales smaller and smaller until it finally reaches the Dock. When maximizing, the window scales larger as it restores itself to its original size.

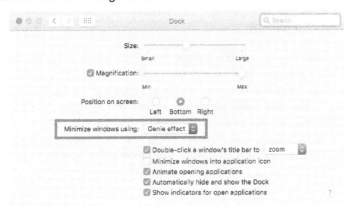

To change how windows minimize, open the **Dock** preference pane in the System Preferences application. Choose either **Genie Effect** or **Scale Effect** for your window minimization effect from the drop-down menu next to **Minimize windows using**.

You can also change how windows minimize from the Dock itself. Position your cursor over the Dock divider. When the cursor turns into a two-headed vertical white arrow, use a secondary click to open the Dock contextual menu. Select **Minimize Using** and choose **Genie Effect** or **Scale Effect**.

Minimize Windows with the Hidden Suck Effect

OS X offers two animations when minimizing windows to the Dock, the Genie and Scale effects with the default being Genie. OS X offers one more hidden animation, the **Suck Effect**, which is not available from the Dock preference pane. As the name suggests, a minimized window appears as if it is being sucked into the Dock by a powerful vacuum cleaner. Maximizing reverses the effect with the window shooting back to its original position as it pushed by a powerful leaf blower.

To enable the suck effect, open Terminal and enter the following commands. Be sure to hit the **return** key after each line. The change takes place immediately, so minimize a window and check it out.

```
defaults write com.apple.dock mineffect -string suck
```

```
killall Dock
```

To revert to the default animations, enter the following commands in Terminal. You can also replace **suck** with either **genie** or **scale** in the above command to configure these window animations directly in Terminal.

```
defaults delete com.apple.dock mineffect
```

```
killall Dock
```

Minimize or Zoom Windows by Double-Clicking

For the El Capitan OS X release Apple added the ability to configure OS X to zoom or minimize a window when you double-click on its Title Bar. Prior to El Capitan, you only had the option of minimizing a window.

Double-clicking the Title Bar to minimize does the exact same thing as clicking the yellow minimize button. Zooming an app by double-clicking causes the window to expand to cover all available desktop space between the Menu Bar and the Dock. If you have chosen to hide both the Menu Bar and Dock when not in use, the window will expand to cover the entire desktop. While this sounds like Full Screen mode, it is not. Mission Control does not recognize zoomed windows as Full Screen apps and you can still take an app to Full Screen mode when zoomed by clicking the green button in its Title Bar.

Double-clicking to minimize or zoom is configured in the **Dock** preference pane in System Preferences. Make your selection from the drop-down menu next to **Double-click a window's title bar to**.

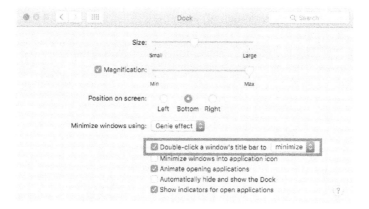

Size the Dock

The Dock will automatically resize itself based on the number of icons docked. As you squeeze more icons into the Dock, it stretches across the bottom of the desktop. The Dock's maximum size is limited by the size of the screen. OS X will not allow you to make the Dock so big that it won't fit on the screen, although the left- and right-most icons will likely slide off screen when using magnification.

Once the Dock reaches the maximum size allowed by the screen, you can continue to add icons. However, each icon will become smaller in order to allow all icons to fit. If your Dock has become overcrowded with app icons, check out the next chapter where I show you a nifty method to group apps into stacks and use them as application launchers.

Sizing the Dock is accomplished through the **Dock** preference pane in the System Preferences application. At the top of the pane is the **Size** slider, which controls the size of the Dock. Making the Dock smaller means it will take up less desktop real estate. Sometimes it seems that sliding the size towards large has no effect. This is because OS X scales the Dock to the maximum size horizontally (or vertically if positioned along the left or right edge of the desktop) that will fit given the number of icons in the Dock.

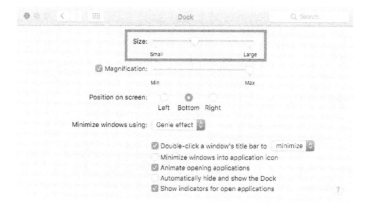

A second option is to change the size of the Dock from the Dock itself. Move your mouse cursor over the divider. It will turn into a double headed vertical white arrow. Click, hold and drag the white arrow up to make the Dock bigger and down to make it smaller. Remember, the maximum size is limited by the size of the screen. And while you can make the Dock very small, OS X limits you here too.

When you resize the Dock, you are essentially changing the size of each of the icons displayed in the Dock. Therefore you can utilize Terminal to more precisely size the icons. Try out the following commands. They will make your Dock small. Don't worry you can resize it.

```
defaults write com.apple.dock tilesize -int 32
```

```
killall Dock
```

OS X will allow you to replace the 32 in the first command to any integer from 1 to 256. The smaller the number, the smaller the Dock. Try using the integer 1.

```
defaults write com.apple.dock tilesize -int 1
```

```
killall Dock
```

Don't worry, your Dock is still there. It's that half-inch long blob where your Dock used to be. A Dock this small is really not useable even with magnification. Let's change the Dock to a more reasonable size.

```
defaults write com.apple.dock tilesize -int 64
```

```
killall Dock
```

There, that's better. You can try other integers between 1 and 256. If you were hoping for a gigantic Dock, you're out of luck. Even if you use 256, the size of the Dock is limited to the maximum size that will fit on the screen.

Sometimes getting the Dock sized properly is like adjusting the driver's seat in your car. It's never quite right. If you want to return the Dock to its default size and start over, open Terminal and enter these commands.

```
defaults delete com.apple.dock tilesize
```

```
killall Dock
```

Clean Up a Cluttered Dock

By default, OS X minimizes windows to the right side of the Dock divider. This can become problematic if you minimize a large number of windows. As you minimize each window, the Dock expands across the Desktop. Once the Dock reaches its maximum size, each successive window minimization causes it to become smaller as OS X crowds more minimized window icons into the right side of the divider. Eventually the overcrowding causes the icons in the Dock to become extremely difficult to differentiate, especially the minimized windows.

OS X has a solution, available in the Dock preference pane. Open the Dock preference pane in the System Preferences application. Click the checkbox next to **Minimize windows into application icon**.

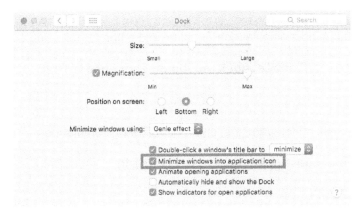

When this option is checked, OS X will minimize windows into their associated application icon. Minimized windows will no longer clutter the right side of the Dock and increase its size. This saves a great deal of Dock real estate. When you want to see all the windows of an application, simply use **App Exposé** on the associated application icon. **App Exposé** is activated by hovering the cursor over an application icon in the Dock and swiping down with either three or four fingers on the trackpad. Note that **App Exposé** has to be activated in the Trackpad preferences.

Stop App Icons from Bouncing

Application icons in the Dock will bounce when one of two events occur: upon launching the app or if the app needs to get your attention. The latter event typically occurs when a dialog box opens with a warning, needs your input, or the app wants to tell you a task has been completed.

Bouncing can be disabled in the **Dock** preference pane in the System Preferences application.

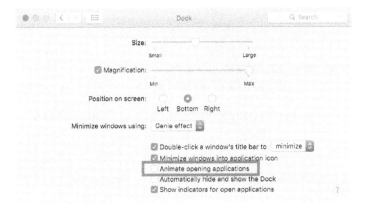

Animate opening apps is enabled by default. Uncheck this box if you do not like this animation. This will stop apps from bouncing when you open them from the Dock. However, some applications will bounce their icon continuously until you respond by clicking the bouncing icon. The incessant bouncing can be irritating if you are busy doing something else and are not at a convenient break point. Stopping icons from bouncing in response to a warning or when the app needs your attention requires configuration using the Terminal application.

To disable application bouncing, launch Terminal and enter the following commands.

```
defaults write com.apple.dock no-bouncing -bool TRUE

killall Dock
```

To turn bouncing back on for warnings, enter the following commands.

```
defaults delete com.apple.dock no-bouncing

killall Dock
```

Turn Off Open Application Indicators

OS X puts a tiny black indicator underneath the icon of open applications. If you moved the Dock to the left or right edge of the Desktop, the indicator will be on the left or right, respectively. If you don't care to know which applications are open, you can disable this feature in the **Dock** preference pane. Uncheck the box next to **Show indicators for open applications**.

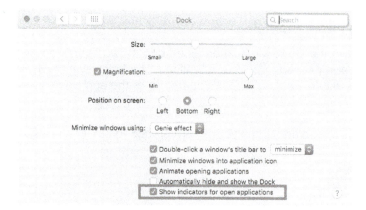

You can also turn off open application indicators using Terminal. To turn off the indicator lights for open applications, launch Terminal and enter the following commands.

```
defaults write com.apple.dock show-process-indicators -bool FALSE

killall Dock
```

To turn the indicator lights back on, enter the following commands.

```
defaults write com.apple.dock show-process-indicators -bool TRUE
```

```
killall Dock
```

Space Out the Apps

All of the application icons are equally spaced next to each other on the Dock. If you'd like to better organize your apps, you can group similar apps together and put a blank space between groups. Launch Terminal and enter the following commands. The first two lines are a single command. **Do not** hit the **return** key until you have entered both lines.

```
defaults write com.apple.dock persistent-apps -array-add '{tile-data={};tile-type="spacer-tile";}'
```

```
killall Dock
```

A blank space will appear at the end of the app icons permanently kept in the Dock. Note the blank space between the icons for System Preferences and Terminal in the picture. Drag the blank space to your desired position. Repeat the Terminal commands if you want to add another space.

Removing the space is rather interesting. Drag it off the Dock to remove. What makes this interesting is it will appear as if you are dragging nothing because the blank space is invisible! If that is too weird for you, secondary click on the blank space to display the **Remove from Dock** option.

Space Out the Trash Can

This command adds a space in front of the Trash on the right side of the divider. By default, the Trash is the very last icon in the Dock. This tweak will place a space to the left of the Trash to separate it from all of the icons located on the right side of the Dock divider.

Open Terminal and enter the following commands. The first two lines are a single command. **Do not** hit the **return** key until you have entered both lines.

```
defaults write com.apple.dock persistent-others -array-add '{tile-data={};tile-type="spacer-tile";}'
```

```
killall Dock
```

A blank space will appear to the left of the Trash. Drag the space to your desired location. Repeat the commands if you want to add more spaces.

Remove the space by dragging it off the Dock past the middle of your desktop and release. Remember the blank space is invisible so it will appear that you are dragging nothing. If you prefer, you can secondary click on the blank space to display the **Remove from Dock** option.

Dim Hidden Apps

How do you know which applications are hidden? An indicator light under the icon denotes a running app, but the Dock provides no feedback to tell you which applications are hidden versus which ones are not. The Dock can be customized to dim the icon of a hidden application, allowing you to spot the applications you have hidden at a glance. Note the difference between the icons for Microsoft Word versus Evernote and iBooks. Word is hidden and its icon appears dimmed compared to the icons for iBooks and Evernote.

To enable this feature, open Terminal and enter the following commands.

```
defaults write com.apple.dock showhidden -bool TRUE
```

```
killall Dock
```

If you hid applications before entering the commands above, you'll notice no change to the icons. Click on the hidden apps and then hide them again. They will now dim.

Use the following commands to change the Dock back to its default behavior.

```
defaults write com.apple.dock showhidden -bool FALSE
```

```
killall Dock
```

Turn the Dock into a Taskbar

The Dock serves a twofold purpose, combining the functions of an application launcher and a taskbar to switch between open apps. OS X lets you change the behavior of the Dock so that it operates only as a taskbar, showing only the applications that are currently open. Enter the following commands into Terminal to switch the Dock to taskbar only mode.

```
defaults write com.apple.dock static-only -bool TRUE
```

```
killall Dock
```

Once the Dock is operating in taskbar mode, you may want to turn off the indicator lights for the running applications. Since the Dock now shows only running apps, the indicator lights are superfluous. You can disable indicator lights from the **Dock** preference pane by unchecking the box next to **Show indicators for open applications**.

Running the Dock in taskbar mode is particularly useful if you don't want to use the Dock to launch applications or you have categorized your applications into App Stacks as described in the next chapter. Often users want to put all of the applications they routinely use into the Dock. The problem is the Dock's maximum size is limited and once reached, each application icon becomes smaller and more difficult to differentiate from the others.

OS X offers several alternative methods to launch applications. First, Launchpad offers a quick and easy method to access and launch any of your applications. Another method is to categorize applications into folders for easy access and to combat sprawl and clutter. Applications can be organized into App Stacks and launched directly from the Dock in taskbar mode. If you are an ex-Windows user, you may want to create aliases on the desktop for your applications. Alternatively, if there is a particular set of applications you use constantly, you can set them to launch when you start or log into your Mac. Another option is to enter ⌘**space** (command+space) to activate **Spotlight** and use it as an application launcher.

To change the Dock back to its default behavior, enter the following commands.

```
defaults write com.apple.dock static-only -bool FALSE
```

```
killall Dock
```

Surprise! OS X remembered what your Dock looked like and restored it back to its original state.

Use App Exposé in the Dock

App Exposé is an OS X feature that lets you see all the windows of an open application regardless on which desktops the windows reside. It differs from Mission Control which only lets you see the windows of every open application a Desktop space at a time. App Exposé is opened by swiping down with either three or four fingers in an application window. The number of fingers is configured in the **Trackpad** preference pane, accessible from > **System Preferences... > Trackpad**.

If you configured a gesture for App Exposé, that gesture will also work in the Dock. Position your cursor over any application icon and swipe down with either three or four fingers (depending on how you configured the gesture). Click on the desired window or swipe with three or four fingers in the opposite direction to close App Exposé.

Activate App Exposé with a Two-Finger Scroll Gesture

App Exposé can only be accessed using a trackpad, so you are out of luck if you use a Magic Mouse unless you activate this tweak. This tweak allows you to open App Exposé using a scroll up gesture on an application icon in the Dock. Scroll up with one or two fingers on an Apple Magic Mouse or with two fingers on a trackpad. Scroll in the opposite direction with the same number of fingers to close App Exposé.

Open Terminal and enter the following commands to activate this feature.

```
defaults write com.apple.dock scroll-to-open -bool TRUE
```

```
killall Dock
```

Once active, you'll be able to open App Exposé by moving the cursor to an application icon in the Dock and scrolling up. Scroll down to close App Exposé. An additional benefit of this feature is that it also allows you to open and close a stack by scrolling up or down, respectively.

Enter the following commands in Terminal to deactivate this feature.

```
defaults delete com.apple.dock scroll-to-open
```

```
killall Dock
```

Single Application Mode

Hiding applications is a handy technique to keep your desktop free of clutter and distractions to help you stay focused. A Dock shortcut allows you to accomplish two commands simultaneously – launching an application while hiding all other apps.

Hold down the ⌥⌘ (option+command) keys while clicking on an application icon in the Dock. The app will open and all other open windows from other running applications will instantly be hidden. You can also use this shortcut even if the application is already open.

If you like this behavior, you can make it permanent by configuring the Dock to operate in single application mode. Anytime you open a new application from the Dock, all other apps will be hidden. Note that this tweak does not affect applications launched from Launchpad, Spotlight, or from the Applications folder.

Enter the following commands in Terminal to turn on single application mode.

```
defaults write com.apple.dock single-app -bool TRUE
```

```
killall Dock
```

To turn off single application mode and return the Dock to its default behavior, enter the following commands.

```
defaults delete com.apple.dock single-app
```

```
killall Dock
```

Change the Hide/Show Animation Speed

If you like keeping your Dock hidden, you'll notice that OS X animates the Dock's disappearance and reappearance to/from underneath the desktop. OS X allows you to completely eliminate this animation, making the Dock hide and unhide instantly.

Enter the following commands in Terminal to eliminate the Dock animation.

```
defaults write com.apple.dock autohide-time-modifier -float 0
```

```
killall Dock
```

OS X also allows you to increase the length of the animation. Setting the animation to a larger number slows the animation down. A smaller number speeds it up. The following commands will set the animation to 2.5 seconds so you can see the Dock animation in slow motion. You can even use decimals like 0.15 and 0.5 to tune the length of the animation to your exact specification.

```
defaults write com.apple.dock autohide-time-modifier -float 2.5
```

```
killall Dock
```

To restore the Dock to its default animation, enter the following commands.

```
defaults delete com.apple.dock autohide-time-modifier
```

```
killall Dock
```

Make the Dock Dark

When you configure the Menu Bar for Dark Mode in the **General** preference pane in System Preferences, it turns the Dock dark too. Do you like the look of a dark Dock, but you're not so happy with the dark Menu Bar? This tweak puts the Dock into Dark Mode while leaving the Menu Bar light gray.

To configure a dark Dock, launch Terminal and enter the following commands. This change takes effect immediately.

```
defaults write NSGlobalDomain AppleInterfaceStyle Dark
```

```
killall Dock
```

```
defaults remove NSGlobalDomain AppleInterfaceStyle
```

This change will also put the Application Switcher into dark mode – enter ⌘**tab** (command+tab) to check it out. The Dock and Application Switcher will remain in dark mode while the Menu Bar stays light gray until you restart your Mac. Unfortunately this tweak doesn't survive a restart, but most Mac users put their Macs to sleep rather than restarting them.

Find an App's Location

Another handy Dock shortcut is to hold the ⌘ (command) key while clicking on an app icon. This shortcut opens the application's location in Finder with the application highlighted.

Spring Loaded Dock Icons

Applications icons in the Dock are spring loaded like folders in Finder. If you drag a file, pause, and hover over an application icon, **App Exposé** will launch, allowing you to drop the file onto the app. Hit **space** if you don't want to wait out the spring load delay.

Add a Preference Pane

If you find yourself frequently using a specific preference pane in the System Preferences application, you may find it convenient to add it to the Dock. A preference pane can only be added to the right side of the Dock.

To add a preference pane to the Dock, open Finder. Enter ⇧⌘G (shift+command+G) to open the **Go to the folder** dialog box. Enter the following into the field and click **Go**.

/System/Library/PreferencePanes/
Locate the preference pane you want to add to the Dock and drag it to the right side of the divider. You are now able to access it directly from the Dock without having to first launch the System Preferences application.

To remove a preference pane from the Dock, drag it off like any other item you wish to remove from the Dock.

Lock the Dock

You spent a significant amount of time customizing the Dock to get it to look and perform exactly the way you like it. However, it is very easy to accidentally reorder or remove icons or resize or reposition the Dock. All it takes is one bad click from your trackpad or mouse to ruin your customization. It is easy to prevent this from happening by locking the Dock. If you are satisfied with the way your Dock looks, OS X allows you to individually lock the Dock's contents as well as its size, position, and magnification settings. Ensure that the Dock preference pane is closed before executing any of the following commands.

To prevent unintentional changes to the contents of the Dock, launch Terminal and enter the following commands. Hit the **return** key after each line.

```
defaults write com.apple.dock contents-immutable -bool TRUE
```

```
killall Dock
```

The following commands will prevent accidental changes to the size of the Dock. After running these commands, you'll notice the **Size** slider in the Dock Preference pane will be grayed out.

```
defaults write com.apple.dock size-immutable -bool TRUE
```

```
killall Dock
```

To lock the Dock's position on the Desktop, enter the following commands.

```
defaults write com.apple.dock position-immutable -bool TRUE
```

```
killall Dock
```

To prevent changes to your Dock's magnification setting, enter the following commands.

```
defaults write com.apple.dock magnify-immutable -bool TRUE
```

```
killall Dock
```

To lock the Dock's autohide feature, enter the following commands.

```
defaults write com.apple.dock autohide-immutable -bool TRUE
```

```
killall Dock
```

After locking the Dock's contents, size, magnification, position, and hiding, OS X will gray out these settings in the Dock preference pane.

Now that your Dock is locked, what do you do if you need to make changes later? I'll show you how to unlock the Dock next.

Unlock the Dock

What happens if you want to make changes to a locked Dock? Well, unlock it, of course! Each of the locks for contents, size, position, magnification, and hiding can be unlocked individually.

To completely unlock the Dock, enter the following commands in Terminal.

```
defaults delete com.apple.dock contents-immutable
defaults delete com.apple.dock size-immutable
defaults delete com.apple.dock position-immutable
defaults delete com.apple.dock magnify-immutable
defaults delete com.apple.dock autohide-immutable
killall Dock
```

7

Stacks

Stacks are another iconic and cool feature of OS X, offering quick access to frequently used folders directly from the Dock. Stacks are located to the right of the divider, the thin black vertical line separating applications from the stacks, minimized windows, and the trash can. Applications go to the left of the divider. Everything else goes on the right.

Unless you upgraded from a previous version of OS X where you customized the Dock, El Capitan gets you started with one stack, which is linked to the Downloads folder. The Downloads stack is the exact same Downloads folder you see under Favorites in the Finder Sidebar. Anything downloaded using Safari, Mail, Messages, or AirDrop will be saved to this folder.

When you click on the Downloads stack, its contents spring from the Dock in a fan. Clicking on any item in a stack opens it. At the very top of the stack is a link to open the Downloads folder in Finder. Of course, you can change this behavior and view the contents as a **Fan**, **Grid**, or **List**. An **Automatic** option lets OS X select the most appropriate view depending on the number of items in the stack. Secondary click on the Downloads stack to access the contextual menu to configure how the stack is displayed and how its contents are viewed and sorted.

OS X offers four options to view stack contents. **Automatic** is the default, automatically switching between **Fan** and **Grid** depending on the number of items in the stack. Choosing Fan will always display the contents as a stack fan, however, only the first ten items will display. OS X will tell you how many more items are available. Clicking the circular icon with the arrow will open the folder in a Finder window so you can see the remaining items.

As their names imply, **Grid** displays stack contents as a grid and **List** as a list. Both the Grid and List options behave differently than the Fan view. Clicking on a folder in a Fan stack will open the folder in Finder. Clicking on a folder in a Grid or List stack will open the sub-folder directly in the Grid or List view, allowing you to navigate through many layers of folders to your intended destination. If you don't want to navigate further in the grid or list, holding down the ⌘ (command) key while clicking a folder will open it in Finder. In addition to changing how you want the contents to display, the menu allows you to change the stack icon to a folder.

OS X offers five sorting options. A stack can be sorted by **Name**, **Date Added**, **Date Modified**, **Date Created**, or **Kind**. The default is to sort by Name. In a Fan, the closest icon to the Dock is based on the sort type. For example, if a Fan is sorted by name, the closest item to the Dock is the first item in alphabetical order. Similarly, when the Fan is sorted by date added, the item with the most recent date will be closest to the Dock.

Add Stacks

You can customize the right side of the Dock by adding stacks for folders like the Applications folder or other frequently accessed folders or devices. Adding folders you frequently use as stacks is much more efficient than navigating through Finder. The picture shows stacks for my Home folder, Applications, Desktop, Downloads, Recent Documents, and Volumes.

To add a folder stack to the Dock, simply locate the folder you wish to add in Finder and drag it to the Dock. It's that easy. Another method is to locate the folder in the Finder Sidebar and secondary click on it to open a contextual menu. Choose **Add to Dock**. Any item in the Finder Sidebar can be added to the Dock as a stack with the exception of **All My Files**, **AirDrop**, and **iCloud Drive**. OS X allows you to create as many stacks as you want or can fit on the Dock.

To add a disk drive, look under **Devices** in the Finder Sidebar. Secondary click the device and select **Add to Dock**. Note that the icon for a removable storage device will turn into a question mark on top of a disk drive icon when the media is removed.

Once your stacks are in the Dock, you can arrange their order. Rearrange stacks by dragging them left or right. Remember, you cannot drag a stack to the left of the vertical divider. OS X will not allow you to move stacks to the left of the divider as that side is reserved for applications.

You can even drag individual documents into the Dock, although technically, a document is not a stack, it is an alias. The only options available with a secondary click are to **Remove from Dock**, **Open at Login**, **Show in Finder**, and to open the document. Despite these limitations, adding a document to the Dock is particularly useful if you frequently access it.

You can drag and drop items in a stack to move them to another folder, stack, onto the Dock, to the Desktop, into the Trash, to an external disk drive, or any other location.

Remove Stacks

Removing a stack is done the same way as you would remove any Dock icon. Simply click, drag, and drop it off the Dock until **Remove** appears above the icon. Release and the stack will disappear in a puff of smoke. Stacks can also be removed by secondary clicking on the stack and selecting **Options > Remove from Dock**.

This Happens All the Time

You think you are dragging a file from the Downloads stack, but you accidentally drag the entire Downloads stack off the Dock and poof, it's gone! Don't panic. You can put the Downloads folder back with one command.

Open Finder, navigate to the missing item and drag it back onto the Dock. If the missing item is located in the Finder Sidebar, secondary click on it and select **Add to Dock**. To avoid accidentally removing or rearranging items in the Dock, lock it. See "Lock the Dock" in the last chapter to learn how to lock and unlock the Dock.

Highlight Stack Items

OS X offers a feature that will highlight an item in a Stack as you hover over it with the cursor. Highlighting is disabled by default. To enable highlighting, open Terminal and enter the following commands. Don't hit the **return** key until you have completely entered the first two lines.

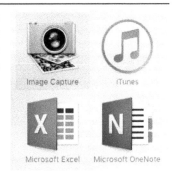

```
defaults write com.apple.dock mouse-over-
hilite-stack -bool TRUE
```

```
killall Dock
```

To turn off highlighting and go back to the default, enter the following commands.

```
defaults delete com.apple.dock mouse-over-hilite-stack
```

```
killall Dock
```

Temporarily Highlight Stack Items

If you don't want to permanently highlight stack items, OS X allows you to use highlighting on an as needed basis. If you want to temporarily highlight items, click and hold the Stack icon. Do not remove your finger from the trackpad or mouse as the Stack expands. With your finger still pressing down on the trackpad or mouse, move up the Stack listing. Whichever item your cursor is hovering over will be highlighted. Continue to hold the trackpad or mouse until you hover over the item you want to open and then release. The highlighted item will open immediately.

Another option is to click and hold the stack icon. Release immediately after the stack expands. Now type the first few letters of the desired item's name. OS X will highlight items as you type. Once the desired item is highlighted, press the **return** key to open it immediately.

Add a Recent Items Stack

To save you the trouble of looking for a recently opened application, document, or server, OS X keeps a list of **Recent Items** under the (Apple) Menu. Select **> Recent Items** to display a list of the last ten applications, documents, and servers. Ten is the default and can be changed in the **General** preference pane. Access the pane by clicking **System Preferences > General**. Look for **Recent Items** near the bottom of the pane and select **None**, **5**, **10**, **15**, **20**, **30**, or **50** items.

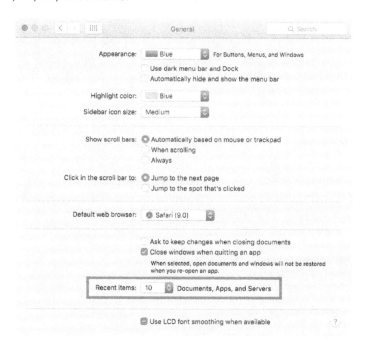

But what if you want to use the Dock instead of the menu to access your recent items? Adding a recent items stack to the Dock is one of the most useful OS X tweaks. Open Terminal and enter the following commands. Do not press the **return** key until you have completely entered the first three lines.

```
defaults write com.apple.dock persistent-others -array-add '{
"tile-data" = { "list-type" = 1; }; "tile-type" = "recents-tile";
}'
```

```
killall Dock
```

OS X will place a recent items stack on the Dock to the left of the trash. By default, the recent items stack will list the most recently accessed applications with the contents viewed as **Automatic**. A secondary click on the stack icon will open a contextual menu of options, allowing you to change the type of recent items in the stack and how the stack is viewed. The recent items stack can show **Recent Applications**, **Recent Documents**, **Recent Servers**, **Recent Volumes**, or **Favorite Items**. Like all stacks, contents can be viewed as a **Fan**, **Grid**, **List**, or **Automatic**.

OS X allows you to create as many stacks as you want. If you want another recent items stack, run the commands again. By default, each new stack will appear as a **Recent Applications** stack. Use a secondary click to change to **Recent Documents**, **Recent Servers**, **Recent Volumes**, or **Favorite Items**. The contents of a newly created Recent Items Stack are viewed as **Automatic**. Secondary click on the Recent Items Stack to set the **View content as** option. To remove a Recent Items stack, drag it off the Dock or secondary click on it and select **Remove from Dock**.

If you ever need to clear the recent items displayed in a stack or set of stacks, go to > **Recent Items > Clear Menu**. If you have a large number of recent items, you will have to scroll down to access the **Clear Menu** command at the very bottom. The recent items stack will look like it disappeared, but it is still there. It just has no contents to display.

Create an App Stack

If your Dock is crowded with applications making it difficult to quickly find the application you are looking for, a solution to the overcrowding is to organize your apps into App Stacks. You can organize your apps by any method imaginable – by application type like productivity, social media, utilities, or browsers or by how often you use them. This feature is particularly useful if you like a neat and tidy Dock or if you switched the Dock to taskbar mode, where it only shows the running applications.

Follow these simple steps to create an App Stack:
1. Create a new folder in your Home Directory called "Stacks."
2. Open the folder.
3. Create and name a new folder for your App Stack using ⇧⌘N or **File > New Folder**.
4. Open a new Finder Window using **⌘N** or **File > New Finder Window**. Click on the Applications folder in the Sidebar.
5. Select an application you wish to add to your App Stack from the Applications folder and drag it into your App Stack folder.
6. Repeat step 5 for each application you want to add to your App Stack.
7. Drag and drop your App Stack folder onto the right side of the Dock.
8. Repeat starting at step 3 to create another App Stack, if so desired.

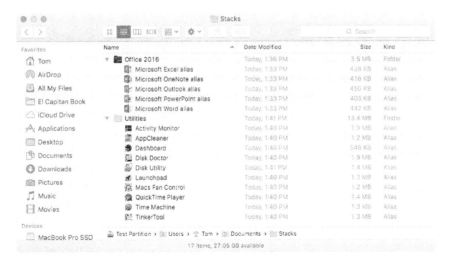

Dragging a folder from the Stacks folder to the Dock creates the App Stack. By default, the contents of an App Stack are sorted by **Name**, displayed as a **Stack**, and content viewed as **Automatic**. Secondary click on the App Stack to set the **Sort by**, **Display as**, and **View content as** options.

To add a new application to an existing App Stack, open the Applications folder and drag the new app to your App Stack in the Dock. To remove apps from an App Stack, open the App Stack in the Dock and drag the app alias to the Trash. To remove an App Stack, simply drag it off the Dock. Release and poof, the stack disappears.

Create a Document Stack

If there are certain folders you frequently access, the quickest and easiest method to open items in these folders is to create a **Document Stack** on the Dock. A Document Stack can be created for any folder in Finder including your Home folder.

To create a Document Stack, simply locate the desired folder in Finder and drag it to the right side of the Dock. By default, the contents of a Document Stack are sorted by **Name**, displayed as a **Stack**, and content viewed as **Automatic**. Secondary click on the Document Stack to set the **Sort by**, **Display as**, and **View content as** options.

To remove a Document Stack, simply drag it off the Dock until **Remove** appears above the icon, release, and poof, the stack disappears.

Create a Desktop Stack

If you like a clean and clutter-free desktop like I do, you probably configured the OS X tweak "Create a Pristine Desktop" in Chapter 3. However, a lot of items are saved to the Desktop by default. If they no longer appear on the Desktop, where do they go? In reality, OS X doesn't save these items to the Desktop. They are saved to a folder in your **Home** directory called **Desktop**. You can access this folder in Finder, but because so many items get saved to the Desktop folder by default, I suggest you add a Desktop Stack to your Dock for quicker access to those items.

To create a Desktop Stack, open Finder. If the Desktop folder is in the Finder Sidebar, drag it to the right side of the Dock. If the Desktop folder is not in the Finder Sidebar, you can find it in your Home directory. Drag it to the right side of the Dock. You may want to also drag the Desktop Folder to the Finder Sidebar to provide another method to quickly access it. By default, the contents of a Desktop Stack are sorted by **Name**, displayed as a **Stack**, and content viewed as **Automatic**. Secondary click on the Desktop Stack to set the **Sort by**, **Display as**, and **View content as** options.

To remove a Desktop Stack, drag it off the Dock until **Remove** appears above the icon, release, and poof, the stack disappears.

Create a Volumes Stack

If you have numerous internal or external drives, wouldn't it be cool to see them all in one stack? While OS X allows you to drag each one individually from the **Devices** list in the **Finder** Sidebar, you have to use this tweak to see them all in a single stack like the one shown in the picture.

If you like a clean, uncluttered desktop, you probably wish OS X wouldn't show all of your disk drives on the Desktop. See Chapter 3 to learn how to disable this feature. Once OS X is no longer displaying your hard drives on the Desktop, a **Volumes Stack** makes accessing any of your internal or external hard drives a breeze.

Creating a Volumes Stack is a multi-step process.
1. Open Finder and enter ⇧⌘G (shift+command+G) to open the **Go to the folder** dialog box.
2. Enter **/Volumes** in the dialog box and hit **return** to open the **Volumes** folder.
3. Click **Column** View in the Finder toolbar. The **Volumes** folder will be highlighted and grayed. This is because **Volumes** is a hidden folder.
4. Drag and drop the hidden **Volumes** folder to the right side of the Dock to create a Volumes Stack.

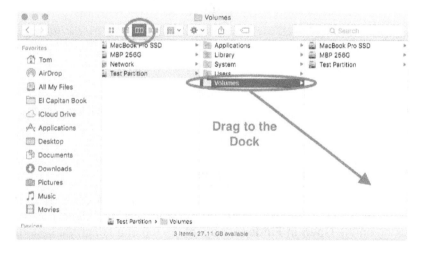

By default, the contents of a Volumes Stack are sorted by **Name**, displayed as a **Stack**, and content viewed as **Automatic**. Secondary click on the Volumes Stack to set the **Sort by**, **Display as**, and **View content as** options.

To remove a Volumes Stack, simply drag it off the Dock until **Remove** appears above it. Release and it disappears. If you changed the **Finder** preferences so external drives no longer display on the desktop, you may wish to turn this feature back on. Otherwise, the only place you will be able to see your external drives is under the **Devices** list in the **Finder** Sidebar. See Chapter 3 on customizing the Desktop to learn how to change the Finder preferences to make external drives appear on the Desktop.

Activate Stacks with a Scroll Gesture

Typically a stack is opened using a single click or click and hold (when using temporary highlighting). Another method available is to use a scroll up gesture using a single finger on a Apple Magic Mouse or two fingers on a trackpad.

To activate this feature, launch Terminal and enter the following commands.

```
defaults write com.apple.dock scroll-to-open -bool TRUE

killall Dock
```

Once active, you'll be able to open a stack by moving the cursor to the stack and scrolling up. Scroll down to close the stack. An additional benefit of this feature is that it also activates **App Exposé** when you use the scroll gesture on an application icon in the Dock. Give it a try on an application with multiple windows open. All open windows of the application will be shown in App Exposé.

Enter the following commands to deactivate this feature.

```
defaults delete com.apple.dock scroll-to-open

killall Dock
```

Slow Motion Stack Animation

Next time you open a stack, hold down the ⇧ (shift) key while clicking on the stack. The stack will open in slow motion. Try holding the shift key while closing the stack.

Quickly Open a Stack in a Finder Window

If you ever need to open a stack in Finder, hold down the ⌥⌘ (option+command) keys while clicking on the stack. The folder linked to the stack will immediately open. This is the same as clicking on the **Open in Finder** control at the top of a fan or the bottom of a grid or list stack. This trick works for any stack except a Recent Items Stack.

Locate a Stack

Another handy Dock shortcut is to hold the ⌘ (command) key while clicking on a stack. This shortcut opens the stack's location in Finder with the item highlighted. This trick works for any stack except a Recent Items Stack and Volumes Stack.

Spring Loaded Stacks

Try dragging a file onto a Stack, pause while hovering over the Stack and suddenly a Finder window will open allowing you to move the file into the folder. If you hold down the ⌥ (option) key while dragging and hovering, you will copy the file instead of moving it. Holding down ⌥⌘ (option+command) will create an alias.

8

Spotlight

After receiving a major overhaul in OS X Yosemite, **Spotlight** again received a makeover in the El Capitan release. Spotlight retains the same overall front and center look and feel from Yosemite, but has added a few new features. It can now provide sports scores, weather forecasts, and find online videos. In addition to finding stuff on your Mac, Spotlight will make suggestions from the Internet, iTunes, the App Store, find movie showtimes, and suggest nearby locations.

The biggest cosmetic change to Spotlight is, believe it or not, the ability to resize the window. Well sort of. You can make the window longer, but not wider. You can't make the window any smaller than its default. But you can move the Spotlight window around your desktop.

Spotlight has the ability to search 22 different categories of data, which is configurable in the **Spotlight** preference pane in System Preferences. To make suggestions more relevant, Spotlight includes your approximate location with its search request to Apple.

Spotlight is accessed by clicking on its icon, located in its usual spot in the upper right corner of the Menu Bar next to Notification Center. Clicking on the Spotlight icon opens a large search window in the center of your desktop. The default keyboard shortcut remains the same as in earlier versions, ⌘**space** (command+space).

As you type into the search field, Spotlight will offer results it thinks are likely matches, refining them as you type and organizing them into categories directly below the search field. Results are displayed in categories, with the **Top Hit**, the result Spotlight determined to be the most likely, highlighted at the top of the list. If you press **return**, OS X will immediately open the Top Hit. Spotlight displays search results in the categories listed in the Spotlight preference pane, skipping categories that lack a result.

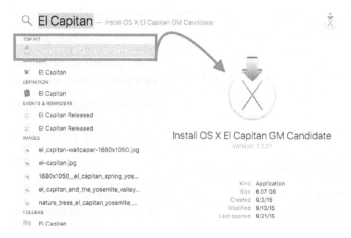

A large preview pane on the right allows you to preview results you select in the left pane. Any item in the search results can be previewed by highlighting it. Clicking on an item in the Spotlight search results opens it. If an item is already highlighted because you were previewing it, pressing the **return** key will open it. To see the location of an item in the file system, hold down the ⌘ (command) key. The file path is shown at the bottom of the preview pane.

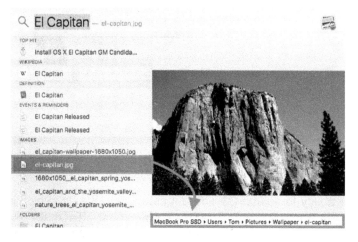

One of the coolest features of Spotlight in El Capitan is its ability to search the Internet without first having to launch Safari. And unlike searching using Safari or another browser, the results are not just links to the results, Spotlight displays the actual webpage in its preview pane. Highlight the result and hit **return** to open Safari and go to the website.

Natural Language Search

Apple added natural language search capability to Spotlight in the El Capitan release. Although this is a welcome improvement, I found it very limited in the beta versions of El Capitan including the Golden Master. While Spotlight was able to understand and successfully provide results for "photos from yesterday," "emails I received today from Petco," and "messages I received today from my daughter," it was unable to find the current price of Apple stock. I could easily find sports scores, standings, rosters, and schedules. Typing "weather" into the Spotlight search field quickly produced the current local weather conditions as well as the hourly and 10-day forecasts. I'm betting Apple will improve Spotlight in subsequent minor releases of OS X 10.11.

Avoid Spotlight Information Overload

By default, **Spotlight** will search 22 different categories including files on your internal and external drives, the web, Maps, Wikipedia, Bing, music, movies, images, bookmarks, web browsing history, events, reminders, contacts, (take a deep breath), mail, messages, music, movies, definitions, applications, system preferences, fonts, documents, folders, presentations, spreadsheets, PDFs, plus an other category for those things not listed above. Spotlight will do unit conversions so you never have to remember that formula to convert temperatures in Celsius to Fahrenheit. Spotlight even makes the best cup of latte you ever had. Okay, I was kidding about the latte, but you can use Spotlight to find the best latte in town.

Depending on your point of view, this could be pretty darn awesome or just information overload. If you think this is information overload, the Spotlight preference pane allows you to remove categories that do not interest you.

To remove Spotlight search categories, open the Spotlight preference pane in the System Preferences application. Next, click **Search Results** at the top of the pane if it is not already highlighted. Feel free to uncheck as many categories as you like. You can always add them back later.

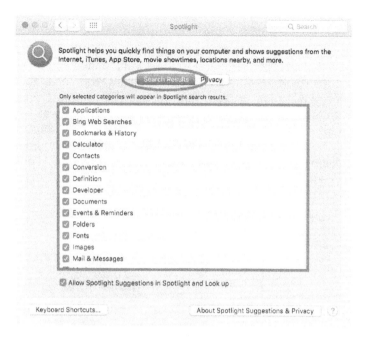

Exclude Volumes or Folders from Spotlight

Spotlight searches everything on your Mac by default. However, OS X El Capitan allows you to exclude specific volumes or folders from being searched.

To exclude a volume or folder, open the Spotlight preference pane in the System Preferences application. Click **Privacy** at the top of the pane if it is not already selected.

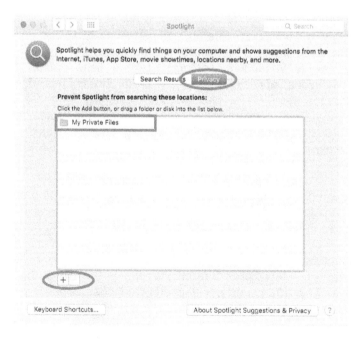

Click the **Add Button**, denoted by the **+** at the bottom left, to open a **Finder** window. Browse to the volume or folder you want to exclude. Click the **Choose** button. Your selection will be added to the exclusion list. To remove a volume or folder previously excluded, highlight it in the list of excluded folders and click the **−** at the bottom left.

Change the Spotlight Keyboard Shortcut

The default keyboard shortcut for **Spotlight** is **⌘space** (command+space). OS X lets you configure any keyboard shortcut you desire for Spotlight.

To change the keyboard shortcut for Spotlight, open the Spotlight preference pane in the System Preferences application. Click the **Keyboard Shortcuts...** button found in the lower left hand corner of the preference pane. This button is available on both the **Search Results** and **Privacy** tabs. The **Keyboard shortcuts..** button will launch the **Keyboard** preference pane in System Preferences.

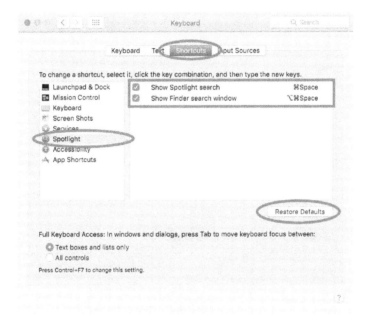

From the **Keyboard** preference pane you can choose any combination of keys as Spotlight's keyboard shortcut. Click on the **Shortcuts** tab if it is not already highlighted. Next, select **Spotlight** in the left-hand column. **Show Spotlight search** is the first choice in the list of shortcuts in the right-hand pane. Click on **Show Spotlight search** to highlight it and click on **⌘space**. You can now enter your own custom shortcut in the field provided. Be sure to select a shortcut that is not already in use. If you select a shortcut already in use, a yellow triangle will appear to warn you of the conflict. A yellow triangle will also appear in the left column next to the category containing the conflict.

You can also change the keyboard shortcut for the Finder search window that is used to search for files located on your Mac. Click on **Show Finder search window** to highlight it and click on **⌥⌘space**. You can now enter your own custom shortcut in the field provided.

To revert back to the OS X defaults for both Spotlight and Finder Search Window, click the **Restore Defaults** button at the lower right of the Keyboard preference pane.

Improve Spotlight Search Results

Spotlight allows you to narrow your search to specific types of files using the search modifier **kind**. For example, if you are looking for a specific file type, such as a spreadsheet created in Excel, you can enter **kind:excel** followed by the name of the file. Spotlight will limit the search results to only Excel files.

The following list of search modifiers can be used to improve your Spotlight searches. Enter the search term after the modifier. Entering a Spotlight search modifier alone without a search term returns all files of that type.

kind:alias	Returns results that are aliases.
kind:app	Used to locate applications.
kind:audio	Returns search results that are audio files.
kind:avi	Returns results that are AVI files.
kind:bookmark	Used to search Safari bookmarks.
kind:chat	Used to search the Messages logs.
kind:contact	Searches Contacts.
kind:developer	Returns results from the developer category.
kind:document	Used to search for document files.
kind:event	Searches Calendar events.
kind:folder	Finds folders.
kind:font	Used to search for fonts.
kind:gif	Returns images in GIF format.
kind:history	Searches your Safari history.
kind:image	Returns results that are image files.
kind:jpeg	Used to search for images in JPEG format.
kind:mail	Used to search Mail.
kind:message	Returns results from Messages.
kind:movie	Returns results that are movies.
kind:music	Used to search for music.
kind:pdf	Used to locate PDF files.
kind:preferences	Used to search for system preferences.
kind:presentation	Returns files that are presentations.

`kind:quicktime`	Used to locate QuickTime movies.
`kind:reminder`	Used to search for Reminders.
`kind:spreadsheet`	Returns files that are spreadsheets.
`kind:tiff`	Returns images in TIFF format.
`kind:webpage`	Searches your Safari history.

Search by Specific Application

Spotlight has the capability to search for files created by specific applications. For example, to search for this book, written in Microsoft Word, I would enter **kind:word Customizing OS X** into the Spotlight search field.

The following list shows search modifiers that you can use to look for specific files produced by Apple's iWork suite and the Microsoft Office productivity suite.

`kind:pages`	`kind:word`
`kind:numbers`	`kind:excel`
`kind:keynote`	`kind:powerpoint`

Search Using Tag Color

If you use Finder tags, **Spotlight** allows you to search for files based on the color of their tag using the search modifier **tag**. For example, to find files with a red tag, you would enter **tag:red** into the Spotlight search field. Valid tag colors in El Capitan are white, red, orange, yellow, green, blue, purple, and gray.

Once you have begun to routinely tag files, you most likely will rename tags to something more descriptive. OS X allows you to search for tags based on their color or their name. Let's say you renamed the green tag to "vacation." Either of the following searches would return all of your files tagged with the green tag "vacation."

`tag:green`

`tag:vacation`

For more information on using tags, see the chapter on Finder.

Search by Document Author

Spotlight allows you to use the search modifier **author** to search for documents written by a specific author. For example, to search for documents written by myself, I would enter the following into the Spotlight search field.

`author:Magrini`

Search by Date

Spotlight has the capability to search for files based on the date they were created or modified using the search modifier **date**. The date can be a specific date, a range, today, or yesterday. For example, entering **date:7/4/15** in the Spotlight search field will return files created or modified on July 4, 2015.

Spotlight also allows you to search for ranges. The following search would return all files created or modified during the month of July 2015.

```
date:7/1/15-7/31/15
```

You can use greater than and greater than or equal to in order to find files created or modified on or after a certain date. The following search would return all files created or modified after September 1, 2015.

```
date:>9/1/15
```

This search returns all files created or modified on and after September 1, 2015.

```
date:>=9/1/15
```

You can also look for files created or modified before a specific date. In this example, Spotlight returns all files created or modified before September 1, 2015.

```
date:<9/1/15
```

This search returns all files created or modified on and prior to September 1, 2015.

```
date:<=9/1/15
```

Spotlight also allows you to search for files created or modified yesterday or today.

```
date:yesterday
```

```
date:today
```

Spotlight understands yesterday and today. What about tomorrow? Yes, Spotlight does understand what tomorrow means. However, results are limited to Calendar events and Reminders since your Mac can't predict the files you will create or modify in the future.

```
date:tomorrow
```

In addition to the **date** search modifier, Spotlight understands **created** and **modified**.

```
created:<=10/1/15
```

```
modified:7/1/15
```

Use Multiple Search Modifiers

Any of the search modifiers can be used together to narrow your search. For example, the following Spotlight search would find all Microsoft Word documents I created or modified during the month of September 2015.

```
kind:word date:9/1/15-9/30/15 author:Magrini
```

This search looks at Safari's history and returns any webpages about El Capitan that I visited after August 1, 2015.

```
kind:history created:>8/1/15 El Capitan
```

Handy Keyboard Shortcuts

Spotlight features a number of useful keyboard shortcuts. Use any of the following shortcuts when Spotlight displays search results.

⌘B	Opens **Safari** and searches the Internet for the terms listed in the Spotlight search field.
⌘D	Opens the **Dictionary** application and looks up the terms in the Spotlight search field.
⌘K	Opens the **Dictionary** application and looks up the terms in Wikipedia.
⌘O	Opens the currently highlighted search result, the same as pressing **return**.
⌘R	Opens the containing folder of the currently highlighted result.
⌘T	Launches the **Top Hit**.
⌘down	Jumps down and highlights the first result in the next category of search results.
⌘up	Jumps up and highlights the first result in the category of search results above.

Show the File Path

Pressing the ⌘ (command) key while a Spotlight search result is highlighted will display the item's path at the lower right of the window. Entering **⌘R** (command+R) or **⌘return** (command+return) will open the containing folder in Finder with the item highlighted.

Save a Spotlight Search

OS X allows you to save **Spotlight** searches to reuse later. To save a Spotlight search, highlight the **Show All in Finder** result at the bottom of the search results and then click on the large Finder icon in the right pane. This will open a Finder window displaying all of the results from the Spotlight search. Click the **Save** button at the upper right of the Finder window to save the search.

A drop-down sheet will appear asking you to specify a name for the search and location to save it. OS X saves searches to the **Saved Searches** folder in your **Home** directory. A checkbox, which is checked by default, allows you to add the saved search to the Finder Sidebar. Click the **Save** button to save your search or **Cancel**. If you left the **Add To Sidebar** box checked, your search will appear in the Finder Sidebar.

What you have just created is a **Smart Folder**, a saved instance of a Spotlight search that will dynamically update its content based on your search criteria. Simply click on the Smart Folder under **Favorites** in the Sidebar to run the search again. We'll cover Smart Folders in more detail in the chapter on Finder.

Use Spotlight as an Application Launcher

Spotlight makes a pretty handy application launcher. This is a great feature if you're trying to launch an application that is not in the Dock or if you're running your Dock in taskbar mode where it only displays running applications. The best part is that your fingers never have to leave the keyboard to launch an app.

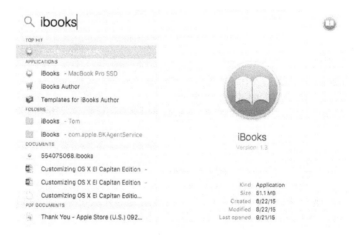

Start Spotlight by clicking on its icon in the Menu Bar, but that defeats the purpose of your fingers never leaving the keyboard; use **⌘space** instead. Begin typing the name of the application into the search field. Spotlight will zero in on the application after you enter a few letters of its name. The application will appear as the **Top Hit**. You can launch the application by pressing **return**, entering **⌘T** (command+T), or clicking on the app within the search results. Spotlight will learn which applications you launch most and will often find your target application after you've typed just one letter.

You can use an application's initials to quickly find and launch it. For example, **Photos** can be launched by entering **ph**. QuickTime can be launched using **qt**. Similarly, you can use **ib** for **iBooks**, **it** for **iTunes**, **wo** for **Word**, **ex** for **Excel**, **pa** for **Pages**, **ev** for **Evernote** and so forth.

Search for Comments

Adding **Comments** to your files is a convenient way to organize related content without having to create folders in Finder. The Comments feature allows you to enter descriptive metadata into a file's **Get Info** window. This metadata will facilitate searching.

For example, if you are working on a large project, you may create or collect a number of different files from several applications. While all are related to your project, they may not be saved in the same location in Finder. Of course, you could create a folder in Finder and save or move your files to that folder. Another option is to use Comments and never care where your files are located.

To add Comments to a file, first locate the file in Finder. Next, highlight it, secondary click, and select **Get Info** or press **⌘i** (command+i). This will open the Get Info window. Expand the Comments section, if necessary, by clicking on the little triangular shaped caret to the left of **Comments**. Enter your comments in the field provided. Enter multiple words by separating them with commas.

To do a Spotlight search using Comments, use the search modifier **comment:** followed by one of your comments.

```
comment:Mac OS X Book
```

To search for files tagged with multiple comments, type **comment:** into the Spotlight search field before each comment.

```
comment:Mac OS X Book comment:Icons
```

Comments are a great way to quickly find files while keeping them organized in their respective folders.

Use Spotlight as a Calculator

An neat feature of Spotlight is that it can also be used as a calculator. Simply type the formula in the Spotlight search field and Spotlight will calculate the answer. If you have no need for this functionality, you can disable it in the Spotlight preference pane in System Preferences. Uncheck the checkbox next to Calculator in the Search Results tab.

Use Spotlight to Convert Currency

Another nice Spotlight feature is that you can use it as a currency converter. For example, if you want to know what 500 euros is in U.S. dollars, simply enter 500 euros in the Spotlight search field. Spotlight will tell you that 500 euros equals $559.82 as of the day of this writing. If you have no need for this functionality, you can disable it in the Spotlight preference pane in System Preferences. Uncheck the checkbox next to Conversion in the Search Results tab. Note that by doing so you will disable all conversions in addition to currency conversion, so you'll have to remember the formula to convert temperatures in Celsius to Fahrenheit.

Rebuild the Spotlight Index

Sometimes you will swear that **Spotlight** is not finding a file you know is on your Mac or on an external drive. You're not crazy. Sometimes the Spotlight index becomes corrupt, causing inaccurate searches. When this happens, it is time to rebuild the index.

To rebuild the Spotlight index, launch Terminal and enter the following commands. The first command erases the existing Spotlight index. While the second command turns Spotlight back on, forcing it to reindex the drive. Enter your password into Terminal when prompted.

```
sudo mdutil -E /

sudo mdutil -i on /
```

You can verify Spotlight is rebuilding its index by launching and looking for the indexing progress bar. The rebuilding process takes some time and is dependent upon the size and speed of the drive and the number of files it contains. Once the rebuilding process is complete, Spotlight will provide more accurate search results.

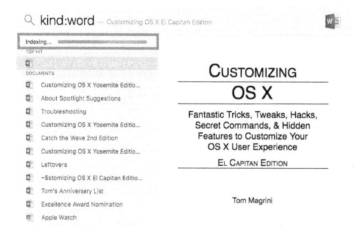

9

Notification Center

Notification Center is a hidden panel on the right edge of the Desktop that collects and displays notifications and alerts from various apps. Similar to the iOS feature of the same name, you can choose which applications will save their alerts to Notification Center. The gesture to display Notification Center seems a little odd at first because you actually start off the trackpad. Starting at the right edge, swipe left with two fingers to reveal the Notification Center panel. Swipe in the opposite direction to hide it. Alternately, you can click on the Notification Center Menu Extra in the Menu Bar. Click the Menu Extra again or press the **esc** key and Notification Center will slide off the right edge of your screen.

Customize Today View

OS X El Capitan lets you customize your **Today** view, choosing the items you wish to display and their order. To edit the Today view, slide out the Notification Center panel and click on **Today** at the top of the panel. Next, click the **Edit** button at the bottom of Notification Center.

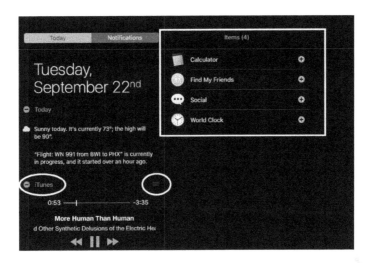

The panel will expand to display a second column to the right of the Today view with any available widgets that you can add. Click on the green **+** button to add a widget. To remove a widget from the Today view, click the red **−** button. Click the **Done** button at the bottom of the panel when finished.

Rearrange Today View Widgets

Don't like the order of the widgets? Simply drag a widget to rearrange it. Open Notification Center and click the **Edit** button at the bottom of the panel. Using the handle to the right of the widget's name, drag the widget to your desired location and drop it in place.

Add Third Party Widgets to Notification Center

OS X lets you add third party widgets to your Today View. Open Notification Center and click the **Edit** button at the bottom of the panel. When the panel expands click the **App Store** button at the bottom center of Notification Center. This will take you to the **Notification Center Widgets** section of the Mac App Store.

Poking around the App Store, I've found a number of handy third party widgets. Let's take a look at a few of the widgets I stumbled upon. All are available in the App Store at the time of this book's publication.

iStat Mini

iStat Mini provides a quick overview of some basic performance statistics. It shows the percentage of CPU, memory, and storage your Mac is currently using as well as the speed of your network connection. iStat Mini, as its name implies is a scaled down version of its big brother, iStat Menus. iStat Mini was available for $2.99 in the Mac App Store at the time of this writing at: https://itunes.apple.com/gb/app/istat-mini/id927292435?mt=12

Wunderlist

Wunderlist, the Mac App of the Year for 2013, is a full featured task list application. It offers native applications for Mac OS X and iOS as well as a full featured web version, allowing you to seamlessly access your task lists regardless of platform. Changes made on one platform are immediately pushed to your other devices, keeping everything synchronized. Each task list can contain a limitless number of tasks.

At the time of this writing, Wunderlist is free to download from the Mac App Store. There is an optional upgrade to the Pro version for $4.99 a month or $49.99 a year. The Wunderlist Pro upgrade provides unlimited access to assignments, subtasks, and attachments. Wunderlist is available in the Mac App Store at: https://itunes.apple.com/us/app/wunderlist-to-do-list-tasks/id410628904?mt=12.

Deliveries

 Do you do a lot of online shopping and receive lots of packages? **Deliveries** will help you keep track of your packages and will always know when they are supposed to be  delivered. Deliveries syncs with iCloud so you can track your packages on all of your Apple devices. Deliveries was available for $4.99 in the Mac App Store at the time of this writing at:

https://itunes.apple.com/us/app/deliveries-a-package-tracker/id924726344?mt=12.

PCalc

 PCalc is a full featured scientific calculator supporting hexadecimal, octal, and binary calculations. It features an extensive collection of unit conversions, programmable functions, and supports RPN mode, which is necessary for many engineering fields. PCalc was available for $9.99 in the Mac App Store at the time of this writing at:

https://itunes.apple.com/us/app/pcalc/id403504866?mt=12.

Countdowns

 Countdowns is a Notification Center widget that keeps track of the days until or since an important event that you configure. The countdown is displayed in the Notification Center. Countdowns syncs with iCloud so  you can keep track of the days to an important event on all of your Apple devices. At the time of this writing, Countdowns is available as a free trial from the Mac App Store and requires a 99-cent in-app purchase to unlock its full functionality. Countdowns is available at: https://itunes.apple.com/us/app/countdowns-widget-for-counting/id926707738?mt=12.

Battery Monitor

 Battery Monitor does just what its name implies, allowing you to access and monitor information about your MacBook's, MacBook Air's, or MacBook Pro's battery from the Notification Center. Battery Monitor also includes a Menu Extra for the Menu Bar and is the same application I recommended in Chapter 5. Battery Monitor displays the current charge level, time remaining, the cycle count, and time remaining in the Notification Center. It's Menu

Extra provides additional information including battery capacity and current charge. Battery Monitor was available for free in the Mac App Store at the time of this writing at: https://itunes.apple.com/us/app/battery-monitor-health-status/id836505650?mt=12.

Select Widgets for Today View

You can also configure the widgets displayed in Notification Center's **Today View**, by opening the **Extensions** preference pane in the System Preferences application. Select **Today** from the left column if not already highlighted. Use the checkboxes in the right side of the pane under **Select widgets for the Today view in Notification Center** to add or remove widgets.

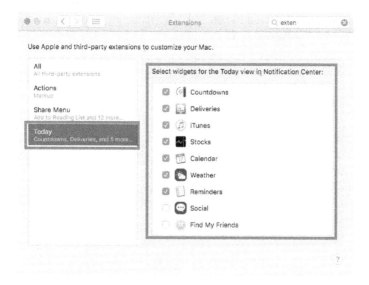

Customize Notifications

The other half of Notification Center should be very familiar to OS X and iOS users. The **Notifications** view is a one-stop shop consolidating all notifications from a variety of Apple applications including Messages, Mail, Calendar, Reminders, iTunes, Safari, FaceTime, Game Center, iMovie, and Maps. Notification Center supports notifications from social media applications like LinkedIn, Facebook, and Twitter, as well as from many third party applications and websites.

Notifications are delivered to the upper right hand corner of your desktop in the form of a **Banner** or **Alert**, depending on the style chosen in the Notifications preference pane in System Preferences. **Banners** appear and disappear automatically after a set period of time. iTunes notifications of the song it is playing are an example of a Banner. **Alerts** stay on your desktop until you dismiss them. Reminders are an example of an Alert, requiring you to take some action to dismiss the notification. All previous notifications, regardless of style, are stored in Notification Center.

To unhide Notification Center, start with two fingers on the right edge of your trackpad and swipe left. Select **Notifications** if it is not already highlighted. Alternately, you can click on the Notification Center Menu Extra in the Menu Bar. Click the Menu Extra again to close Notification Center or press the **esc** key.

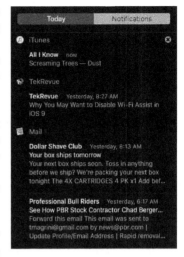

Clicking on a notification launches the application that created it. For example, clicking on a Mail notification takes you to the Mail application. Doing so will mark the notification as read and the notification will be removed. Clicking the **X** at the top right of any application dismisses all notifications associated with that application.

Any application utilizing Apple's push notification service or local notifications can send notifications to Notification Center. OS X allows you to customize which applications are allowed to send notifications to the Desktop and Notification Center via the **Notifications** preference pane located in the System Preferences application.

Choose Which Apps Will Notify

By default, all of the applications listed in the **Notifications** preference pane will display alerts in the upper right-hand corner of your desktop and deposit a notification in **Notification Center**. The number of applications configured in Notification Center could easily inundate you with annoying and superfluous alerts. OS X allows you to turn off notifications from any of the apps listed in the Notifications preference pane.

To turn off notifications, open the **Notifications** preference pane in System Preferences. This preference pane is split into a left column and a right pane. The left column lists the applications that are able to send an alert or banner to your desktop and deposit a notification in your Notification Center.

To stop an application from placing a notification in Notification Center, first highlight the application in the left column. Next, uncheck the checkbox next to **Show in Notification Center**. With the checkbox unchecked, the application will not save its alerts to Notification Center. However, the application will continue to send notifications to your desktop. This is a completely valid configuration. Another valid configuration is for an application to not send notifications to the desktop and only save them in Notification Center.

If you want to stop an application from sending notifications to your desktop, you must click on **None** under the **alert style** at the top of the right-hand pane. When **None** is selected as the notification style, the application will stop sending notifications to your desktop.

If you want the application to save notifications in Notification Center but not send them to the desktop, choose the **None** alert style and ensure the checkbox next to **Show in Notification Center** is checked.

Choose the Notification Style

The OS X **Notification Center** can be configured to send banners or alerts to your desktop. There is a difference between a banner and an alert. A **Banner** is a notification that will appear and disappear after a set amount of time. An **Alert** is a notification that will stay on your desktop until you respond or dismiss it. Alert styles and options such as history, badging, and sound are configured on a per application basis in the Notifications preference pane.

To choose a notification style, open the Notifications preference pane in the System Preferences application. Click on an application in the left column. Once an application has been selected, the right-hand pane will change to show the alert style currently configured, which is highlighted in blue, and any available configuration options. Choose **Banners** or **Alerts** to change the alert style that will appear on your desktop. If you choose **None**, the application won't send notifications to your desktop.

Once you have chosen your alert style, you can configure the various options shown below the alert style. Depending on the application, there may be 2 to 5 options available. Generally, the options are: **Show notifications on lock screen**, **Show message preview**, **Show in Notification Center**, **Badge app icon**, and **Play sound for notifications**. All of the checkboxes are usually checked by default.

OS X will show alerts when your Mac is locked. This creates a potential privacy issue since anyone can read your notifications when your Mac is locked and you are away from it. If you want to disable this feature, uncheck the checkbox next to **Show notifications on lock screen**.

The **Show message preview** option is only applicable to apps such as **Mail** and **Messages**. OS X will show a preview of your messages only **when unlocked**. The **always** option will show message previews regardless of whether your Mac is locked or not, presenting a potential privacy issue. Uncheck the checkbox to turn message preview off.

By default, the **Show in Notification Center** option is checked and the 5 most recent notifications will be available in Notification Center. OS X allows you to choose the number of recent items saved, which is configurable to 1, 5, 10, or 20 items.

The **Badge app icon** option will show the number of notifications in a red circular badge on the app's icon in the **Dock**. The app must be in the Dock for badges to appear. If you don't want the application icon to get badged, uncheck this checkbox.

Some notifications play a sound when they appear. If you prefer silence, uncheck the checkbox next to **Play sound for notifications**.

Change the Notification Sort Order

Notification Center displays notifications using the sort order configured in the Notifications preference pane. Notifications are sorted with the most recent ones on top.

To change the sort order for notifications displayed in Notification Center, open the **Notifications** preference pane in the System Preferences application. Change the sort order using the drop-down menu next to **Notification Center sort order**. You can sort by **Recents**, where the most recent notifications regardless of application will appear at the top of Notification Center. This is the OS X default. Another sort option is to sort **Recents by app**, which places the most recent notifications organized by application at the top of Notification Center.

The final option, **Manually by app**, allows you to reorder the list of applications displayed in the left column of the Notifications preference pane. When selecting this option, you'll notice the list of applications in the left column will rearrange themselves to what Apple suggests is a logical sort order. You don't have to accept Apple's suggestion. Simply drag and drop the applications in the left column into the order in which you want to see your notifications. Once finished, close the preference pane. The notifications will be displayed in your desired order. Any application without a notification is skipped.

Keep Banners Around Longer

Banners delivered to the upper right hand corner of your desktop automatically disappear after 5 seconds. Often this is not enough time to glance at them. I find myself forced to check Notification Center to read the Banner I just missed. This tweak allows you to set the amount of time in seconds that Banners will stay on your desktop before they disappear.

To increase the Banner time, launch Terminal and enter the following command. This command will increase the Banner time to 30 seconds. You can change the 30 in the command below to any whole number you wish. You will have to log out and log back in for the change to take effect.

```
defaults write com.apple.notificationcenterui bannerTime 30
```

If you want Banners to stick around until you dismiss them, enter the following command in Terminal. You will have to log out and log back in for the change to take effect.

```
defaults write com.apple.notificationcenterui bannerTime 86400
```

To return to the OS X default of 5 seconds, enter the following command in Terminal. Log out and log back in for the change to take effect.

```
defaults delete com.apple.notificationcenterui bannerTime
```

Set Up Social Media Accounts

Notification Center can be set up so you can receive alerts from and post messages to LinkedIn, Facebook, and Twitter. To add your social media accounts open the **Internet Accounts** preference pane in the System Preferences application.

To add a social media account, click on the account type you wish to add. Once configured, you'll receive notifications from and be able to post to your social media accounts directly in Notification Center.

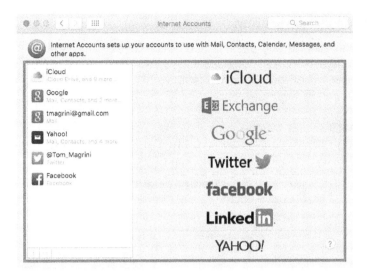

Post to Social Media Directly from Notification Center

You can post to your social media accounts or send a Message directly from Notification Center's Today view. To add social media to the Today view, open the Notification Center panel. Click **Today**, if not already highlighted. Click the **Edit** button at the very bottom of the pane. The Notification Center pane will expand to reveal a column of available widgets. Click the green button with the **+** sign next to **Social** to place buttons for Linkedin, Facebook, Twitter, and Messages in Notification Center's Today view.

Clicking any one of the Social buttons will open a window in Notification Center for you to create your post. If you haven't configured any of the social media accounts, OS X will provide an **Add Account...** button. Clicking this button will take you to the Internet Accounts preference pane where you can enter your credentials for the account.

Swipe to Dismiss a Notification

OS X allows you to dismiss any desktop notification by swiping on the notification from left to right with two fingers on your trackpad. If you are using a Magic Mouse, swipe left to right with one finger. The notification will fade away as it moves towards the right edge of the screen.

Some desktop notifications include controls. For example, the iTunes notification allows you to skip a song. Hover your cursor over the iTunes notification and a **Skip** button will appear to the right. Click to skip the current song.

Enable Do Not Disturb

Finding all those desktop notifications a little distracting? The **Do Not Disturb** feature turns Notification Center off for the remainder of the day. To enable the **Do Not Disturb** feature, first open Notification Center. Next, swipe in a downward motion with two fingers with your cursor located anywhere within Notification Center to reveal the Do Not Disturb switch at the very top.

Click the switch to the **ON** position. When Do Not Disturb is enabled the Notification Center Menu Extra turns gray. Any notifications received while Do Not Disturb is enabled are still available in Notification Center, but Banners and Alerts will not be sent to your desktop when Do Not Disturb is enabled. OS X will automatically turn Do Not Disturb off tomorrow. To disable Do Not Disturb, switch the Do Not Disturb switch to **OFF**.

There is a quicker way to enable the Do Not Disturb feature. Hold down the ⌥ (option) key while clicking the Notification Center Menu Extra to enable Do Not Disturb. Click again while holding the ⌥ (option) key to disable Do Not Disturb.

Schedule Do Not Disturb

OS X allows you to schedule the **Do Not Disturb** feature to turn on and off automatically at a scheduled time each day. To schedule Do Not Disturb, open the **Notification** preference pane in the System Preferences application. Click on **Do Not Disturb** in the left column if not selected already.

To schedule Do Not Disturb, check the box next to **From:** and **to:** and select the times during which you do not want to be disturbed by banners and alerts.

OS X enables Do Not Disturb while your Mac is sleeping and when it is mirroring its display to TVs and projectors. Enabling Do Not Disturb when you are mirroring your display to a TV or projector is quite handy if you are streaming a video to your AppleTV or giving a presentation to a group of people and don't want notifications interrupting you. However, if you do want to receive banners and alerts when mirroring, you can disable this behavior by unchecking the checkbox next to **When mirroring to TVs and projectors**.

Your Mac will not disturb you if you receive a FaceTime call when Do Not Disturb is enabled. If you would like to accept all FaceTime calls, check the checkbox next to **Allow calls from everyone**. Another option is to accept only repeated calls by checking the **Allow repeated calls** checkbox. If a second call is received from the same person within 3 minutes, you will be notified. Both of these options are disabled by default.

Safari Push Notifications

Websites supporting Apple's push notification service can send notifications to you of breaking news, sports, a new post, or other relevant info. These notifications will appear on your desktop and in Notification Center. Before a website can send you push notifications, you must choose to opt in. If a website supports push notifications, you'll be asked if you would like to receive notifications when browsing to the website in Safari. Click **Allow** to opt in or **Don't Allow** to opt out. Don't worry, you can always change your mind later. You can configure how you receive these notifications in the Notifications preference pane in System Preferences.

If you no longer find notifications from a particular website useful, you can opt out. Similarly, if you opted out, you can opt back in.

To change your Safari notification choice, launch **Safari** and open the Safari preference pane by selecting **Safari > Preferences...** or by entering ⌘, (command+comma). Once the Safari preferences launch, select **Notifications**. The websites that have asked for permission to send you push notifications will be listed. Next to each website are two radio buttons for **Allow** and **Deny** with the radio button with the current status selected.

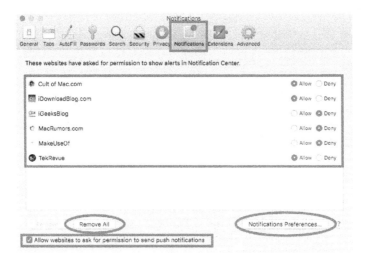

If you want to delete a website from the list, highlight it and click the **Remove** button. You also have the option of removing all websites from the push notification list by clicking the **Remove All** button. Doing so turns off Safari push notifications until you opt in to another website. If you would prefer that websites not ask you to opt in to their push notification service, uncheck the checkbox next to **Allow websites to ask for permission to send push notifications**. Checking this checkbox stops websites from asking you if you want to receive notifications from them.

Clicking **Notification Preferences...** in the lower right corner of the Safari preferences opens the **Notification Center** preference pane. Scroll down the left-hand column and select **Safari**. By default, Safari push notifications will appear on your desktop and in Notification Center. To configure notifications to appear on your desktop, but not in Notification Center, uncheck the checkbox next to **Show in Notification Center**.

Conversely, you can configure notifications to appear in Notification Center, but not on your desktop. Change the **Safari alert style** to **None** and ensure the checkbox next to **Show in Notification Center** is checked and choose the number of recent items.

You can configure the notification style, whether you want notifications to appear when your Mac is locked, and the number of recent items in Notification Center.

Assign a Hot Corner to Notification Center

The OS X **Hot Corners** feature allows you to assign a specific action to each of the four corners of your desktop. The command assigned to a Hot Corner is activated by moving your cursor to the corner associated with the command. Sometimes it's quicker to use a **Hot Corner** than to use a keyboard shortcut or to click on an icon.

To assign a Hot Corner to Notification Center, open the **Mission Control** preference pane from System Preferences. Click **Hot Corners...** at the lower left of the pane to reveal the configuration sheet. Since the Notification Center Menu Extra is located at the top right of the desktop, it may make sense to assign the top right-hand Hot Corner to Notification Center. Click **OK** when finished, then close the Mission Control preference pane.

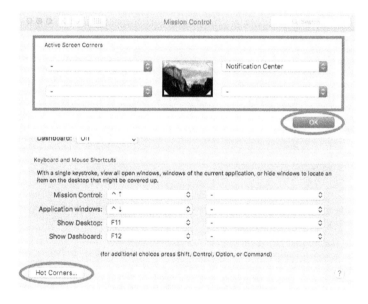

To turn off Hot Corners, open the **Mission Control** preference pane and click the **Hot Corners...** button in the lower left corner. Select the − from the drop-down menu for each corner that you want to turn off.

You can also configure Hot Corners using the **Desktop & Screen Saver** preference pane.

To learn how to avoid accidentally triggering the Notification Center Hot Corner, see "Avoid Accidentally Triggering a Hot Corner" in Chapter 3.

Create a Keyboard Shortcut for Notification Center

OS X allows you to assign keyboard shortcuts to execute any number of actions. If you would like to create a keyboard shortcut to open Notification Center, open the **Keyboard** preference pane from System Preferences. Click on the **Shortcuts** tab.

Select **Mission Control** from the left column. By default, the **Show Notification Center** checkbox is not checked. Check the checkbox and select a shortcut in the field provided. Be sure to select a shortcut that is not used by another function. If you select a shortcut that is already assigned, a yellow triangle will appear to the right of the shortcut. The yellow triangle will also appear in the left column. I use the keyboard shortcut ⌥⌘tab (option+command+tab) since it isn't assigned to another shortcut.

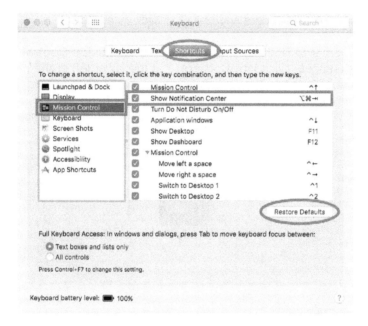

To remove the shortcut, simply uncheck the checkbox next to **Show Notification Center**. If you want to restore all keyboard shortcuts to their OS X defaults, click the **Restore Defaults** button at the lower right of the preference pane.

Create a Keyboard Shortcut for Do Not Disturb

In addition to creating a keyboard shortcut to open Notification Center, OS X allows you to assign a shortcut to toggle **Do Not Disturb** on and off. Open the **Keyboard** preference pane in the System Preferences application. Click on the **Shortcuts** tab.

Next, select **Mission Control** in the left column. By default, **Turn Do Not Disturb On/Off** is not checked. Check the box and select a shortcut key combination. Once configured, the shortcut will act as a toggle to enable and disable Do Not Disturb. Remember that you can check the status of Do Not Disturb by looking at the Notification Center icon in the Menu Bar. If it is grayed out, Do Not Disturb is enabled.

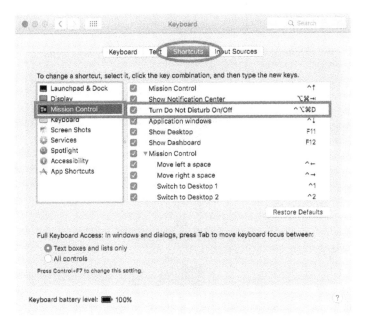

Disable Notification Center

Don't like Notification Center? OS X lets you completely disable it. Launch Terminal and enter the following command. Note that this command is a single line and there is a space after **–w**. Be sure to enter the entire command before pressing the **return** key. This change takes effect immediately. The Notification Center icon remains in the Menu Bar, but clicking on it does nothing. In addition to disabling Notification Center, this tweak will also disable desktop notifications.

```
launchctl unload –w
/System/Library/LaunchAgents/com.apple.notificationcenterui.plist
```

If you miss Notification Center, you can bring it back by entering this command in Terminal. Note that this command is a single line and there is a space after **–w**. Be sure to enter the entire command before pressing the **return** key. You will have to log out and log back in for this change to take effect. Note that Do Not Disturb may be enabled when you log back in. Look for the grayed out Notification Center icon.

```
launchctl load –w
/System/Library/LaunchAgents/com.apple.notificationcenterui.plist
```

10

Dashboard

 The **Dashboard** is an OS X feature that runs mini-applications called widgets on a dedicated desktop space or as an overlay with the widgets appearing in the foreground. The Dashboard is disabled in OS X El Capitan. When enabled, the Dashboard can be accessed using the **F12** key or by clicking on the Dashboard icon in the Dock or Launchpad. Note that you will have to hold the **fn** (function) key while pressing **F12**. On older Macs, use the **F4** key.

Enable the Dashboard

The **Dashboard** is off by default in OS X El Capitan. To turn it on, open the **Mission Control** preference pane in the System Preferences application. From the drop-down list, choose either **As Space** or **As Overlay**.

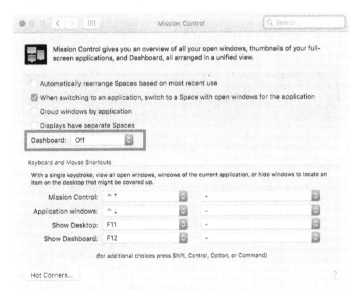

As the name implies, **As Space**, enables the Dashboard as a separate dedicated desktop space. Press **F4** or **F12**, depending on the age of your Mac and keyboard to reveal the Dashboard. The picture below shows the Dashboard running in its own space to the left of Desktop 1. Press **F4** or **F12** again to hide the Dashboard.

Dashboard Desktop 1 Desktop 2 Desktop 3 Desktop 4

With OS X El Capitan, Apple added the ability to rearrange the Dashboard space. Initially, the Dashboard will always appear to the left of Desktop 1. The Dashboard is accessed like any other space in Mission Control by clicking on it to make it active.

As Overlay allows you to display the widgets in the foreground of any desktop. Launching the Dashboard will dim your desktop and the widgets will appear in the foreground. Configuring the Dashboard to run in the foreground provides convenient access to the widgets without changing Desktop Spaces. Press **F4** or **F12** to hide the Dashboard.

Disable the Dashboard

Dashboard is getting a bit long in the tooth and appears to be on its last legs. The fact that Apple disabled it by default in OS X El Capitan is an admission that it is less than useful. I'm surprised Apple didn't kill it outright, especially considering the more functional widget feature Apple added to Notification Center. Browsing Apple's Dashboard widget page, which is not incorporated into the Mac App Store, is like taking a trip back in time before iPhones and iPads. Most of the widgets haven't been updated in years and few are being actively developed or maintained. Many Mac users feel that the Dashboard has outlived its usefulness and wonder when Apple will eliminate it for good. I'm hoping that El Capitan is the last release where we'll see the Dashboard. RIP. The Dashboard widget page is located at: http://www.apple.com/downloads/dashboard/.

If you want to disable the Dashboard, open the **Mission Control** preference pane in the System Preferences application and select **Off** in the drop-down menu next to **Dashboard**.

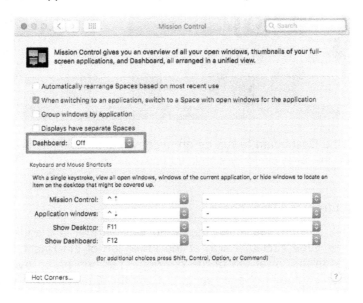

You can also remove the Dashboard by entering the following commands in Terminal.

```
defaults write com.apple.dashboard mcx-disabled -bool TRUE
```

```
killall Dock
```

If you change your mind and want Dashboard back, launch Terminal and enter the following commands.

```
defaults write com.apple.dashboard mcx-disabled -bool FALSE
```

```
killall Dock
```

Add New Widgets

OS X El Capitan comes with a rather spartan **Dashboard** containing only four widgets: a calculator, calendar, clock, and weather, which shows the weather in Cupertino, of course.

You add widgets by clicking on the large, circled **+** sign located at the lower corner of the Dashboard. This will open what appears to be a Launchpad for widgets, listing the available widgets installed on your Mac.

If these widgets aren't enough for you, Apple's website has a page dedicated to Dashboard widgets: http://www.apple.com/downloads/dashboard/. This page contains thousands of widgets, organized into categories.

If you configured the Dashboard to run as an overlay, adding widgets is done in a similar fashion. You'll find the large circled **+** sign in the lower left corner of your Desktop.

Remove a Widget from the Dashboard

Dashboard widgets are deleted much the same way as they are added. To delete a widget, click on the large circled **–** sign at the lower left of the Dashboard, if run as a separate space, or at the lower left of the desktop when run as an overlay. An **X** will appear at the upper left corner of each widget. Click the **X** to remove a widget. Widgets are only removed from the Dashboard. They are not deleted and can be added back later.

Rearrange Widgets

Dashboard widgets can be rearranged by dragging them to a new location. This method works in both space and overlay modes.

Open Duplicate Widgets

If you haven't tried to open multiple copies of the same widget, you may never know this feature exists. OS X doesn't limit you to one instance of a Dashboard widget. One obvious use is to open multiple weather or clock widgets so you can see the weather or time in different locations.

To open duplicate widgets, repeatedly add the same widget as many times as needed. This method works in both space and overlay modes.

Assign a Keyboard & Mouse Shortcut to the Dashboard

The default keyboard shortcut for the **Dashboard** is **F12** or **F4** on older Macs. You can assign another keyboard shortcut for the Dashboard by opening the **Mission Control** preference pane in the System Preferences application. Select your desired **F** key from the drop-down list next to **Show Dashboard** or choose − to disable the keyboard shortcut for the Dashboard. The following modifier keys are supported: ⇧, ^, ⌥, or ⌘ (shift, control, option, and command). You can use one, two, three, or all four modifier keys together.

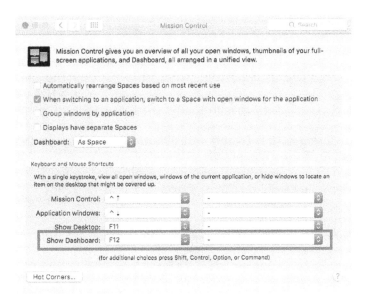

You can also configure a mouse shortcut from the Mission Control preference pane using the drop-down list in the second column next to **Show Dashboard**. You have a choice of the **Secondary Mouse Button** or the **Middle Mouse Button**.

What if you want to use a keyboard shortcut other than the **F** keys? Easy. Configure your keyboard shortcut using the **Keyboard** preference pane. Open the Keyboard preference pane in the System Preferences application. Click on **Shortcuts** if not highlighted already.

Choose **Mission Control** from the left column and check the checkbox next to **Show Dashboard** if it is not checked. Next, click on the shortcut (**F12**, by default) in the right column. Change the shortcut by entering your desired keyboard shortcut.

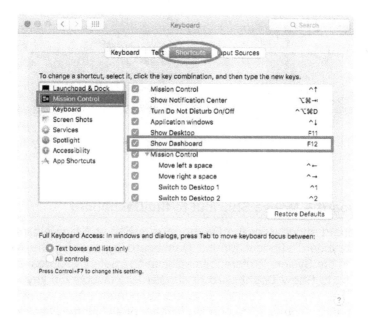

Assign a Hot Corner to the Dashboard

The **Hot Corners** feature allows you to assign a specific action to each of the four corners of your desktop. A **Hot Corner** is activated by moving your cursor to one of the corners to execute the associated command. It is sometimes quicker to use a **Hot Corner** than to use a keyboard shortcut or to click on an icon.

To assign a **Hot Corner** to the **Dashboard**, first open the **Mission Control** preference pane in the System Preferences application.

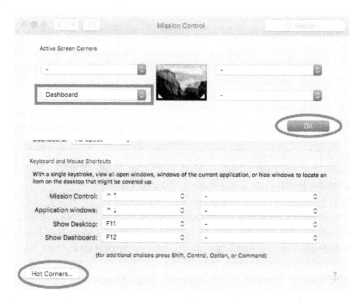

Next, click the **Hot Corners...** button at the lower left of the pane to reveal the drop-down configuration sheet. Choose which corner you want to use to launch the Dashboard and select **Dashboard** from the drop-down list. Click **OK** when finished, then close the Mission Control preference pane.

To turn off Hot Corners, open the **Mission Control** preference pane and click the **Hot Corners...** button in the lower left corner. Select the – from the drop-down menu for each corner that you want to turn off.

You can also configure a Hot Corner using the **Desktop & Screen Saver** preference pane.

To learn how to avoid accidentally triggering the Dashboard Hot Corner, see "Avoid Accidentally Triggering a Hot Corner" in Chapter 3.

Move the Dashboard to Another Display

You can move the **Dashboard** to another display in a multiple display system. In order to move the Dashboard to another display, you have to configure separate spaces on each display and run the Dashboard as a space.

Open the **Mission Control** preference pane in the System Preferences application. Select **As Space** from the drop-down list next to **Dashboard**. Next, check the checkbox next to **Displays have separate Spaces**. You will have to log out and log in for this change to take effect.

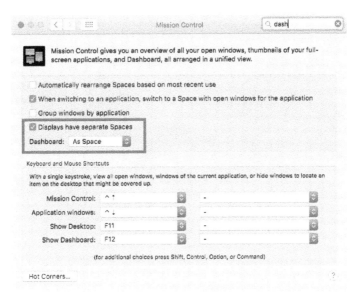

To move the Dashboard to another display, simply drag it over to the destination display via the right or left edge of the screen.

The following is a picture of my main display. Note the absence of the Dashboard.

That is because I moved it to my second display as shown below.

11

Launchpad

 Launchpad is a feature that blurs the line between iOS and OS X. Similar to iOS, Launchpad allows you to see every application installed on your Mac on one or more full screen pages. Launchpad serves as an application launcher, providing an alternative method to launch applications. From Launchpad, you can search, launch, organize, and delete apps.

To open Launchpad, click on its icon in the Dock, press the **F4** key (on newer Macs), or pinch your thumb and three fingers together using the trackpad. When you open Launchpad, your desktop background will blur and any windows will disappear and reveal a grid of application icons similar to the home screen on an iPad or iPhone. The Dock, if hidden, will reappear.

Launchpad provides a search field at the top center allowing you to easily find applications, particularly ones that may be hidden in a folder. Small dots at the bottom center represent pages. You can swipe left or right with one finger on a Magic Mouse or two fingers on a trackpad or hold down the ⌘ (command) key while pressing the left or right arrow keys to navigate between pages. You also can click on one of the dots to jump directly to that page. All four arrow keys can be used to move up, down, left, or right within the grid to highlight an application. Pressing the **return** key launches the highlighted application, as does clicking on its icon.

Folders can be created the same way they are in iOS, by dragging one icon on top of another. Once a folder is created, it can be renamed and other applications can be dragged into it. Folders are opened by clicking on them. Close an open folder by clicking anywhere outside the folder.

You can close Launchpad by clicking on the desktop wallpaper, pressing the **F4** key again, pressing the **esc** key, or using the Show Desktop gesture by spreading your thumb and three fingers apart.

Rearrange the App Icons

The application icons in **Launchpad** can be rearranged by dragging them into the order you desire. To move an icon between pages, simply drag it to the edge of the screen and hold it there until the page flips. Drop the icon on the desired destination page.

Delete an App Using Launchpad

Some applications can be deleted from your Mac using **Launchpad**. To delete an app, click and hold on an icon until all of the app icons begin shaking. Some icons will have an **X** in the upper left corner. Clicking the **X** will delete that application.

Add Finder to Launchpad

Open **Launchpad**. Now type **Finder** in the search field. No Results. Noticeably absent from Launchpad is one of the most critical apps in OS X, Finder.

To add Finder to Launchpad, first open a **Finder** window. Enter ⇧⌘G (shift+command+G) to open the **Go to the folder** dialog box. Enter the following into the field and click **Go**.

```
/System/Library/CoreServices/
```

Locate **Finder** in this folder and drag and drop it onto the **Launchpad** icon in the Dock. Now, check out Launchpad and there's Finder.

Change the Number of Apps per Page

OS X lays out a 7 column by 5 row grid in Launchpad, displaying 35 icons per page. If you want more application icons to appear on each Launchpad page, you do so by making the grid larger by adding more columns and more rows.

For example, if you want Launchpad to display 60 application icons per page, you would need to resize the grid to 10 columns by 6 rows. To resize Launchpad, open Terminal and enter the following commands.

```
defaults write com.apple.dock springboard-columns -int 10

defaults write com.apple.dock springboard-rows -int 6

killall Dock
```

I suggest you experiment, trying different combinations of column and row sizes until you find the right combination. Simply replace the number after **-int** in each command with an integer to find the perfect size for you.

Increasing the size of the grid decreases the size of each icon. With Launchpad displaying more icons per page, it takes less pages to display all of your applications. In the picture below, Launchpad is configured to display 60 icons in a 10 column by 6 row grid. Why aren't there 60 icons on this page? I only have 35 applications installed.

Conversely, you can make the Launchpad grid smaller – i.e., fewer columns and rows – so that fewer application icons are displayed on each page.

For example, if you want Launchpad to display 20 application icons per page, you would need to resize the grid to 5 columns by 4 rows. To resize Launchpad, enter the following commands in Terminal.

```
defaults write com.apple.dock springboard-columns -int 5
```

```
defaults write com.apple.dock springboard-rows -int 4
```

```
killall Dock
```

Decreasing the size of the grid increases the size of each icon. With Launchpad displaying less icons per page, it takes more pages to display all of your applications. In the example, it now takes 5 pages to display all of the application icons.

To revert back to the OS X default of 7 columns by 5 rows, enter the following commands.

```
defaults delete com.apple.dock springboard-columns
```

```
defaults delete com.apple.dock springboard-rows
```

```
killall Dock
```

You probably noticed that as you changed the Launchpad grid size, your application icons spread out across multiple pages. Launchpad does not automatically rearrange the icons for you as you experimented with different grid sizes. Unfortunately, you'll have to rearrange the app icons manually.

Remove the Launchpad Show & Hide Delays

When opening **Launchpad**, you'll notice an ever-so-slight delay before it appears. The same slight delay in animation also occurs when you exit Launchpad. If you would like Launchpad to appear and disappear immediately, enter the following commands in Terminal. The first command removes the delay when opening Launchpad, while the second removes the delay when closing it.

```
defaults write com.apple.dock springboard-show-duration -int 0
```

```
defaults write com.apple.dock springboard-hide-duration -int 0
```

```
killall Dock
```

To revert back to the OS X default Launchpad animation delay, enter the following commands in Terminal.

```
defaults delete com.apple.dock springboard-show-duration
```

```
defaults delete com.apple.dock springboard-hide-duration
```

```
killall Dock
```

Remove the Page Scrolling Delay

OS X introduces a delay when scrolling between pages in Launchpad. If you prefer pages appear immediately without the delay, enter the following commands in Terminal.

```
defaults write com.apple.dock springboard-page-duration -int 0
```

```
killall Dock
```

To restore the default scroll animation between Launchpad pages, enter the following commands.

```
defaults delete com.apple.dock springboard-page-duration
```

```
killall Dock
```

Change the Launchpad Keyboard Shortcut

The default OS X keyboard shortcut for Launchpad is the **F4** key on newer Macs. (Older Macs use the **F4** key to launch the Dashboard.) If you would like to change this keyboard shortcut, open the **Keyboard** preference pane in the System Preferences application.

Next, select **Shortcuts** if not already highlighted. Select **Launchpad & Dock** from the left-hand pane. **Show Launchpad** is the second choice in the list of shortcuts in the right-hand pane. To change the shortcut, enter a shortcut key combination in the field at the right.

Be sure to select a shortcut that is not used by another function. If you select a shortcut that is already assigned to another function, a yellow triangle will appear to the right of the shortcut. The yellow triangle will also appear in the left column to denote a conflict with one of the assigned shortcuts.

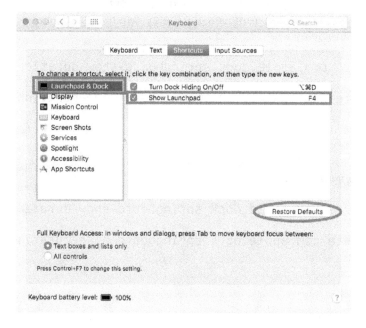

To remove the shortcut, simply uncheck the checkbox next to **Show Launchpad** or click the **Restore Defaults** button at the lower right of the preference pane.

Assign a Hot Corner to Launchpad

You can assign a specific action to each of the four corners of your desktop using the **Hot Corners** feature. A **Hot Corner** is activated by moving your cursor to one of the corners to execute the associated command.

To assign a Hot Corner to Launchpad, first open the Mission Control preference pane in the System Preferences application.

Next, click the **Hot Corners...** button at the lower left of the pane to reveal the drop-down configuration sheet. Choose which corner you want to use to open Launchpad. Click **OK** when finished.

To turn off Hot Corners, open the **Mission Control** preference pane and click the **Hot Corners...** button in the lower left corner. Select the – from the drop-down menu for each corner that you want to turn off. You can also configure a Hot Corner for the Launchpad using the **Desktop & Screen Saver** preference pane.

To learn how to avoid accidentally triggering the Launchpad Hot Corner, see "Avoid Accidentally Triggering a Hot Corner" in Chapter 3.

Need to Start From Scratch?

If you need to revert back to the OS X **Launchpad** defaults for any reason, enter the following commands in Terminal. This will reset Launchpad to its out-of-the-box settings. Any tweaks, including folders you may have created, will be reset to their defaults.

```
defaults write com.apple.dock ResetLaunchPad -bool TRUE

killall Dock
```

12

Finder

 Finder is the OS X file manager application, providing a graphical user interface to manage files, disk drives, and network drives, and to launch applications. A Finder window has three major components. At the very top of the Finder window is the **Toolbar**, which contains various tools to manipulate the window and its contents. The **Sidebar** is located at the left and is divided into four sections. **Favorites** lists shortcuts to favorite or frequently used items such as your Home, Desktop, Applications, Documents, Movies, Music, and Pictures folders. The Favorites category also allows access to AirDrop and iCloud Drive. Underneath Favorites is the **Devices** list, a list of internal and external drives. Below Devices is **Shared**, a list of shared computers and network shares to which your Mac is connected. The final section is the list of **Tags**, which are useful method of organizing your files. Finally, the right pane displays the contents of the selected folder.

Clicking on the Finder icon in the Dock launches a Finder window showing the **All My Files** view, which displays files organized by file type and chronologically with the most recent at the top of the window. You can return to this view by clicking **All My Files** under **Favorites** in the Sidebar.

Modify the Sidebar

The **Finder** Sidebar offers one-click access to items that you use the most, organized into four categories – **Favorites**, **Devices**, **Shared**, and **Tags**.

The **Favorites** category provides quick, single-click access to folders and files that you access frequently. Your **Home** folder, denoted by a house, **All My Files**, **iCloud Drive**, and **AirDrop** are listed first. You can add any folder to Favorites by locating the folder in Finder and then dragging it into the Sidebar.

The order of the items listed under favorites can be rearranged by dragging items until the list is arranged the way you want it. Any item in the Favorites list can be removed by dragging it off the Sidebar until a gray circle containing an **X** appears underneath its title. Simply release and the item disappears.

Secondary clicking on an item in the **Favorites** list opens a submenu allowing you to **Open in New Tab**, **Show in Enclosing Folder**, **Get Info**, **Remove from Sidebar**, or **Add to Dock**.

Open in New Tab

Show in Enclosing Folder

Get Info

Remove from Sidebar

Add to Dock

The **Devices** category includes internal drives, external drives, or other devices connected to your Mac. A secondary click on items in the list of **Devices** provides a different set of options allowing you to **Open in New Tab**, **Show in Enclosing Folder**, **Eject**, **Get Info**, **Encrypt**, **Rename**, **Remove from Sidebar**, or **Add to Dock**.

The **Shared** category includes other computers, network drives, or shared devices on your network.

The **Tags** category lists the Finder Tags. Clicking on a Finder Tag populates the Finder window with all files tagged with the selected tag. Secondary clicking offers options to **Open in New Tab**, **Remove from Sidebar**, **Delete Tag**, or change its color.

Hiding Sidebar Lists

Hovering your mouse over any of the Sidebar categories (Favorites, Devices, Shared, or Tags) reveals a **Hide/Show** toggle switch to the right of the category name. Clicking **Hide** collapses the category while clicking **Show** expands it.

Devices — Hide

MacBook Pro SSD

MBP 256G

Choose Which Items Appear in Sidebar

OS X lets you customize the Sidebar, choosing which items you want to display.

To customize the Sidebar, select **Preferences...** from the **Finder** menu in the Menu Bar. You can also access the preferences by entering ⌘, (command+comma). Once the preference pane appears, make sure **Sidebar** is selected from the set of four icons at the top of the pane. Using the checkboxes, check and uncheck items until you have configured the Sidebar to your liking.

Checked items are displayed in Sidebar, while unchecked items are hidden. Hidden items can be unhidden later by accessing the Finder preferences and checking their associated checkbox.

Add the Trash to the Sidebar

Missing from the **Finder** Sidebar is one of the most often used folders on OS X, the **Trash**. It only takes a couple of steps to add the Trash to the Sidebar.

First, open a Finder window. Enter ⇧⌘G (shift+command+G) to open the **Go to the folder** dialog box. Enter the following into the field and click **Go**.

~/Trash

Next, switch to **Column** view. The Trash folder will be highlighted, but it will be grayed to indicate that it is a hidden folder. Simply drag it into the Sidebar. I recommend placing it at the bottom as shown, but its location is your choice.

You now can use the Trash folder in the Sidebar to drop files into the Trash. However, the Sidebar Trash folder doesn't quite operate like the Trash in the Dock. Besides the fact that the icon is wrong (it's a folder instead of a trash can), you cannot empty the Trash by secondary clicking on the Trash folder. If you want to empty the trash from Finder, click on the Trash folder in the Sidebar and then click the **Empty** button in the upper right.

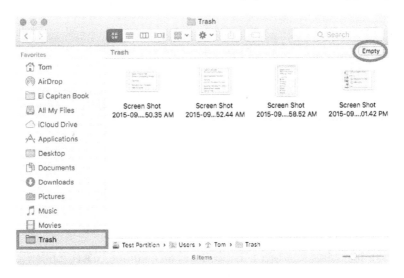

To delete the Trash folder from the Sidebar, drag and drop it off the Sidebar.

Rename Sidebar Items

Any folder added to the Finder **Sidebar** can be renamed by secondary clicking on it to display a contextual menu. From that menu, you can open the folder in a new tab, show its enclosing folder, get info, rename it, remove it from the Sidebar, or add the item to the Dock. Renaming an item in the Sidebar not only renames the Sidebar shortcut, but it also renames the original folder.

Change the Sidebar Icon Size

By default, OS X sets the size of the icons in the Sidebar to medium. If you have a lot of items in the Sidebar, you may want to set the icons to a smaller size to avoid having to scroll. Conversely, you may like the Sidebar to display larger icons to make the items easier to read.

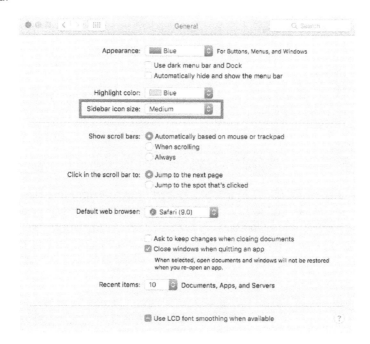

To change the icon size in Sidebar, open the **General** preference pane in the System Preferences application. Use the drop-down menu next to **Sidebar icons size** to choose **Small**, **Medium**, or **Large**.

Hide the Sidebar

OS X offers a number of features to change the look of your Finder windows. Various bars can be toggled on or off as needed. You can choose to show or hide the Path Bar, Status Bar, Tab Bar, and Sidebar.

To hide the Sidebar, choose **View > Hide Sidebar** or enter ⌥⌘S (option+command+S). The Sidebar can be toggled back on by selecting **View > Show Sidebar** or by entering ⌥⌘S (option+command+S). Another method is to hover your cursor over the dividing line between the Sidebar in the right-hand pane until the resizing cursor appears. Sliding the resizing cursor left or right will make the Sidebar width smaller or larger, respectively. The resizing cursor can also be used to hide the Sidebar by moving it all the way to the left until the Sidebar disappears.

Show the File Preview Panel

The Preview Panel comes in handy when you want to see a preview of a file or image without having to use Quick Look. The Preview Panel also shows the file name, size, date created, date modified, date last opened, and tags. You can even add tags directly from the Preview Panel.

To show the Finder Preview Panel, select **View > Show Preview** or enter ⇧⌘P (shift+command+P). Select any file to see it in the Preview Panel. Once you have enabled the Preview Panel, it is enabled for any new Finder window.

You can zoom into the Preview Panel by holding the ⌥ (option) key while clicking on the image and using the pinch zoom gesture.

To hide the Preview Panel, select **View > Hide Preview** or enter ⇧⌘P (shift+command+P).

Customize the Toolbar

The Finder **Toolbar**, located at the top of the Finder window, provides a number of tools to manipulate the contents of folders displayed in the Finder window's right-hand pane. The picture below shows the default Finder Toolbar in OS X El Capitan.

From left to right, the Toolbar provides forward and back buttons to navigate through folders similar to navigating forward and back in Safari. The next set of four icons change how the contents of a folder are viewed – by **Icon**, by **List**, by **Column**, or by **Cover Flow**.

The **Arrange** button offers a drop-down list where you choose how to sort files in the Finder window. The sorting options are: by **Name**, **Kind**, **Application**, **Date Last Opened**, **Date Added**, **Date Modified**, **Date Created**, **Size**, or **Tag**. The final option, **None**, leaves the folder unsorted.

The **Action** button provides a contextual drop-down menu that changes based on the item that is selected.

The **Share** button lets you share an item via Mail, Messages, Airdrop, or through a number of third party extensions. OS X will list your recent shares under **Recents**, allowing you to quickly share an item. To configure the third party extensions available in the **Share Menu**, click the Share button and select **More...** or by opening the **Extensions** preference pane from System Preferences. Select **Share Menu** in the left column if not already selected. Use the checkboxes to select which third party extensions you wish to make available in the Share drop-down menu.

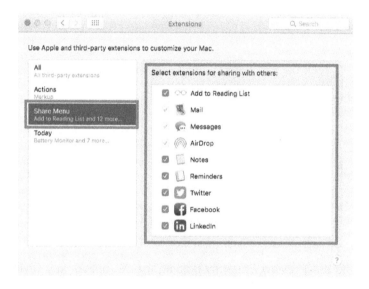

Back to the Finder toolbar, the **Edit Tags** button allows you to add, change, and remove tags. Finally, at the upper right corner of the Finder window is a Spotlight search field that we will cover later in this chapter.

OS X allows you to customize the Finder **Toolbar**, adding, removing, and rearranging tools as you see fit. Secondary click in any open area of the Toolbar to reveal a contextual menu. This menu allows you to choose how the tools appear. Tools can be displayed using both their **Icon and Text**, **Icon Only**, or **Text Only**. The current setting has a checkmark next to it. An option to completely hide the toolbar is also available.

Icon and Text
✓ Icon Only
Text Only
Hide Toolbar

Customize Toolbar...

The final option, **Customize Toolbar...** allows you to add, rearrange, and remove tools using the drop-down tools palette with the entire selection of tools available. Simply drag and drop the tools from the palette into the Toolbar. Rearrange as you see fit. You can choose how the tools will be displayed – **Icon and Text**, **Icon Only**, or **Text Only**. Click the **Done** button when finished. You can also access the palette by selecting **Customize Toolbar...** from the **View** menu.

The additional tools that are available include the **Path** tool, which displays the full path to the location shown in Finder's right-hand pane. You can also see the path by holding down the ⌘ (command) key while clicking on the title shown at the top of the toolbar. The **Eject** tool will eject optical media from the optical drive and will unmount any drive whose contents are displayed in Finder's right-hand pane. The **Burn** tool is used to burn files and folders to optical media such as a CD or DVD. The **Space** and **Flexible Space** tools are used to space out the tools in the toolbar by adding a blank space between them. The **New Folder** tool does what its name implies. It creates a new folder in the current folder displayed in the right-hand pane. The **Delete** tool sends the selected items to the Trash. The **Connect** tool is used to connect to network servers and shared drives.

The **Get Info** tool opens the Get Info window with displays information about the selected file such as its tags, kind, size, location, date created, date modified, its file extension, Spotlight comments, the default application which opens the file, and a file preview. The Get Info tool can be used on multiple files.

The **Quick Look** tool opens a preview of the selected file without launching the application in which it was created. Quick Look allows you to preview a file before deciding to open it. The Quick Look window provides a **Open with** button, allowing you to launch the application that created the file, as well as a **Share** button. You also can open Quick Look by clicking on a file and pressing the spacebar.

The **Share** button allows you to share a selected item using the third party extensions configured in the **Extensions** preference pane in System Preferences.

To add a tool to the Toolbar, drag it from the palette and drop it onto the toolbar. Existing tools located on the Toolbar can be rearranged by dragging them. A tool is removed by dragging it off the Toolbar and onto the tools palette. Click the **Done** button when finished customizing your toolbar.

Tools located on the Toolbar can be rearranged without having to use the drop-down tools palette. To move a tool, hold the ⌘ (command) key down while dragging the tool to its new location. You can also use the ⌘ (command) key to remove a tool. Hold down ⌘ while dragging the tool off the Toolbar. The tool will disappear in a puff of smoke.

To revert back to the default set of tools, drag the default set onto the Finder Toolbar and click **Done**.

Tag Files & Folders

Tagging files is a major shift in the way you work with the OS X file system. Files no longer need to be saved in a specific folder in order to create a relationship between them. Tags remove the need to have deeply nested folders within the file system in order to create relationships between different files. It doesn't matter where files are saved because Tags can be used to relate them to each other. The OS X search capabilities in both Finder and Spotlight allow you to immediately locate files based on their Tags regardless of where they reside in the file system.

Tagging files with a color and name is a convenient way to organize related files, such as files from a project, without having to create a special folder or modify the locations of the files. You can customize the name to something like "Kitchen Remodel Project" or "FY15 Budget" instead of categorizing only by color.

To tag a file that is open, move the cursor to the right of the filename in the Title Bar, click on the drop-down arrow, and click on the Tags field. You can choose a tag from the list or create a new one. This method does not work on all applications, most notably the Microsoft Office productivity suite.

There are several methods to tag an item in Finder. The first is to select the item, click the **Edit Tags** button in the toolbar, and select the appropriate tag. Another method is to select the file, secondary click on it, and add a Tag. Files can be tagged with one or more tags as needed. A third method is to select the file or files you want to Tag and select a Tag from the bottom of the Finder **File** menu. The fourth method is to select the files in Finder and click on the appropriate Tag in the Sidebar. The fifth method is to choose a Tag when saving a file for the first time.

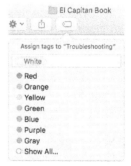

To change or remove a Tag from an open file, click on the arrow next to the file name in the title bar to reveal the drop-down menu. Remove or modify any existing Tags.

To change or remove a tag from an item in Finder, select the file and click the **Edit Tags** button in the Toolbar. Remove or modify any existing Tags. An alternate method is to secondary click on an item and remove or change any existing Tags from the contextual menu that appears. A third method is to use **File > Tags...** to remove existing Tags.

Customize Tags

You can rename **Tags** in the Finder preference pane. Select **Preferences...** from the **Finder** menu. You can also access the preferences by entering ⌘, (command+comma). Once the Finder preferences appear, make sure **Tags** is selected from the set of four icons at the top of the pane.

To rename a tag, click on its name and rename it. The tag will appear under **Tags** in the Sidebar if its checkbox is checked. Drag the Tags to rearrange their order.

To add a new Tag, click the **+** button. To remove a Tag, click the **–** button or secondary click on the Tag and choose **Delete**. You can also rename a tag by secondary clicking on it and choosing **Rename**.

The bottom section of this preference pane is used to configure which tags appear in Finder menus. To remove a Tag, drag it off the preference pane. To add a Tag, drag it from the list at the top into the **Tags...** box at the bottom.

A quicker way to create a Tag is to click the **Edit Tags** button in the toolbar to reveal an option to enter the name of a new Tag. Begin typing in the field, and you will be given the option to create a new Tag. Press **return** when finished.

Search for Tags

All files associated with a Tag can be easily and quickly retrieved using the Sidebar in Finder. However, there is no easy way to find files and folders tagged with multiple Tags in the Sidebar. The only method is to perform a tag search using Spotlight.

To search for a file that is tagged with both a blue and a purple tag, open Spotlight and enter the following search.

```
tag:blue tag:purple
```

You can also search for tagged files by the Tag name. For example, I have named the blue tag "OS X" and the purple tag "El Capitan." The following Spotlight search will return the same result as the search above.

```
tag:OS X tag:El Capitan
```

Create a Smart Folder

After selecting **Show all in Finder...**, you can save your search by clicking the **Save** button located in the upper right of the Finder window below the Tabs. In actuality, you are creating a **Smart Folder**, a dynamic list of items meeting your search criteria. By saving a search as a Smart Folder, you save time by not having to rebuild a search from scratch each time. When you click the **Save** button, a drop-down sheet will appear allowing you to name the Smart Folder, save it, and display it in the Sidebar. I recommend saving frequently used searches to the Sidebar so you can access them quickly.

Smart Folders remain current as you add and delete items matching the search criteria. All items are conveniently displayed in a Smart Folder as if they were located in a single folder regardless of where they actually reside. While the items only appear to be located in one folder, they remain safely tucked away in the folders in which you saved them.

OS X offers several ways to create a Smart Folder. The first is to execute a search using Spotlight, selecting **Show all in Finder...** and then clicking **Save**. Other methods include selecting **File > Find**, using the ⌘**F** (command+F) shortcut, or typing search criteria into the **Search** field of an open Finder window. Another method is to select **File > New Smart Folder** or use the shortcut ⌥⌘**N** (option+command+N) when Finder is the active application.

To add additional search criteria, click the **+** button next to **Save**. You can choose the search scope with **This Mac** being the default. You also have the option of only searching within the current folder. That option is directly to the right of **This Mac**. Any search line can be removed by clicking the **–** button. Select **Other...** to reveal a list of over 100 attributes against which you can search.

Once you have perfected your search criteria, click the **Save** button to reveal a drop-down sheet allowing you to name your Smart Folder, save it to a folder, and add it to Sidebar. By default, all Smart Folders are saved to the **Saved Searches** folder, however, you can choose where to save your Smart Folder. By default, the checkbox next to **Add to Sidebar** is checked. Uncheck it if you do not want your Smart Folder to appear in the Sidebar, otherwise your new Smart Folder will appear at the bottom of the list of Favorites.

Open a File & Close Finder

Holding down the ⌥ (option) key while double-clicking on a file or folder in Finder will open the file while simultaneously closing the current Finder window. You can also accomplish the same thing with the keyboard shortcut ⌥⌘**O** (option+command+O).

Disable Opening Folders in Tabs

By default, El Capitan opens all folders in a new tab. It is sometimes more convenient to have multiple tabs available, particularly if you are copying or moving files between them. In the past you would have had to open multiple Finder windows, cluttering your desktop. However, if you prefer not to open folders in Tabs, you can disable this feature.

To change the OS X El Capitan default to behave like older versions of OS X, open the **Finder** preferences by selecting **Finder > Preferences...** or by entering ⌘, (command+comma). Next, select **General** if not selected already. Uncheck the checkbox next to **Open folders in tabs instead of new windows**.

Changing how folders are opened in Finder does not disable the Finder Tabs feature. You can still open new Tabs with ⌘T (command+T) or by choosing **File > New Tab**.

When you disable opening folders in tabs, you also change another OS X behavior. Double clicking to open a folder while holding down the ⌘ (command) key will open the folder in a new Finder window. Holding down the ⌘ (command) key when tabs are enabled opens the folder in a new Tab.

Merge Multiple Finder Windows into Tabs

If you have multiple Finder windows open, you can merge them all into a single window with each window becoming its own Tab. To merge all windows, click on any Finder window then select **Window > Merge All Windows**.

Make a New Finder Window from a Tab

Any of the Tabs in a Finder window can be moved to a separate, new Finder window. Secondary click on the tab you want to move to a new window and select **Move Tab to New Window**. Alternately, you can drag and drop a tab out of a Finder window onto the desktop to make it open in a new Finder window.

The contextual menu revealed when secondary clicking on a Tab also allows you to create a **New Tab**, **Close Tab**, **Close Other Tabs**, or **Move Tab to New Window**.

Hide the Tab Bar

The **Tab Bar** appears just below the Finder toolbar. You can only hide the Tab Bar when Finder is displaying a single tab. Once multiple tabs are opened, OS X will automatically unhide the Tab Bar. To hide the Tab Bar, select **View > Hide Tab Bar** or enter ⇧⌘T (shift+command+T). Hiding the Tab Bar when you have a single tab open makes the Finder interface appear cleaner. The Tab Bar will automatically unhide when a second tab is opened.

Change the Icon Size, Spacing, Arrangement, & Sort

The default icon size in OS X is 64 x 64 pixels. While this is good for most applications, you may find it too small when trying to view pictures or movies in Finder. OS X allows you to change the default icon size to make it smaller or larger.

To change the default icon size, secondary click any open space in a Finder window to reveal a contextual menu. Choose **Show View Options**. You can also select **Show View Options** from under Finder's **View** menu or enter **⌘J** (command+J). The Finder View panel appears with the name of the folder located in the Title Bar at the top of the window. If the checkbox next to **Always open in icon view** is checked, this folder will always open in icon view.

The next section allows you to change the arrangement of the icons and how they are sorted. Use the drop downs to choose your desired arrangement and sorting methods.

In the next section, you can change the icon size using the slider. Icons can be made as small as 16 x 16 pixels or as large as 512 x 512 pixels. The OS X default is 64 x 64. The largest size is handy when sorting through a folder containing pictures or movies.

The next section allows you to change the text size for the label shown at the bottom of files and folders. The default text size is 12 points. Supported text sizes are 10, 11, 12, 13, 14, 15, and 16 points. By default, the label position is at the bottom of files and folders. OS X lets you display the label at the bottom or to the right of an item.

The next section contains two checkboxes. The first, **Show item info**, will display the size of the file or the number of items a folder contains. The second checkbox, **Show icon preview**, is checked by default and will render a preview of the file content. If you uncheck it, OS X will display only default icons rather than rendering previews of file content.

The next section allows you to change the background upon which icons are displayed. The default is white and you have the choice of choosing a color or a picture.

Clicking on the **Use as Defaults** button located at the bottom of the window makes your selections the default for the folder and all of its sub-folders.

Show the User Library Folder

OS X allows you to toggle a switch to make the **Library** folder in your **Home** directory visible. To make the **Library** folder visible, open **Finder** and navigate to your **Home** directory.

Secondary click any open space in the Finder window showing your Home directory. Choose **Show View Options**. You can also select **Show View Options** from under Finder's **View** menu or enter **⌘J** (command+J). Check the checkbox next to **Show Library Folder**.

If you do not want to permanently show your Library folder and need only temporary access, hold down the ⌥ (option) key while selecting the **Go** menu. The **Library** folder will appear while you are holding down the ⌥ (option) key. Select **Go > Library**.

Change the Spring Load Delay

Try dragging a file or folder onto another folder, pausing for a moment without releasing your hold on the file. Suddenly the folder will spring open to reveal its contents. This is an OS X feature called spring-loaded folders. Once a spring-loaded folder opens, you can repeat to drill down through the directory structure until you reach your desired destination folder. The delay, the amount of time you must pause on a folder before it springs open, can be tweaked or turned off all together.

To adjust the spring load delay, open the **Accessibility** preference pane in the System Preferences application. Next, select **Mouse & Trackpad** in the left-hand pane. Adjust the spring load **Delay** using the slider located next to **Spring-loading delay**. If you want to disable the spring load delay feature entirely, uncheck the checkbox next to **Spring-loading delay**.

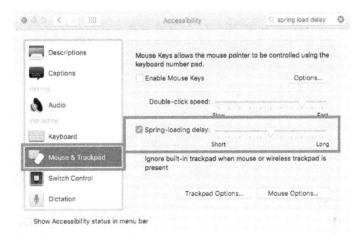

The **Tab Bar** appears just below the Finder toolbar. Like OS X folders, tabs are spring-loaded meaning the tab will expand if you drag a file or folder and hover over it until the spring load delay timer expires. If you are in a hurry and don't want to wait for the spring load delay timer to expire, hit the **spacebar** to bypass the spring load delay to open a folder or tab immediately.

Select the Folder Displayed in New Windows and Tabs

OS X displays the **All My Files** view when new **Finder** windows and tabs are opened. If you prefer new windows and tabs display another folder, such as your **Home** directory, you can set this attribute in the Finder preferences.

To set the location for new Finder windows and tabs, open the Finder preferences by selecting **Finder > Preferences...** or by entering **⌘,** (command+comma). Next, select the **General** tab if not already highlighted. Use the drop-down menu under **New Finder windows show** to set your desired location. This attribute will set the location for both new Finder windows and tabs.

Close All Finder Windows

Sometimes you'll end up with a lot of open Finder windows. Wouldn't it be great if there was an easy and quick way to close all of them? Hold down the ⌥ (option) key while clicking the red **Close** window button in the upper left-hand corner of any Finder window. All Finder windows will close. You also can enter ⌥⌘W (option+command+W) to close all Finder windows. By the way, this trick works for any application. You can also minimize all open windows of an application by holding down the ⌥ (option) key while clicking the yellow **Minimize** window button in the Title Bar.

Show the Path Bar

There are a number of ways to view the path taken to arrive at the folder currently displayed in Finder. You could press and hold the **Back** button in the upper left of the toolbar to display the path taken to reach the folder. Another method is the hold the ⌘ (command) key down while clicking on the name of the folder in the title bar. This will reveal the path taken to reach the folder displayed in Finder.

Yet another method is to display the Finder **Path Bar** at the bottom of every Finder window. To turn on the Finder Path Bar, select **View > Show Path Bar** or enter ⌥⌘P (option+command+P). When the Path Bar is enabled, every Finder window will display the Path Bar at the bottom of its window.

To turn the Finder Path Bar off, select **View > Hide Path Bar** or enter ⌥⌘P (option+command+P).

Shorten the Path Bar

OS X lists the path from the root of the disk drive to the current directory, which, depending on the depth of your directory structure can result in ridiculously long paths. If most of your file browsing is done in your **Home** directory, it would be better if the path was shortened to reflect your location as it relates to your Home directory.

To shorten the path shown in the **Path Bar**, open Terminal and enter the following commands. This change takes effect immediately.

```
defaults write com.apple.finder PathBarRootAtHome -bool TRUE

killall Finder
```

To revert to the OS X default and show the longer path, enter the following commands.

```
defaults delete com.apple.finder PathBarRootAtHome

killall Finder
```

Path Bar Tips & Tricks

You can drag files into any folder listed in the **Path Bar** to move them. If you want to copy the file instead, hold down the ⌥ (option) key while dragging. To create an alias, hold down ⌥⌘ (option+command) while dragging. You can even drag between different Finder windows. While dragging, hover the cursor over the Path Bar of the inactive Finder window and it will become active after a few moments.

You can see the contents of any folder in the **Path Bar** by double-clicking on it. Its contents will replace the items displayed in the current Finder window. If you hold down the ⌘ (command) key while double-clicking, the folder will open in a new tab. Holding down the ⌥ (option) key while double-clicking opens the folder in a new Finder window while simultaneously closing the source window or tab.

A folder can be moved by dragging it off the Path Bar and into another folder, window, tab, or onto the Desktop. Holding down the ⌥ (option) key while dragging will make a copy of the folder. Holding down ⌥⌘ (option+command) will create an alias in the new location. A folder can even be dragged within the Path Bar to move it to its new location.

If you change your mind while dragging, press the **esc** key to cancel the operation. If you change your mind after completing the move, copy, or alias creation, select **Edit > Undo** or type ⌘**Z** (command+Z) to undo.

Sometimes a path is so long that it cannot fit in the Path Bar. In that case, OS X will truncate the folder names. Simply pointing to a truncated folder name will expand it so you can read it.

Show the Path in the Title Bar

If you prefer to not use the Path Bar, OS X allows you to configure Finder's Title Bar to display the path. By default, the Title Bar simply shows the name of the folder currently displayed. If you would like to show the path instead, open Terminal and enter the following commands. This change takes effect immediately.

```
defaults write com.apple.finder _FXShowPosixPathInTitle -bool TRUE

killall Finder
```

To revert back to the OS X default, enter the following commands.

```
defaults delete com.apple.finder _FXShowPosixPathInTitle

killall Finder
```

Show the Status Bar

The Finder **Status Bar** shows the number of items contained within a folder and the amount of free space left on the drive in which the folder is located.

To turn the Finder Status Bar on, select **View > Show Status Bar** or enter ⌘/ (command+/). When the Status Bar is enabled, every Finder window will display the Status Bar at the bottom, below the Path Bar.

Another handy feature of the Finder Status Bar is that it provides a slider in the lower right corner that you can use to change the size of the icons displayed in the Finder window. Slide the slider left or right to make the icons smaller or larger, respectively.

To hide the Finder Status Bar, select **View > Hide Status Bar** or enter ⌘/ (command+/).

Show File Extensions

For those of you switching from a Microsoft Windows PC to a Mac and are worried because you miss the comfort of seeing those 3- and 4-letter file extensions after every filename, OS X allows you to turn on file extensions. They are disabled in OS X by default.

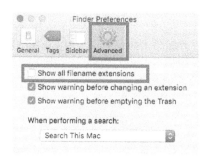

To have OS X show the file extensions, open the Finder preferences by selecting **Finder > Preferences...** or by entering ⌘**,** (command+comma). Next, select the **Advanced** tab if not already highlighted. Check the checkbox next to **Show all filename extensions**.

Note that OS X will also warn you if you change a filename extension. To disable this warning, uncheck the checkbox next to **Show warning before changing an extension**. However, changing a file extension could make a file unusable.

Quickly Duplicate a File

OS X offers a number of methods to duplicate a file. You can select a file in Finder, secondary click to reveal the contextual menu and choose **Duplicate**. Or you could select **File > Duplicate**. A quicker method is the hold down the ⌥ (option) key and drag the file to a blank space in the Finder window and release.

Cut & Paste Files

There are a few things that freak out Microsoft Windows users who are moving to a Mac. First, there is no right mouse button (there isn't a left either). Second, the **delete** key on a Mac keyboard acts like the backspace key on a PC. So how do you delete? On a Mac, the **delete** key works both ways. Hold down the **fn** key while pressing **delete**. Third, OS X doesn't display file extensions by default, proving that learning the difference between all of those 3- and 4-letter extensions was a terrible waste of your time. Fourth, windows do not have scroll bars. You'll see what to do about that soon. Finally, the **Cut** command and ⌘**X** doesn't work in Finder. OMG! How do you cut and paste a file?

No need to panic. Since OS X is based on the UNIX operating system, there is no concept of cut and paste. Cut and paste is equivalent to a move in OS X. To accomplish a cut and paste in OS X, you would simply move a file by dragging and dropping it in its new location.

If you really, really can't live without cut and paste, there is a workaround. Select the file in Finder, then copy it by selecting **Edit > Copy** or by entering ⌘**C** (command+C). Navigate to the file's new location and hold down the ⌥ (option) key while selecting the **Edit** menu. When the ⌥ (option) key is held down, **Paste Item** will become **Move Item Here**. You can also enter ⌥⌘**V** (option+command+V) to move the file. This effectively is the same thing as cut and paste in the PC world.

Rename a Group of Files

OS X features the ability to rename a list of files using a batch rename tool in Finder.

Launch **Finder** and select the documents you want to rename. Next, secondary click on one of the files in the group and choose **Rename**. The number of items will be listed as in **Rename 10 Items...** in the contextual menu.

The drop-down configuration sheet offers several renaming options: **Replace Text**, **Add Text**, or **Format**.

Replace Text is used when the files all have a common element within their name. For example, files from a digital camera may be named "img" followed by a number. You could replace "img" with something more descriptive like "vacation."

The **Add Text** option allows you to add text before or after the existing file name.

The **Format** option lets you completely change the file name to one of three different formats: **Name and Index**, **Name and Counter**, or **Name and Date**. For example a group of files could be renamed "Vacation" with an index, counter, or date appended.

For all options, click the **Rename** button when finished.

Delete a File Immediately

A new feature Apple added to the El Capitan release of OS X is the ability to delete files immediately without having the first send them to the Trash.

To delete a file immediately, highlight the file you want to delete in Finder and hold down the ⌥ (option) key while selecting **File > Delete Immediately...** or enter ⌥⌘delete (option+command+delete). A dialog box will appear to confirm the deletion and warn that this action cannot be undone. Click the **Delete** button to delete the file immediately or **Cancel**.

Note that the Delete Immediately option will only appear in the **File** menu when you are holding down the ⌥ (option) key. When the ⌥ (option) key is held down, **Move to Trash** will change to **Delete Immediately**.

Change the Scroll Bar Behavior

Scroll bars only appear when you are actually scrolling. This is very different from Microsoft Windows where scroll bars are an ugly and permanent blight on the right and bottom edge of every window. If you are a former Windows PC user and really miss your scroll bars, OS X can be configured so those ugly scroll bars are permanently tacked to the right and bottom edges of every OS X window. To change the behavior of the scroll bars, open the **General** preference pane from System Preferences.

When set to **Automatically based on mouse or trackpad**, scrollbars will not appear unless the document requires scrollbars and you have placed either one finger on the mouse or two fingers on a trackpad in preparation to scroll. This is the OS X default. If you like your scroll bars hidden until you are actually scrolling, choose **When scrolling**. Once you're done scrolling, the scrollbars will hide themselves. If you are a former Windows user suffering from scroll bar separation anxiety, select **Always**.

You have two options for clicking within a scroll bar – **Jump to the next page**, which is the default behavior, or **Jump to the spot that's clicked**. When **Jump to the next page** is selected, clicking within the scroll bar will page up or page down a single page at a time.

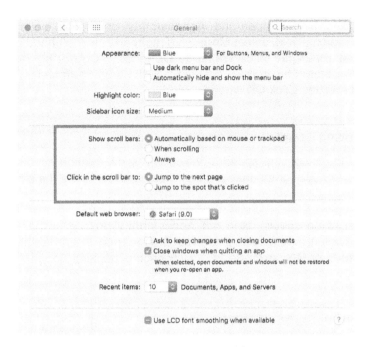

When **Jump to the spot that's clicked** is selected, clicking within the scroll bar will take you to that spot in the document. For example, clicking the very bottom of the scroll bar will take you to the end of a document. Clicking ¼ of the way down the scroll bar, will allow you to jump about a quarter way through the document. This feature is quite handy when you need to navigate quickly through a long document.

Disable Scrolling Inertia

OS X mimics the scrolling experience of iOS devices where a flick of your fingers causes the window to scroll rapidly. This feature is called **Scrolling Inertia** and is enabled by default. Flicking your fingers across your trackpad will cause the window to scroll rapidly. Compared to normal scrolling, it appears the window was scrolling about 100 mph. If you don't like Scrolling Inertia, OS X allows you to disable it.

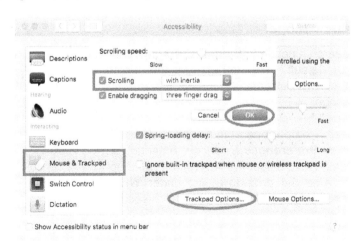

To disable Scrolling Inertia, open the **Accessibility** preference pane in the System Preferences application. Next, select **Mouse & Trackpad** in the left-hand pane. To turn off Scrolling Inertia on a trackpad, click **Trackpad Options…**. **Do not uncheck** the box next to **Scrolling** as it will turn off scrolling. Instead, use the drop-down menu next to **Scrolling** to select **without inertia**. Click **OK** when finished.

Change the Scrolling Speed

OS X allows you to change the speed at which you scroll through documents. If you find the default setting too slow or too fast you can tweak it until you get the scrolling speed just right.

To change the scrolling speed, open the **Accessibility** preference pane in the System Preferences application. Next, select **Mouse & Trackpad** in the left-hand pane. Click **Trackpad Options…** or **Mouse Options…** to configure the scrolling speed on each.

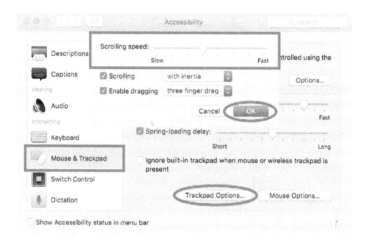

Both the trackpad and mouse options will reveal a drop-down configuration sheet. Use the slider at the top to adjust the scrolling speed. Click **OK** when finished.

Change the Search Scope

When using the search function in **Finder**, OS X searches your entire Mac by default. You can change the search scope to limit it to the currently displayed folder or a previous search scope.

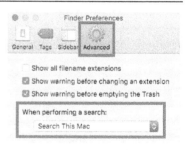

To change the search scope, open Finder preferences by selecting **Finder > Preferences…** or by entering ⌘, (command+comma). Next, select the **Advanced** tab if not selected already. Use the drop-down list under **When performing a search** to select your desired search scope.

Remove the Empty Trash Warning

Every time you empty the **Trash**, OS X asks you if you are sure you want to permanently erase the items in the Trash. If you find this warning unnecessary, you can turn it off.

To tell OS X to stop confirming that you want to empty the Trash, open Finder preferences by selecting **Finder > Preferences...** or by entering ⌘, (command+comma). Next, select the **Advanced** tab if not already highlighted.

Uncheck the checkbox next to **Show warning before emptying the Trash**.

Quiet the Trash

OS X makes a noise that sounds like the crinkling of paper when emptying the **Trash**. This can be annoying if you're working in a quiet office environment or are listening to music. The sound of the trash emptying can disturb your concentration or the concentration of others.

To quiet the Trash when emptying, open Terminal and enter the following commands. This change takes effect immediately.

```
defaults write com.apple.finder FinderSounds -bool FALSE

killall Finder
```

Enter the following commands in Terminal to revert to the OS X default. This change takes effect immediately.

```
defaults delete com.apple.finder FinderSounds

killall Finder
```

Change the Columns Displayed in List View

OS X displays the following three columns in the **Finder List View**: **Date Modified**, **Size**, and **Kind**. The Finder List View also supports other attributes such as **Date Created**, **Date Last Opened**, **Date Added**, **Version**, **Comments**, and **Tags**.

To change the columns shown in the Finder List View, select **View > Show View Options** from the Finder View menu or enter ⌘J (command+J) to display the View Options preference pane. Check the checkboxes next to the items you want to display. Be sure your Finder window is in list view otherwise you will not see these options.

Multiple Item Inspector

The Get Info feature provides information about a file. If you select multiple files and choose **File > Get Info** or enter ⌘i (command+i), OS X will open a Get Info pane for each file. That might not be what you intended if you wanted to see the combined size of a group of files.

To launch the **Multiple Item Inspector**, hold down the ⌥ (option) key while selecting **File > Show Inspector** or enter ⌥⌘i (option+command+i). Additional files can be added to an open Multiple Item Inspector window by holding down the ⌘ (command) key while clicking on them. The Multiple Item Inspector will dynamically update as new files are added.

Change the Title Bar Font Size

OS X allows you to change the size of the Title Bar font. To change the font size, enter the following commands in Terminal. The number equals the font size. In the example, the new font size is 14 points.

```
defaults write com.apple.finder NSTitleBarFontSize 14

killall Finder
```

To revert back to the OS X default, enter the following commands.

```
defaults delete com.apple.finder NSTitleBarFontSize

killall Finder
```

Calculate Folder Sizes

When you're viewing items in **List View** in **Finder**, you will notice that only files have an entry under the **Size** column. OS X does not calculate the size of folders. Therefore, you will see a pair of dashes in the size column.

If you would like to see the amount of disk space your folders are taking up, you need to tell OS X to **Calculate all sizes**.

To enable this feature, select **View > Show View Options** from the Finder View menu or enter ⌘J (command+J) to display the View Options preference pane. Check the checkbox next to **Calculate all sizes**.

This attribute is set on a per-folder basis. So if you would like to make this the default for all folders click the **Use as Defaults** button at the bottom of the preference pane. However, be careful to ensure that the other attributes on the preference pane are set to properly display folders the way you want to see them.

Increase the Window Resize Area

Any application window can be resized by hovering your cursor over any of its borders until the cursor changes to the resizing cursor, which looks like a double headed black arrow. Dragging the resizing cursor allows you to resize the window. The area in which the cursor changes to the resizing cursor is quite thin and it is sometimes difficult to get the cursor in exactly the right spot to make the resizing cursor appear.

This tweak increases the size of the area in which the cursor will change into the resizing cursor. Open Terminal and enter the following command. You will need to logout and log back in for the change to take effect.

```
defaults write -g AppleEdgeResizeExteriorSize 15
```

Feel free to try different numbers at the end of the command to make the area larger or smaller as you see fit.

To revert back to the OS X default, enter the following command. You will have to logout and log back in for the change to take effect.

```
defaults delete -g AppleEdgeResizeExteriorSize
```

Add a Quit Command

Finder is the one application that you simply can't quit. The reason for this is that Finder is responsible for managing the OS X file system. If you check out the **Finder** menu you will not find a **Quit** command. That is because other than relaunching Finder through **Force Quit** or with a **killall Finder** command, Finder must run continuously.

So why would you want to add a Quit command to the Finder menu? Having a Quit command in the Finder menu is a quick and easy way to execute the **killall Finder** command or to force quit and restart Finder.

Open Terminal and enter the following commands to add a Quit command to Finder's File menu.

```
defaults write com.apple.finder QuitMenuItem -bool TRUE
```

```
killall Finder
```

To revert back to the OS X default and remove the Quit command from the Finder menu, enter the following commands.

```
defaults delete com.apple.finder QuitMenuItem
```

```
killall Finder
```

13

Window Snapping

There is only one feature I miss when switching between my Windows PC at work and my MacBook Pro at home – Microsoft's window snapping feature. Drag a window to the right edge of the screen and it will snap to exactly half the size of your desktop. Drag another window to the left edge and it will snap to the other half. This feature is great when comparing two documents. While Apple added Split View mode in OS X El Capitan, it just isn't quite the same as the window snapping features of Microsoft Windows. Another nice feature is the ability to maximize a window by dragging it to the top of the desktop. I know I can maximize a window with the green Full Screen button, but doing so hides the Menu Bar and the Dock. Often it's more productive to not have to unhide the Menu Bar or the Dock when you need them. Luckily there is an application in the Mac App Store that offers window snapping, and like everything on a Mac, it is more powerful and more fully featured than Microsoft's implementation.

 BetterSnapTool is a full featured, highly customizable window snapping tool available for $1.99 on the Mac App Store. As I write this sentence, all versions of this app have 2,964 five-star ratings. Written by Andreas Hegenberg, BetterSnapTool allows you to instantly change the size of your windows by simply dragging them to the top, left, or right edge, or the 4 corners of your desktop. BetterSnapTool is available from the Mac App Store at: https://itunes.apple.com/us/app/bettersnaptool/id417375580?mt=12.

Similar to Microsoft's window snapping feature, you can snap a window to the left edge and another to the right edge of your desktop to compare two documents side-by-side. Windows can be maximized by dragging them to the top edge of the desktop. This differs from OS X's maximize function as the Menu Bar and Dock do not hide when using BetterSnapTool.

Everything is just better on a Mac, even window snapping. BetterSnapTool lets you create your own custom Snap Areas anywhere on your desktop and it supports 19 different window resizing and snapping options. It also allows you to create keyboard shortcuts to move and resize windows.

The description on the Mac App Store states that, "BetterSnapTool is very customizable and will change the way you work with your Mac!" I couldn't agree more. I recommend you download it from the Mac App Store now. Buying this productivity tool was probably the best $1.99 I've spent on any application for my Mac.

Enable Snap Areas

BetterSnapTool is pre-configured to snap to 7 locations on your desktop. Snapping a window to the top maximizes it without hiding the Menu Bar and the Dock. Snapping a window to the left or right edge of the desktop, pins the window to the selected edge and resizes it to take up half the desktop. Snapping a window to any of the desktop's four corners pins it to the corner and resizes it to take up a quarter of the desktop.

BetterSnapTool will provide a preview of how the window will resize when the cursor touches the corner or edge of the desktop. Drag and hold a window to one of the snap areas. Releasing your hold will cause the window to resize. If you don't release your hold, you can drag the window off the edge or corner and release to cancel the resizing.

To open the BetterSnapTool preference pane, click on its Menu Extra in the Menu Bar and select **Preferences**. Click on **General Settings**, if not already highlighted.

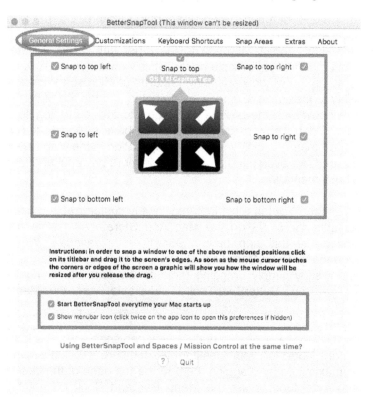

The top part of the preference pane shows the seven snap locations with a check in each checkbox indicating they are active. Uncheck any checkbox next to a snap location you do not want to use.

The two checkboxes at the bottom of the pane are checked by default. The **Start BetterSnapTool everytime your Mac starts up** ensures that BetterSnapTool is available for you every time you restart your Mac. If you uncheck this box, you'll have to manually launch the BetterSnapTool everytime you want to use it.

The checkbox next to **Show menubar icon** toggles the Menu Extra on and off. This provides easy access to the BetterSnapTool preference pane. Once you have completely configured BetterSnapTool to your liking, you can uncheck this box to remove the Menu Extra. To access the preferences again, launch BetterSnapTool from Launchpad, Spotlight, or from your Applications folder or stack.

Do not press the **Quit** button at the bottom of the preference pane as it quits the application. To close the preference pane, click on the red close button in the upper left.

Clicking the button labeled **Using BetterSnapTool and Spaces / Mission Control at the same time?** opens a window with instructions on how to adjust the drag delay when dragging windows to another desktop space located to the left or right of your active desktop space. The issue here is that too small a delay will interfere with BetterSnapTool's ability to snap to the left or right edge. If the delay is too small, the desktop space will change as OS X assumes you want to move the window to another space. The recommendation is to set the window edge delay between desktop spaces to 2 seconds, giving you sufficient time to drag a window to the left or right edge and release your hold to resize. If you want to drag the window to an adjacent desktop space, simply hold the window along the edge until the window edge delay timer expires and the desktop space changes. BetterSnapTool will preview the window resize, but will not resize the window unless you release your hold.

To adjust the drag delay between spaces, open Terminal and enter the following commands.

```
defaults write com.apple.dock workspaces-edge-delay -float 2
```

```
killall Dock
```

This will adjust the delay timer to 2 seconds. I've used BetterSnapTool for a long time and I've found a 1 second delay works fine for me. You can adjust the time by changing the number after **–float** in the first command to find the right delay that works best for you. Decimals are allowed so you can try 1.5 or 2.5 seconds. Setting the number to 0 completely removes the workspace edge delay and effectively eliminates the edges of your desktop as snap areas for BetterSnapTool.

For more information on the workspace edge delay timer, see the section "Move a Window to Another Desktop."

Customizing the Preview Overlay

When you drag a window to one of the snap locations configured in the **General Settings** tab, BetterSnapTool provides a preview overlay to show you what the window will look like when resized. If you don't like the default of a white border and gray background, you can change these settings as well as the border width, corners, and animation.

Select **Preferences** from the BetterSnapTool Menu Extra in the Menu Bar. If you chose to not show the Menu Extra, launch BetterSnapTool from Launchpad, Spotlight, or from your Applications folder or App Stack. Click on **Customizations** if it is not already highlighted.

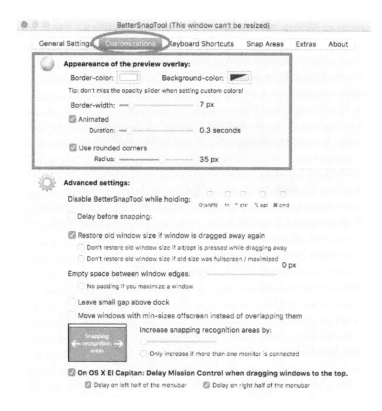

Clicking the white box next to **Border-color** launches a color wheel that lets you change the color of the border around the preview overlay. To change the preview overlay background from the default, click the black/gray box next to **Background-color**. Similarly, you will be presented with a color wheel to select your desired background color.

You can customize the width of the preview overlay border using the slider next to **Border-width**. Valid widths are from 0 to 50 pixels with the default being 7 pixels. You can also click on **7 px** to directly enter the width in the box provided.

The corners of the preview overlay border are rounded with a default radius of 35 pixels. You can use the slider next to **Use rounded corners** to change the radius to any value between 0 and 60 pixels. Similar to the border width, you can click on **35 px** to directly enter the width in the box provided. Unchecking the checkbox changes the preview overlay corners to 90-degree angles.

The preview overlay's animation duration can be adjusted from 0 to 2 seconds with the default being 0.3 seconds. The duration is how long it takes the preview overlay to expand to show you how the window will resize. Unchecking the checkbox next to **Animation** disables the preview overlay animation. In this case, BetterSnapTool will instantly show you how the window will resize when you drag a window to a snap location.

Temporarily Disable Window Snapping

You can configure a modifier key or combination of modifier keys to temporarily disable BetterSnapTool. This is handy if you intend to drag a window to another desktop space and don't want BetterSnapTool to engage. You can choose any one or a combination of the following modifier keys: ⇧ **fn** ^ ⌥ ⌘ (shift, function, control, option, command).

To configure modifier keys to temporarily disable BetterSnapTool, open the BetterSnapTool preference pane and click on **Customizations** if not already highlighted. Check the checkboxes above your desired modifier keys in the **Advanced settings** section.

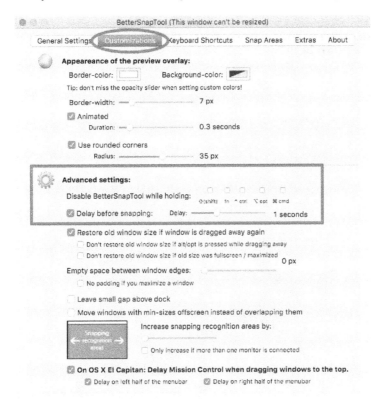

Configure the Snap Delay

BetterSnapTool displays the preview overlay animation the moment your cursor touches a defined Snap Area. If you would like to add a delay before the preview overlay is displayed, open the BetterSnapTool preference pane and click on **Customizations** if not already highlighted. Check the checkbox next to **Delay before snapping** to reveal a slider that supports values between 0 and 2 seconds. You can also click on the **second** box to directly enter the delay.

Be careful setting this delay timer as it can conflict with the workspace edge delay between desktop spaces. If the workspace edge delay is set to a smaller delay than the snap delay, BetterSnapTool will never display the preview overlay. The workspace edge delay timer will expire and your window will be moved to the adjacent desktop space.

Disable Window Size Restoration

After resizing a window with BetterSnapTool, you can resize it back to its original size by dragging it away from the Snap Area. For example, if you resized a window to occupy half your desktop by dragging it to the right edge, dragging it away will restore the window to its original size. This function is enabled by default.

To disable window size restoration, open the BetterSnapTool preference pane and click on **Customizations** if not already highlighted. Uncheck the checkbox next to **Restore old window size if window is dragged away again.**

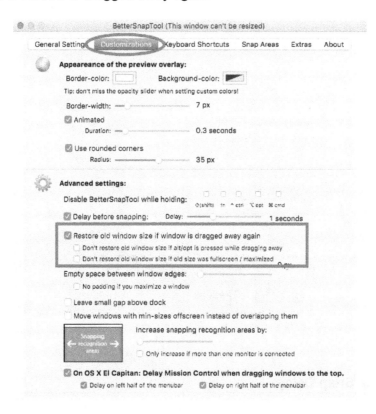

Another available option is to disable window size restoration when the original window size was Full Screen or maximized. To enable this feature, check the checkbox next to **Don't restore old window size if old size was fullscreen / maximized.**

Add Padding Around Windows & the Dock

BetterSnapTool leaves no space between the edge of the desktop and the window when resizing. BetterSnapTool allows you to configure the amount of padding around a window after it is resized.

If you would like some padding around a window, open the BetterSnapTool preference pane and click on **Customizations** if not already highlighted. Use the slider next to **Empty space between window edges** to select a value between 0 and 100 pixels. You can click on the **0 px** to directly enter the padding size in the box provided. Note that the padding will be applied around all four sides of the window.

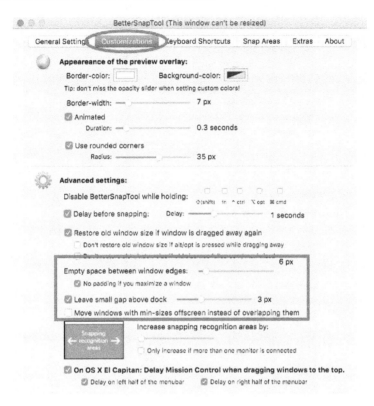

You can check the checkbox next to **No padding if you maximize a window** to avoid adding padding around maximized windows. If you do not check this option and have padding configured, windows will not fully maximize as they will be surrounded on all sides by the padding configured by the slider.

BetterSnapTool will not resize a window over the Dock. You can increase the separation between the bottom edge of a window and the Dock by checking the box next to **Leave small gap above dock** and moving the slider to your desired gap. Valid entries are 0 to 10 pixels. Similar to other configuration items, you can click the setting and directly enter a value into the configuration box.

A final option is to ensure windows with minimum sizes do not overlap. When this option is enabled, minimum sized windows will be pushed off screen.

Increase the Snap Recognition Area

BetterSnapTool will play the preview overlay animation or resize a window the moment your cursor reaches an active Snap Area. You can increase the snap recognition area up to 100 pixels (the default is 0). The increased snap recognition area means that you will no longer have to move your cursor all the way to the edge of an active Snap Area. You only have to move your cursor near it.

To increase the snap recognition area, open the BetterSnapTool preference pane and click on **Customizations** if not already highlighted. Use the slider next to **Increase snapping recognition areas by** to select a value between 0 and 100 pixels.

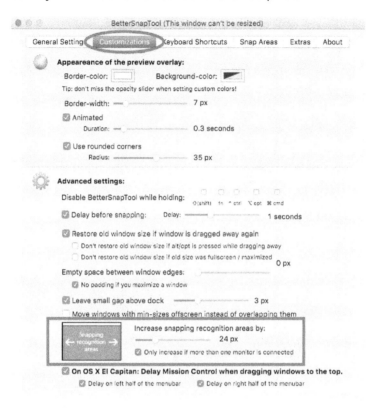

If you have a multiple monitor system, you will have to configure a larger snap recognition area in order for BetterSnapTool to resize windows dragged to the edge of the desktop. In a dual monitor setup, you will notice that only one edge resizes windows. Dragging a window to the opposite edge of the desktop moves the window to the other monitor. By increasing the snap recognition area, BetterSnapTool will resize the window without the cursor actually having to touch the edge of the desktop.

You can configure larger snap recognition areas to enable only when more than one monitor is connected. This is handy if you have a MacBook, MacBook Air, or MacBook Pro and are using it in a dual monitor setup. When docked in dual monitor mode the larger snap recognition area is enabled. When undocked, the larger snap recognition area is disabled. Check the box next to **Only increase if more than one monitor is connected** to enable this option.

Delay Mission Control

A new feature in OS X El Capitan is a handy shortcut that lets you simultaneously open Mission Control and drag a window to another desktop. By simply dragging a window to the very top of your screen, Mission Control will launch. Unfortunately, this interferes with BetterSnapTool's ability to snap a window to full size by dragging it to the top of the screen.

The solution is to configure a delay before Mission Control launches. This can be done in the BetterSnapTool preference pane

To delay Mission Control, open the BetterSnapTool preference pane and click on **Customizations** if not already highlighted. Check the checkbox next to **On OS X El Capitan: Delay Mission Control when dragging windows to the top**.

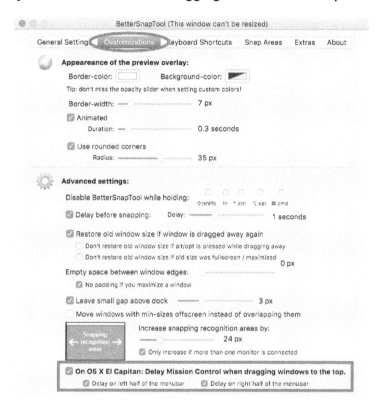

You can configure delays for the entire screen or for only the left or right half of the Menu Bar. Check the checkboxes next to **Delay on left half of the menubar** or **Delay on the right half of the menubar** to configure a delay for only half the screen. This allows you to take advantage of both El Capitan's Mission Control feature and the BetterSnapTool's full screen window snap.

Create a Pop-up Window Resizing Menu

BetterSnapTool supports a total of 20 window resizing options. Only 7 of the options are available by dragging a window to a snap recognition area. The additional 13 window resizing options can only be accessed by configuring BetterSnapTool to display its pop-up resizing menu using a keyboard shortcut. You can also configure keyboard shortcuts for each resizing option.

To access the 13 additional resizing options, open the BetterSnapTool preference pane and click on **Keyboard Shortcuts** if not already highlighted. Choose your desired keyboard shortcut in the **Click to record shortcut** box next to **show menu with all selected actions**. You can optionally check the box next to **also duplicate the menubar**

preferences to this menu. This option lets you access this menu from BetterSnapTool's Menu Extra under **Change Window Position / Size**.

To use the pop-up menu to resize a window, hover your cursor over the window you want to resize and enter the keyboard shortcut you configured. The pop-up resizing menu will appear. All you need to do is select your desired resizing choice.

BetterSnapTool lets you configure which resizing options are displayed on the pop-up resizing menu. Uncheck the options you don't want to appear. You can optionally assign keyboard shortcuts to any or all of the resizing options.

Create Custom Snap Areas

If 20 resizing options and 7 Snap Areas aren't enough for you, BetterSnapTool offers virtually limitless resizing and Snap Area options through an advanced feature called **Snap Areas**. This feature lets you define a specific window size and a customized snap recognition area.

Creating a custom Snap Area is a multi-step process.
1. Resize an arbitrary window to the desired position and size. Make sure this window is the active window.
2. Click on the BetterSnapTool Menu Extra and select **Snap Areas (Advanced Feature)**.
3. Select **Create New Snap Area (Use Active Window As Template)**.

4. BetterSnapTool will enter editing mode. The active window will be grayed out and bordered by a dotted red line. A dialog box will appear in the center of your monitor instructing you to click the box to define a new Snap Area.

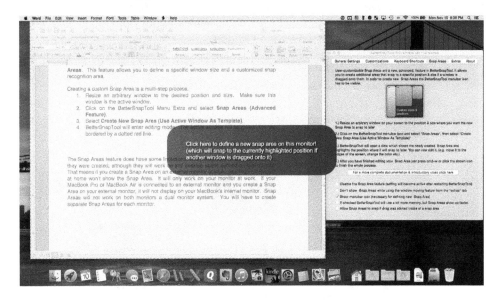

5. The light blue Snap Area box shown below will appear on your desktop. Resize it using the resizing handles and move it to the area of your desktop where you want your Snap Area to be located.

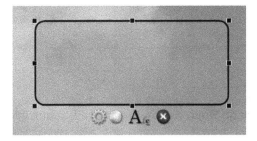

6. There are four tools under the Snap Area. From left to right, the first tool (the one that looks like a gear) allows you to require one or more of the following modifier keys: ⇧ fn ^ ⌥ ⌘ (shift, function, control, option, command) to be held down to show the custom Snap Area. Configuring this option will prevent the Snap Area from displaying every time you move a window. You can also configure BetterSnapTool to display the Snap Area only when a window from a specific application or set of applications are being moved.

7. The color wheel allows you to select the background and border colors. You can also configure border type and width and corner radius if you do not like the defaults. There is also an option to make the Snap Area invisible. When invisible, the Snap Area will only appear when you hover over it with your cursor. Finally, the tool lets you configure the length of the preview overlay animation.

8. You can add custom text to your Snap Area with the text tool. Note that clicking the **X** in the last tool will delete the Snap Area and exit edit mode without creating your custom Snap Area.

9. Once you have finished configuring the Snap Area options, enter ⌘**W** (command+W) or click the gray box in the center of your desktop to exit edit mode. Your custom Snap Area is now ready to use.

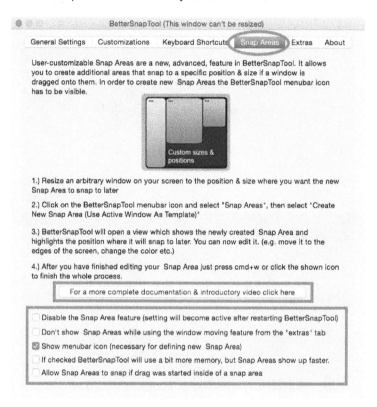

To access a video showing how to create a custom Snap Area, open the BetterSnapTool preference pane and click on **Snap Areas** if not already highlighted. Click the introductory video button. Your default browser will open and will navigate to the page containing the video. There are also 5 additional configuration options at the bottom of this tab.

The Snap Areas feature does have some limitations. Snap Areas only work on the display where they were created, although they will work on any desktop space defined on that display. That means if you create a Snap Area on an external display at work, your external display at home won't show the Snap Area. The Snap Area will only work on your monitor at work. If your MacBook, MacBook Air, or MacBook Pro is connected to an external monitor and you create a Snap Area on your external display, it will not work on your MacBook's internal display. Snap Areas will not work on both monitors in a dual monitor system. You will have to create separate Snap Areas for each monitor.

Edit or Delete a Custom Snap Area

To edit or delete a previously configured custom Snap Area, click the BetterSnapTool Menu Extra and select **Snap Areas (Advanced Feature) > Edit Snap Areas**. Click on the custom Snap Area you want to edit and make your desired changes. To delete a Snap Area, click the **X** and confirm you want to delete. When finished enter ⌘**W** (command+W) or click the gray box in the center of your desktop to exit edit mode.

Define the Window Control Buttons

BetterSnapTool has a feature that lets you define a resizing option for the window control buttons in the upper left of a window when you secondary click on them or use a mouse with a middle button. You have 19 different resizing options to choose from.

To define resizing options for the window control buttons, open the BetterSnapTool preference pane and click on **Extras** if not already highlighted. Select options for each window control for a secondary click, or middle button if your mouse has one. You will need to check the checkbox next to **Block the right-click from passing through to the window button**. If you fail to do so, you will be disappointed. BetterSnapTool will execute the resize command and immediately afterward OS X will execute the command associated with the window control.

Resize by Double-Clicking the Title Bar

You can configure BetterSnapTool to resize a window when you double-click on the window's title bar. Similar to the window controls, you have 19 different resizing options from which to choose.

To configure resizing by double-clicking the title bar, open the BetterSnapTool preference pane and click on **Extras** if not already highlighted. Choose the desired resizing action. If you have already configured OS X to minimize a window by double-clicking the title bar, a dialog box will warn you of the conflict. You can choose to **Cancel** or have BetterSnapTool open the **Dock** preference pane so you can resolve the conflict.

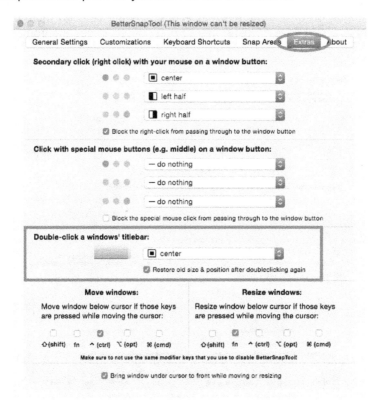

Check the box next to **Restore old size & position after doubleclicking again** if you want a second double-click on the title bar to restore the window's original size and location.

Move & Resize Windows with a Modifier Key

The OS X default is that a window must be active for you to move or resize it. Not with BetterSnapTool. All you have to do is hover your cursor over the window you want to move or resize, hold down the configured modifier key, and move your cursor to move or resize it. It doesn't matter if the window is active or not.

To configure modifier keys to move and resize a window, open the BetterSnapTool preference pane and click on **Extras** if not already highlighted. Select the desired modifier keys for each action. Optionally, you can configure BetterSnapTool to make the window active while moving or resizing it. Check the checkbox next to **Bring window under cursor to front while moving or resizing** to configure this option.

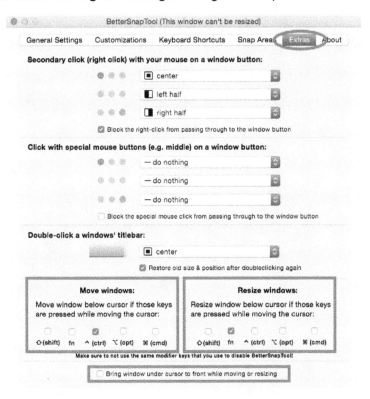

Change App Specific Settings

BetterSnapTool allows you to change the size of the standard resize areas on a per application basis. App specific settings only change the horizontal width of the window when resizing to the left or right edges or the left or right corners of the desktop. Click the BetterSnapTool Menu Extra and select **Specific Settings For Current Application**. Use the sliders to change the horizontal width or type the desired setting directly in the % box.

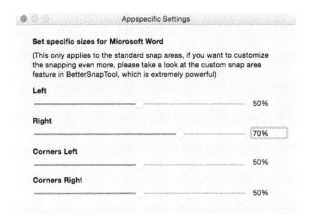

14

Safari

For most users, **Safari** requires little customization and can be operated in an "out-of-the-box" mode. But if you have made it this far, you and I both know that you are not like most users. There is a lot of customization that can be done to fine tune Safari, change its appearance, and make it perform better.

Customize the Toolbar

The **Toolbar**, located at the top of the Safari window, provides a number of tools to enhance your web browsing experience. You can customize the **Toolbar**, adding, removing, and rearranging the tools as you see fit. Secondary click in any open area of the Toolbar to reveal a contextual menu with a single option to **Customize Toolbar...**, which reveals a drop-down tools palette with the entire selection of tools available.

The tools palette allows you to add additional tools to the Toolbar by dragging and dropping them onto the Toolbar. Any extensions that offer their own tool will also be shown on the tools palette. To add a tool to the Toolbar, drag and drop it. Existing tools located on the Toolbar can be rearranged by dragging them. A tool is removed by dragging it off the Toolbar and onto the drop-down tools palette.

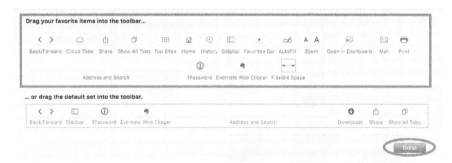

The tools are available include the **iCloud Tabs** tool, which displays the websites open in tabs on other devices associated with your iCloud account including your iPhone and iPad.

The **Share** button lets you share an item via Mail, Messages, Airdrop, or through a number of third party extensions. OS X will list your recent shares under **Recents**, allowing you to quickly share an item. To configure the third party extensions available in the **Share Menu**, click the Share button and select **More...** or by opening the **Extensions** preference pane from System Preferences. Select **Share Menu** in the left column if not already selected. Use the checkboxes to select which third party extensions you wish to make available in the Share drop-down menu.

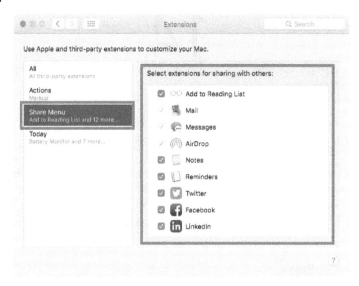

Back to the Safari toolbar, the **Show All Tabs** button allows you to view the tabs in Safari or a tab open one one of your iOS devices. Clicking on any tab takes expands the tab in Safari. The **Top Sites** tool shows you your Top Sites, which are websites you frequently visit. The **Home** tool will take you to the Home page configured in Safari's General preferences. The **History** tool displays a history of webpages you have previously visited. The **Sidebar** tool toggles the Safari sidebar on and off. Safari's sidebar displays your bookmarks, reading list, and shared links. The **Favorites Bar** tool toggles the Safari's favorites bar on and off. The Favorites Bar conveniently lists the websites in your Favorites bookmark folder in a bar just below the Safari toolbar. The **Autofill** tool tells Safari to automatically fill website forms with data such as your name and address. The **Zoom** tool does what you would expect it to do – zooming in and out. The **Mail** tool lets you share a webpage via Mail. The **Print** tool lets you print a webpage. Any third party tools that you have added are located after the search bar. In the picture of the toolbar palette, you will see that I have added tools for 1Password and Evernote. The **Flexible Space** tool is used to space out the tools in the toolbar by adding a blank space between them. Click the **Done** button when finished customizing your Safari toolbar.

To revert back to the default set of tools, drag the default set onto the Finder Toolbar and click **Done**.

Tools located on the Toolbar can be rearranged without having to use the drop-down tools palette. To move a tool, hold the ⌘ (command) key down while dragging the tool to its new location. You can also use the ⌘ (command) key to remove a tool. Hold down ⊛while dragging the tool off the Toolbar. The tool will disappear in a puff of smoke.

Change the Default Browser

Safari 9.0 is the default browser in OS X El Capitan. The default browser is the browser that is launched when you click on a link in an email or another application. While it may seem odd, Apple allows you to choose another browser installed on your Mac as the default. If you want to change the **Default web browser**, open the **General** preference pane in the System Preferences application.

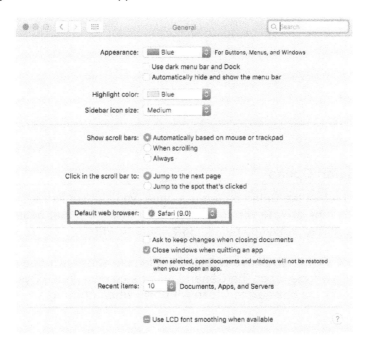

Note that you will have to install other browsers first. Firefox and Chrome are the usual suspects. Both are available at no cost. Firefox is available at https://www.mozilla.org and Chrome can be downloaded at https://www.google.com/chrome/. Once you have other browsers installed on your Mac, they will be listed in the menu next to **Default web browser**.

Configure Your Home Page

Your **Home Page** is the page your browser will navigate to when you click the **Home** button in Safari's toolbar. You also can configure Safari to open new windows and tabs using your Home Page. To configure your Home Page, browse to the site you want as your home page. Next, open the Safari preferences by choosing **Safari > Preferences...** or enter ⌘, (command+,). Click the **General** icon at the top of the pane if it is not already selected.

Safari is configured with Apple's home page as the Home Page. Click **Set to Current Page** or type the URL of your desired Home Page in the field next to **Homepage**.

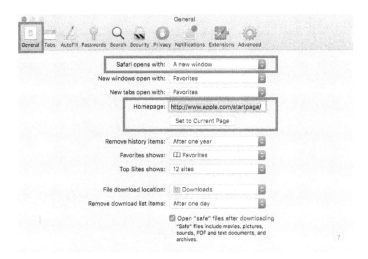

Choose How Safari Opens

From the General tab of the Safari preference pane, you can configure Safari to start with **A new window**, **A new private window**, or **All windows from last session**. Make your selection from the drop-down menu next to **Safari opens with**.

If this option is not shown, you have disabled the feature **Close windows when quitting an application**. To enable, open the **General** preference pane in the System Preferences application and check the box next to **Close windows when quitting an application**.

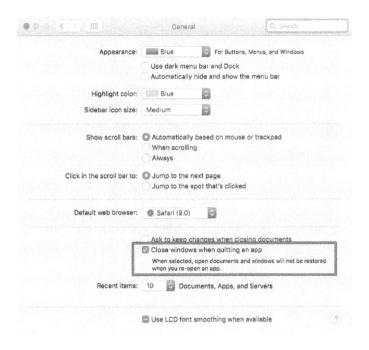

Choose How New Windows & Tabs Open

Safari offers a number of choices with which to open new windows. To configure how Safari opens new windows and tabs, open the Safari preferences by choosing **Safari > Preferences...** or enter ⌘, (command+,).   Click the **General** icon at the top of the pane if it is not already selected.

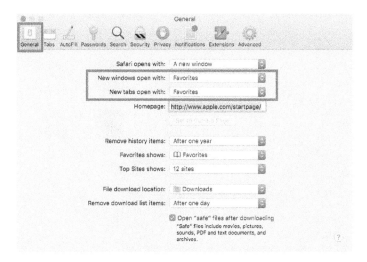

The drop down menu next to **New windows open with** allows you to choose from **Favorites**, a **Homepage** of your choosing, an **Empty Page**, the **Same Page** which you most recently viewed, with **Tabs for Favorites**, or a set of tabs using a **Tabs folder** of your choosing. The default is for Safari to open new windows with Favorites from your Favorites bookmarks folder.

The drop down menu next to **New tabs open with** allows you to choose from **Favorites**, a **Homepage** of your choosing, an **Empty Page**, or the **Same Page** which you most recently viewed. By default, Safari opens new windows and new tabs with your Favorites.

Add a Website to your Favorites

To add a website to your Favorites, click on the URL/search bar to reveal your Favorites list. Drag and drop the website into your Favorites.

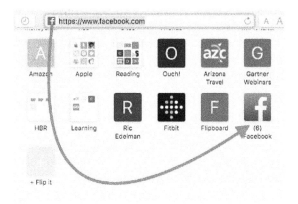

Organize Your Favorites

To rearrange, organize, and delete your Favorites, open a new browser window or tab or click the **Show Top Sites** tool on the Safari toolbar.

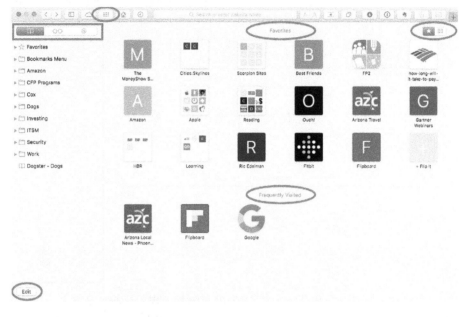

Drag a website bookmark to rearrange it. To delete a site, drag its bookmark out of Safari until you see an **X** appear and drop it. The bookmark will disappear in a puff of smoke. If you accidentally delete the wrong bookmark, select **Edit > Undo Remove Bookmark** or enter **⌘Z** (command+ Z).

You also can edit your Favorite sites by clicking the **Show Sidebar** tool to toggle it on. The Safari sidebar will show your bookmarks, reading list, and shared links. Click on the bookmark icon on the left if it is not already highlighted. Next, click the **Edit** button at the bottom left to open the **Bookmarks Editor** to edit your **Favorites** bookmark folder.

Manage Bookmarks

To manage your **Bookmarks**, select **Bookmarks > Edit Bookmarks** or enter **⌥⌘B** (option+command+B) to launch the Bookmarks Editor. From the Bookmarks Editor, you can drag, drop, rearrange, delete, and add Bookmarks or Bookmark folders. To hide the Bookmark Editor when finished, select **Bookmarks > Hide Bookmarks Editor**, enter **⌥⌘B** (option+command+B), click on a Bookmark to go to a website, or enter a URL in the address and search field.

Hide Frequently Visited Sites

Safari collects your **Frequently Visited** websites automatically, keeping track of the sites you visit most frequently and displaying them under your **Favorites**. If you do not want to see your most frequently visited sites, you can hide them by selecting **Bookmarks > Show**

Frequently Visited in Favorites. When there is a checkmark next to this option in the drop-down menu, your Frequently Visited sites will be shown underneath your Favorites.

Show the Favorites Bar

Safari displays your Favorites when opening a new window or tab, but what if you want quick access to your Favorites without having to open a new window or tab. If you want your Favorites available at all times, select **View > Show Favorites Bar** or enter ⇧⌘B (shift+command+B). The Favorites Bar will appear directly below the Safari toolbar.

Select Your Favorites Source

Safari sources the websites for **Favorites** from the Favorites folder in your Bookmarks. You can change the default source for Favorites to any of your other Bookmark folders. This comes in handy if you have configured Safari to display the Favorites Bar and want another Bookmarks folder to be used as your Favorites when opening a new window or tab.

To change the Bookmark folder used for Favorites, open the Safari preferences by choosing **Safari > Preferences...** or enter ⌘, (command+,). Click on the **General** tab if it is not already highlighted. Select your desired Bookmarks folder using the drop-down menu next to **Favorites shows**.

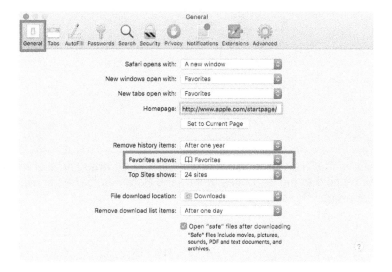

Configure Top Sites

Top Sites is another method Safari uses to collect sites that you visit most often. You can configure Safari to keep 6, 12, or 24 sites in the Top Sites list.

To configure the number of sites in the Top Sites list, open the Safari preferences by choosing **Safari > Preferences...** or enter ⌘, (command+,). Click the **General** icon at the top of the pane if it is not already selected. Choose 6, 12, or 24 sites in the drop-down list next to **Top Sites show**.

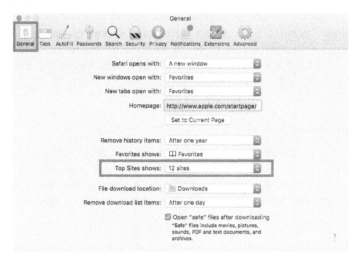

If you have Safari configured to show your Favorites in a new window or tab, you can toggle between your Favorites and Top Sites using the control in the upper right corner of the Safari window.

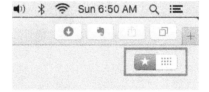

Add a Top Site

Adding a website to the **Top Sites** list is accomplished by dragging the website from the address and search field to the Top Sites tool on the Safari toolbar as shown below. When the big green **+** appears release your hold.

Organize your Top Sites

To rearrange, organize, and delete your Top Sites, click on the Top Sites button from the Safari Favorites view.

Drag and drop the website thumbnails to rearrange them. To pin them permanently, click and hold until you see a blue stick pin appear in the upper left corner of the thumbnail. Click on the stick pin to pin the website to your Top Sites list. Click the **X** to delete a site.

Remove Your Browsing History

Safari will maintain a history of all websites you have visited. This is a handy feature if you want to return to a website but didn't bookmark it. You can view your browsing history by date in Safari by selecting **History > Show History** or by entering ⌘Y (command+Y). Select **History > Hide History** or enter ⌘Y (command+Y) to hide your web browsing history. You can also search your web browsing history using Spotlight.

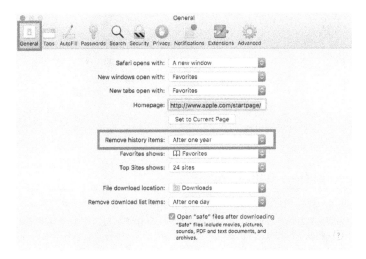

The length of time Safari will keep your history is configurable to one day, one week, two weeks, one month, or one year. Make your selection from the drop-down list next to **Remove history items** in the **General** tab of the Safari preference pane.

Choose Where to Save Downloaded Files

Safari saves downloaded files to the **Downloads** folder. You can change this location to any folder by choosing **Other...** in the drop-down list next to **Save downloaded files to**. Navigate to your desired location and press the **Select** button. You can also configure Safari to ask you for the save location each time you download a file. Choose **Ask for each download** to select this option.

Safari maintains a list of all files downloaded. By default, this list is cleared after one day. You can configure Safari to remove this list when Safari quits, upon successfully downloading the file, or manually in the drop-down list next to **Remove download list items**.

Safari will automatically open movies, pictures, sounds, PDF files, text documents, and archives upon downloading. You can change this behavior by unchecking the checkbox next to **Open "safe" files after downloading** in the General tab in the Safari preference pane.

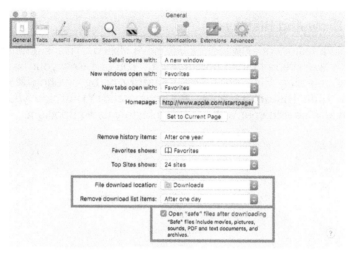

Open Web Pages in New Windows

Safari opens new pages in tabs unless the page is designed for a specially formatted window. To configure how Safari opens new pages, open the Safari preferences by choosing **Safari > Preferences...** or enter ⌘, (command+,). Click the **Tabs** icon at the top of the pane if it is not already selected.

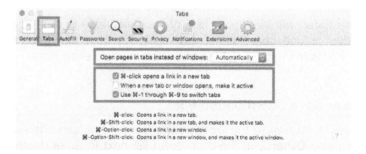

Open pages in tabs instead of windows is set to **Automatically** by default. Two other configuration options are available – **Never** or **Always**. **Never** will open all pages in a new Safari window. If you choose **Always**, Safari will create a new tab even if a website requests a window of a particular size.

Holding down the ⌘ (command) key while clicking on a link opens a new tab. To turn this feature off uncheck the checkbox next to ⌘-**click opens a new link in a new tab**. Holding the ⇧⌘ keys (shift+command) when clicking on a link opens a new tab and makes it the active tab. Holding the ⇧⌥ keys (shift+option) while clicking a link opens it in a new window. Holding the ⇧⌥⌘ keys (shift+option+command) while clicking a link opens it in a new window and makes it active.

You can choose to make a new tab or new window active when it opens by checking the checkbox next to **When a new tab or window opens, make it active**. This feature is disabled by default.

A new option in El Capitan is the ability to switch tabs using the ⌘ (command) key combined with the numbers 1 through 9. This option is enabled by default. Uncheck the checkbox next to **Use ⌘-1 through ⌘-9 to switch tabs** to disable this feature.

Edit Autofill

Safari's **Autofill** feature automatically inserts data into online forms including your name, address, user name, password, credit card, or other information you previously entered in a web form. If you need to change this information because you moved, changed your login credentials, or received a new credit card, you can edit the information saved in Autofill from the Safari preference pane. Click on the **Autofill** tab if not selected already.

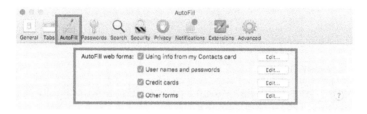

Safari will autofill information from your contacts card, which consists of your name, address, city, state, zip code and phone number. This feature is handy when filling out shipping information when making an online purchase. To edit your contact information, click the **Edit** button next to **Using info from my Contacts card**.

Safari securely saves your login credentials and will automatically enter your user name and password when you revisit a website. To edit your login credentials, click the **Edit** button next to **User names and passwords**. The tab will immediately jump to the **Passwords** tab and list all websites for which user names and passwords have or have not been stored. Double-click any item to edit your stored credentials. Enter your user name and password when challenged.

Safari securely saves your credit card number, expiration date, and cardholder name and automatically enters this information when needed to complete a purchase. To edit your credit card information, click the **Edit** button next to **Credit cards**. Double-click on a stored credit card to edit it. Enter your user name and password when challenged. You can also **Add** new credit cards or **Remove** old ones. Click **Done** when finished.

The **Other forms** attribute allows Safari to save information entered on web forms and automatically enters the information when you revisit the same webpage. To view or edit, click the **Edit** button next to **Other forms**. Safari will provide a list of all websites where you filled out a webform of some type. You can **Remove** any site or **Remove All**. Click **Done** when finished.

If you use **iCloud Keychain**, the information stored by Safari is available to your iOS devices and other Macs using the same Apple ID. Information modified on any device is updated on other devices using that same Apple ID. Similarly, if you change your address or phone number in the **Contacts** application in either OS X or iOS, the changes will be updated through iCloud to all your Apple devices. This is the reason why it is very important to use only a single Apple ID for all your Apple devices.

Turn Off Autofill

Autofill automatically fills online web forms with your name, address, user name, password, credit card, or other information. All of these options are enabled by default. Any option can be disabled by unchecking the checkbox next to the category.

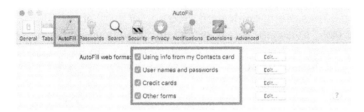

Manage Login Credentials

Safari securely saves your user names and passwords, automatically entering your login credentials the next time you visit a website.

Open the Safari preferences by choosing **Safari > Preferences...** or enter ⌘, (command+,). Click the **Passwords** tab at the top of the pane if it is not already selected. The **Passwords** tab lists all websites for which login credentials have been stored. Highlight any site to edit the user name or password or to **Remove** your credentials. Enter your user name and password when challenged. You can also use the search field to find websites, user names, or passwords.

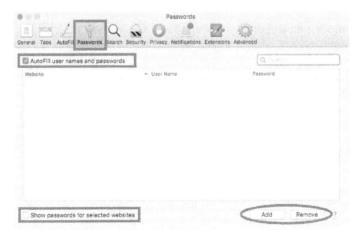

To add credentials for a website, click the **Add** button. Enter the website address, user name, and password in the fields provided.

To see the password for any site, check the checkbox next to **Show passwords for selected websites**. Click on any site to see the password.

Stop Safari from Saving Login Credentials

Safari saves user names and passwords you enter on websites. If you do not want Safari to save your login credentials, uncheck the box next to **AutoFill user names and passwords** to disable this feature.

Recall a Forgotten Password

If you cannot recall a password for a particular website, you can retrieve your lost password from the Passwords tab of the Safari preference pane. Check the checkbox next to **Show passwords for selected websites**. Enter your user name and password when challenged. When you click on any of the websites, Safari will display your password.

Change the Search Engine

You can choose the search engine Safari uses for web searches. Open the Safari preferences by choosing **Safari > Preferences...** or enter ⌘, (command+,). Click the **Search** tab at the top of the pane if it is not already selected.

Choose your preferred search engine from the drop-down list next to **Search engine**. You can choose from **Google**, **Yahoo**, **Bing**, or **DuckDuckGo**.

Checking the checkbox next to **Include search engine suggestions** allows Safari to query your chosen search engine for suggestions based on your search terms.

Enable Quick Website Search lets Safari record information about your searches to speed up future searches. With this feature enabled, you can search within a website by entering the site's name followed by the search term in Safari's search field. You can see and remove the site for which Safari recorded search information by clicking the **Manage Websites...** button. Click on any website to highlight it and click **Remove.** You have the option of removing all websites by clicking **Remove All**. Click **Done** when finished.

When **Preload Top Hit in the background** is enabled, Safari will begin to load the top search hit.

Disable Favorites View

The **Favorites View** is enabled by default and will display your favorite websites as icons below Safari's address and search field. Simply click the address and search field to display your favorite and frequently visited sites. Safari can also be configured to open all of your Favorites in tabs when opening a new Safari window. This feature is enabled in the General tab of the Safari preference pane using the drop-down list next to **New windows open with** and selecting **Tabs for Favorites**.

To disable the Favorites View, open the Safari preference pane by choosing **Safari > Preferences...** or enter ⌘, (command+,). Click the **Search** tab at the top of the pane if it is not already selected. Uncheck the box next the **Show Favorites**.

Block Fraudulent Websites

Safari warns you if a website you are attempting to visit is suspected to be a fraudulent website running a phishing scam. Phishing is an attempt by cyber criminals to trick you into divulging personal information such as your user name, password, social security number, credit card numbers, or banking information. Most phishing attempts start as a fake email that appears to be from a bank, credit card company, or major retailer alerting you that you must take care of something immediately otherwise your account will be suspended or closed. The links in the email direct you to a fraudulent website that appears to be the real thing. If you enter your login credentials or other personal information, it will be captured by a cyber criminal, who will use your information to make fraudulent purchases, steal money from your accounts, or steal your identity.

Safari will warn you if you visit a website that has been reported as fraudulent when the checkbox next to **Warn when visiting a fraudulent website** is checked. I strongly recommend you do not disable this security feature.

Allow Pop-Up Windows

Safari blocks annoying pop-up windows by default. However, some websites use pop-up windows to display essential content. If you want to allow pop-up windows, open the Safari preference pane by choosing **Safari > Preferences...** or enter ⌘, (command+,). Click the **Search** tab at the top of the pane if it is not already selected. Uncheck the box next to **Block pop-up windows** when you want to view pop-up windows from certain websites.

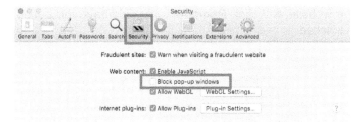

Check the checkbox when you want Safari to again block pop-up windows.

Restrict Website Cookies

Safari allows you to restrict websites, third parties, and advertisers from storing cookies on your Mac. Cookies are small amounts of data that a website sends and stores on your Mac. Every time you go back to a website that sent Safari a cookie, Safari will send the cookie back. Cookies can be used to compile records of your browsing activity and can store passwords and credit card information and are therefore, a privacy concern. Safari allows you to remove and block cookies that websites and third parties use to track you.

To limit or restrict websites, third parties, and advertisers from storing cookies on your Mac, open the Safari preference pane and select the **Privacy** tab if not already selected.

You can control cookies by selecting how restrictive you want Safari to be. There are 4 options available. **Always block** will not allow any website, third party or advertiser to store cookies on your Mac. However, this setting can prevent some websites from working properly. When **Allow from current website only** is selected, Safari will accept cookies only from the current website you are visiting. Safari will not allow embedded content from sources other than the current website from storing or accessing cookies on your Mac. **Allow from website I visit** tells Safari to accept cookies only from websites you visit. This option prevents embedded content from other websites from storing or accessing cookies on your Mac and is the default setting. **Always allow** lets all websites, third parties, and advertisers to store and access cookies on your Mac.

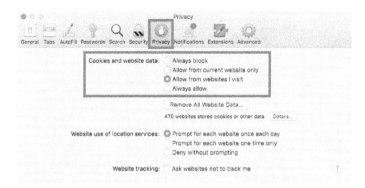

You probably already have cookies stored on your Mac. Safari will let you see which websites have stored cookies on your Mac and remove some or all of them. Click **Details** to see which websites have stored cookies on your Mac. To remove individual website cookies, select the website and click **Remove**. You also have the option to **Remove All**. Click **Done** when finished.

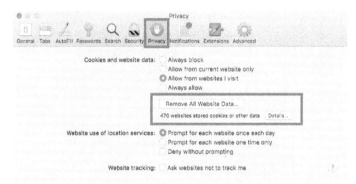

Clicking **Remove All Website Data** from the Privacy tab of the Safari preference pane will remove all cookies and website data from your Mac.

Stop Websites from Snooping on Your Location

Websites can spy on your location. This can be quite handy because location information can be used to deliver relevant content. However, sometimes there is absolutely no reason why a particular website needs to know your location. Safari can be configured to ask your permission before providing your location information to a website that asks for it.

To stop websites from snooping on your location, open the Safari preference pane by choosing **Safari > Preferences...** or enter ⌘, (command+,). Click the **Privacy** tab at the top of the pane. Select **Deny without prompting**. The other two options allow a website to prompt you either once a day or a single time for your location information.

Some websites will keep track of your browsing activity. Safari can be configured to ask websites and their third party content providers and advertisers to not track you by checking the box next to **Ask websites not to track me**. Each time you visit a website, Safari will send a request to not track you. However, it is up to the website to honor this request.

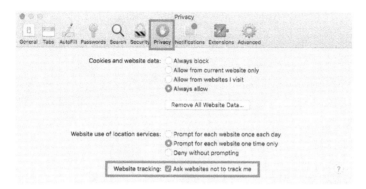

Browse the Web in Private

If you prefer to browse the web in private, you can enable Safari's **Private Browsing** mode by selecting **File > New Private Window** or by pressing ⇧⌘N (shift+command+N) to open a new Private Browsing window. Safari will not save your browsing history and asks all websites you visit to not track you. When in Private Browsing mode, each tab is isolated from the others, so a website in one tab cannot track your browsing in another tab. Note that Autofill does not work when in Private Browsing mode and Safari will not store open webpages in iCloud or save your browsing history.

When Private Browsing, the address and search field will change to white letters on a dark background.

To stop using the Private Browsing feature, close the Private Browsing window and open a new Safari window by selecting **File > New Window** or by entering ⌘N (command+N).

Change Website Notifications

Websites that have asked for permission to send you notifications using Apple's push notification service are displayed in the Notifications tab of the Safari preference pane. Select **Safari > Preferences...** or by entering ⌘, (command+,). Click the **Notifications** tab at the top of the pane if it is not already selected.

The Notifications tab displays a list of websites that have asked for your permission to send notifications and their current status, either **Allow** or **Deny**, based on how you originally answered when queried by the website. You can change the permission of any website by clicking on it and selecting **Allow** or **Deny**.

You can delete a website by highlighting it and clicking **Remove**. The **Remove All** option deletes the entire list.

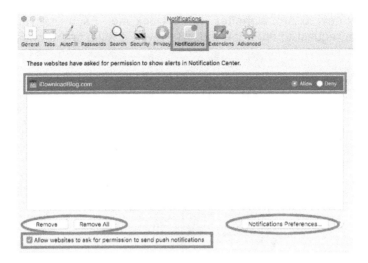

Clicking the **Notifications Preferences...** button at the lower right will open the Notifications preference pane in the System Preferences application, where you can modify the notification type, how the website is allowed to notify you, and whether notifications are saved to Notification Center. See the chapter on Notification Center to learn how to modify notifications in the Notifications preference pane.

Stop Websites from Asking Permission to Send Notifications

If you want to stop websites from asking your permission to send push notifications, uncheck the box next to **Allow websites to ask for permission to send push notifications** at the bottom of the **Privacy** tab in the Safari preference pane.

Manage Third Party Extensions

Extensions are small applications created by third party developers to enhance your web browsing experience.

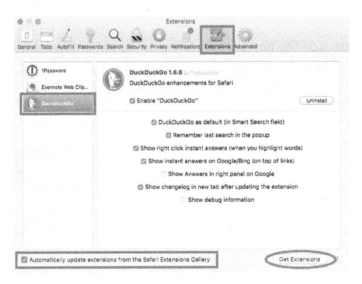

The **Extensions** tab in the Safari preference pane allows you to selectively enable or disable an extension, configure them if they have options, or uninstall them. Until you have installed Extensions, this pane will be empty.

The Extensions list in the left column shows which extensions have been installed. You can select an extension to show any available options or to uninstall it.

The checkbox next to **Automatically update extensions from the Safari Extensions Gallery Updates** is checked by default. Apple recommends that automatic updates be enabled so that your extensions are kept up to date with the latest release.

The **Get Extensions** button at the lower right opens the **Safari Extension Gallery** website at https://extensions.apple.com, where you can find extensions to add new features to Safari. Extensions can be installed with one click and there is no need to restart Safari.

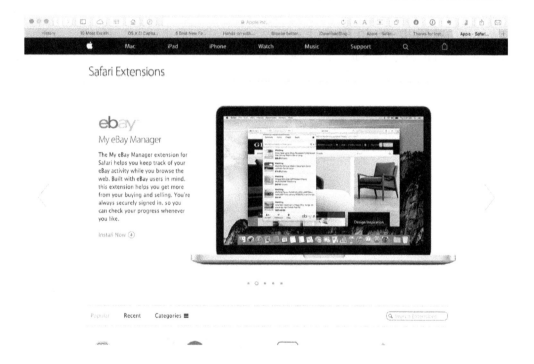

Make Safari Show the URL

Safari 8.0, which was introduced with the previous release of OS X, featured a more streamlined and simple design. One of the default features is that Safari no longer shows the full URL (website address) in its address and search field. Instead Safari only displays the domain name, such as amazon.com. Clicking on the address and search field forces Safari to show the full URL, but what if you want the full URL to always be displayed?

Before I show you how to change this feature, a word of caution. Cyber criminals have figured out that we are so used to seeing incredibly long URLs, that we no longer pay much attention to them. Therefore, it is easy for a cyber criminal to trick us into thinking their fake website is actually the real thing. By displaying only the top level domain name, Safari makes it plain and clear what website you have visited. Also, the padlock, which indicates you are on a secure site using HTTPS, is now front and center.

To configure Safari to permanently display the full URL, select **Safari > Preferences...** or by entering ⌘, (command+,) to open the Safari preference pane. Click the **Advanced** tab at the top of the pane if it is not already selected. Check the box next to **Show full website address**.

Show the Develop Menu

The **Develop Menu** allows you to access commands for developing websites with Safari. By default, the Develop Menu is hidden. To unhide the Develop menu, click **Show Develop menu in menu bar** in the **Advanced** tab of the Safari preference pane.

Allow Internet Plug-Ins to Run

Safari freezes Internet Plug-ins, such as embedded Quicktime content to save power. Clicking the frozen plug-in content starts the plug-in for the website.

If you prefer to have plug-ins start automatically, select **Safari > Preferences...** or by entering ⌘, (command+,) to open the Safari preference pane. Click the **Advanced** tab at the top of the pane if it is not already selected. Uncheck the box next to **Stop plug-ins to save power**.

If you leave this feature enabled, you can view the list of websites that you have allowed to start plug-ins automatically by clicking **Details**. To delete a website, highlight it and click **Remove**. Click **Remove All** to delete all the sites in this list. Click **Done** when finished.

Set a Policy for Internet Plug-Ins

You can control whether Safari will show plug-in content on websites. Plug-ins are used to show pictures, music, and videos. To see which plug-ins have been installed in Safari, open the Safari preference pane by selecting **Safari > Preferences...** or by entering ⌘, (command+,). Click the **Security** tab at the top of the pane if it is not already selected. Next, click on the **Plug-in Settings...** button next to **Allow Plug-ins**.

Clicking on **Plug-in Settings...** will display a list of which plug-ins are installed in Safari and which of the websites that you have visited are using each of the plug-ins. From this sheet, you can configure global or per-website blocking policies for each Internet plug-in.

To set a blocking policy for a plug-in, select the Internet plug-in from the column at the left. Any previous websites you have visited will be displayed in the right pane. Blocking policies can be set on a per website basis. Choose **Ask**, **Block**, **Allow** from the drop-down list next to each website listed. When **Ask** is selected, Safari will display a placeholder in place of the content. Clicking the placeholder will allow the website to use the plug-in. **Block** also displays a placeholder that allows you to run the plug-in by clicking on it. **Allow** always lets the website use the plug-in. Click **Done** when finished.

To configure a global policy for an Internet plug-in, select **Ask**, **Block**, or **Allow** from the drop-down list next to **When visiting other websites**. Click **Done** when finished.

Stop Squinting & Make Website Fonts Bigger

Tired of squinting when trying to read web pages? There are three methods to increase the font size. You can temporarily increase the font size by using the ⌘+ (command +) keyboard shortcut or use the Zoom button in the Safari toolbar. Conversely, the ⌘- (command -) decreases the font size.

If you desire a more permanent fix, open the Safari preference pane by selecting **Safari > Preferences...** or by entering **⌘,** (command+,). Click the **Advanced** tab at the top of the pane if it is not already selected. Check the box next to **Never use font sizes smaller than** and select your desired font size from the drop-down list.

Pin a Web Site to the Tab Bar

El Capitan introduced a new feature to Safari called **Pinned Sites** that allows you to pin your most frequently visited sites to the left side of the tab bar. Pinned sites refresh in the background, so they are always up to date. This feature is especially useful if you have a website or two that you like to revisit throughout the day, like Facebook or a news site.

To pin a site to the Tab Bar, open the website in a Safari tab. Secondary click on the tab and select **Pin Tab** from the contextual menu. The pinned site will move to the left to join your other pinned sites. Pinned sites can be rearranged by dragging and dropping them into place.

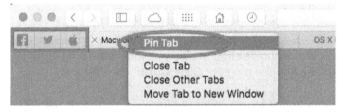

You can also pin a site by dragging the site's tab to the left to join your other pinned tabs and dropping it there. Once a site is pinned, you can quickly access it from any Safari window.

To unpin a site, secondary click on it and select **Unpin Tab**. The tab will move to the right to join your other unpinned tabs. Selecting **Close Tab** will close the tab.

Mute Annoying Website Video Ads

There is nothing worse than opening a bunch of tabs in Safari and then being assaulted by a cacaphony of several video ads playing simultaneously. Before El Capitan, your only response was to hunt down each one by opening each and every tab to kill or mute the annoying advertisement.

Apple introduced two new features in Safari with the El Capitan release of OS X. The first is the ability to quickly identify which tabs are playing sound. Tabs currently playing sound will be denoted by a sound icon. Clicking on the sound icon on the tab will mute the sound. The second feature is the ability to mute all sound in all tabs by clicking the blue sound icon at the far right in the Safari search and URL field. Click this blue sound icon and the cacaphony is silenced. Your ears will appreciate this.

AirPlay Videos in Safari

A new feature in El Capitan is that Safari now features an AirPlay button that lets you AirPlay video from Safari to your AppleTV without having to AirPlay the entire Safari window. Check out a video on YouTube. You'll now see an AirPlay button at the lower right of the video. Click it and pick the device on which you want to play the video.

15

Mail

The default mail client in OS X El Capitan is an application simply called **Mail**. Other than configuration of mail accounts, Mail requires little customization and can be operated in an "out-of-the-box" mode for most users. However, there is a large amount of customization that can be done to fine tune Mail, change its appearance, and make it perform a little better.

Change the Mail Application

Mail is the default mail client in OS X El Capitan. The default mail client is the application that launches when you want to send an email from another application or web link. If you prefer to use another email client Apple allows you to choose one. To change the default email client, open the Mail preference pane by choosing **Mail > Preferences...** or enter ⌘, (command+,). Click the **General** icon at the top of the pane if it is not already selected.

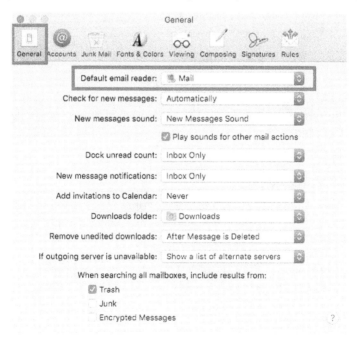

Choose your desired mail client from the drop-down list next to **Default email reader**. For email clients to populate the list, you will first need to download and install them. Mozilla Thunderbird (https://www.mozilla.org/en-US/thunderbird/), Microsoft Outlook, and Postbox (http://postbox-inc.com) are good alternatives. Choosing **Select...** will open a Finder window so you can locate your email application if it is not listed in the drop-down menu.

Change How Frequently Mail Checks for New Email

To change the frequency with which **Mail** checks for new email, open the Mail preference pane by choosing **Mail > Preferences...** or enter ⌘, (command+,). Click the **General** icon at the top of the pane if it is not already selected.

Your choices are **Automatically** (the default), **Every minute**, **Every 5 minutes**, **Every 15 minutes**, **Every 30 minutes**, **Every hour**, or **Manually**. If you select **Manually**, you will have to click the **Get Mail** button in the Toolbar to check for new email.

Change the New Mail Sound

The **New messages sound** allows you to select from a number of sounds to play when a new message arrives. Mail can also be configured to make no sound. Use the drop-down list in the General tab in the Mail preference pane to make your desired selection.

Uncheck the checkbox next to **Play sounds for other mail actions** if you want to disable sounds for other mail actions such as the sound when Mail sends email.

Control the Dock Badge

The **Mail** icon in the Dock displays a red badge showing the count of unread messages. The unread message count can be limited to those messages in the **Inbox Only**, unread messages received **Today**, or all unread messages across **All Mailboxes**.

Change How Mail Notifies You

When new email arrives, OS X will display a notification on your desktop. You can configure the Mail application to notify you when your receive new email in the **Inbox Only**, from **VIPs**, from your **Contacts**, or **All Mailboxes**. The Mail notification style can be configured in the Notifications preference pane in System Preferences.

Automatically Add Invitations to Calendar

Invitations you receive in email can be added to the **Calendar** application. To enable this feature, open the Mail preference pane by choosing **Mail > Preferences...** or enter ⌘, (command+,). Click the **General** icon at the top of the pane if it is not already selected. Select **Automatically** or **Never**.

Choose Where to Save Downloaded Files

By default, Mail saves downloaded attachments to the **Downloads** folder. You can change this location to any folder by choosing **Other...** in the drop-down list next to **Downloads folder** in the General tab of the Mail preference pane. Navigate to your desired location and press the **Select** button.

Mail temporarily saves attachments to the Mail Downloads folder in the Library folder in your **Home** directory. Mail will delete the attachments stored here when you delete the email that contained the attachment. Two other options are **Never** or to delete attachments **When Mail Quits**.

Don't Download Attachments

Mail will automatically download attachments by default. If you prefer to manually download attachments, open the Mail preference pane by choosing **Mail > Preferences...** or enter ⌘, (command+,). Click the **Accounts** icon at the top of the pane if it is not already selected. Next, click on **Advanced.**

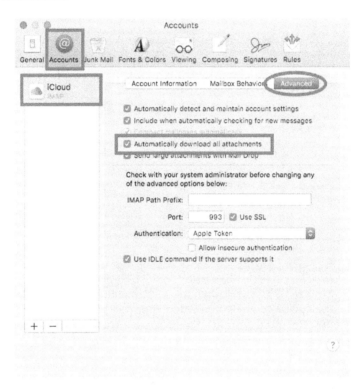

Downloading of attachments is configured on a per mailbox basis. Select the mail account in the column on the left. Next, uncheck the box next to **Automatically download all attachments**. Do the same for other email accounts if desired.

Change the Mail Search Scope

When searching mailboxes, you can choose to include results from the **Trash**, **Junk**, or **Encrypted Messages**. By default, only search results from inboxes and the Trash are included. Configure these attributes in the **General** pane of the Mail preferences.

Change Mailbox Behavior

You can configure how you want the **Mail** to handle email drafts, sent email, junk email, and email you delete. To configure mailbox behaviors, open the Mail preference pane by choosing **Mail > Preferences...** or enter ⌘, (command+,). Click the **Accounts** icon at the top of the pane if it is not already selected. Next, click on **Mailbox Behaviors**.

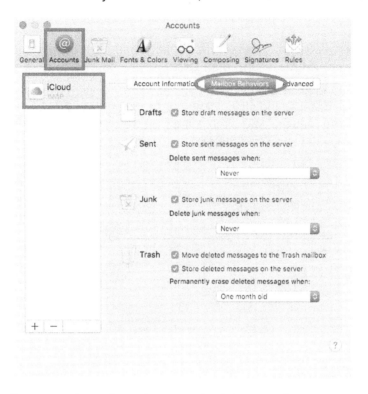

Select an email account from the column at the left to configure its mailbox behavior. **Drafts** can be stored on the server by checking the box next to **Store draft messages on the server**. When this box is unchecked, email you are drafting will be stored locally. Storing drafts on the server is handy because you can later access a draft email using your web browser, iPhone, iPad, or a mail client on another Mac.

Similarly, email that you have sent can be stored on the server by checking the checkbox next to **Store sent messages on the server**. When this box is unchecked, sent email will be stored locally. You can also configure how long you want sent email to be stored. Mail will automatically delete sent email after 1 day, 1 week, 1 month, or when you quit the Mail application. You also have the option to never delete sent email.

You can configure the Mail application to store junk email on the server by checking the box next to **Store junk messages on the server**. When this box is unchecked, junk email will be stored locally. Mail will automatically delete junk email after 1 day, 1 week, 1 month, or when you quit the Mail application. If you'd like to keep your junk email forever, choose the never option.

There are 2 options when you delete an email. You can temporarily leave it in your inbox or move it to the trash mailbox. Unchecking the box next to **Move deleted messages to**

the trash mailbox will leave deleted email in your inbox and dim it. Deleted messages can be stored on the mail server by checking the checkbox next to **Store deleted messages on the server**. When this box is unchecked, deleted email will be stored locally. Mail will automatically erase deleted email after 1 day, 1 week, 1 month, or when you quit the Mail application. If you'd like to keep your deleted email, choose the never option. However, doing so could cause your email account to exceed its storage quota. It's best to have Mail erase deleted messages automatically.

Send Large Attachments using Mail Drop

Have you ever tried to send a video to a friend or relative only to have your email provider reject the message because the attachment was too large? Apple fixed this problem in OS X with the **Mail Drop** feature. Mail Drop is enabled by default in the **Advanced** tab under the **Accounts** icon in the Mail preference pane.

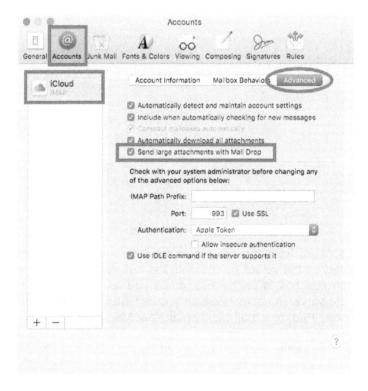

Mail will automatically send attachments larger than 20 MB to your iCloud account where they are encrypted and stored for up to 30 days. Mail Drop attachments do not count against your iCloud storage quota. If the person you sent your email to is using the Mail application on OS X, the large attachment will be automatically downloaded and included in the email like any other attachment. For those using a different operating system or email client, a link is provided in the email along with its expiration date.

If you use DropBox, Box, or OneDrive to share large attachments, you may wish to disable this feature. To do so, uncheck the checkbox next to **Send large attachments with Mail Drop**.

Change the Mail Drop Threshold

When you try to send an email with an attachment larger than 20 MB, Mail will automatically send the attachment to your iCloud account. If the person you sent your email to is using the Mail application on OS X, the large attachment will be automatically downloaded and included in the email like any other attachment. For those using a different operating system or email client, a link is provided in the email along with its expiration date. The attachment will expire after 30 days.

Some organizations have some pretty draconian limits to attachments. I've seen some companies limit the size of email attachments to 10 MB and even 5 MB. OS X allows you to change the default threshold for **Mail Drop** to a lower threshold. To change the default threshold for Mail Drop, launch Terminal and enter the following commands.

```
defaults write com.apple.mail minSizeKB 10000
```

The 10000 at the end of the command is the Mail Drop threshold in KB. Since 1 MB equals 1,000 KB, 10 MB equals 10,000 KB.

To revert back to the OS X default of 20 MB, enter the following command in Terminal.

```
defaults write com.apple.mail minSizeKB 20000
```

Get Rid of Junk Email

Junk email is annoying and fills up your inbox. Mail has a number of configuration options to make junk email less of an annoyance. To configure junk mail handling rules, click on the **Junk Mail** icon in the Mail preference pane.

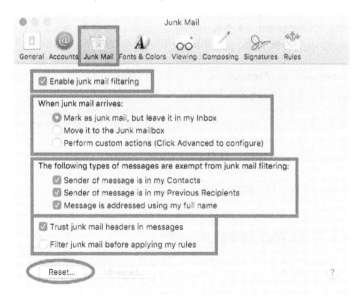

Junk email filtering is enabled by default. Uncheck the checkbox next to **Enable junk mail filtering**. You may wish to do so if your email provider already filters junk email or if you want to see all email, junk or not.

Junk email is left in your inbox where you are given a choice to mark an email as **Not Junk** if it was mistakenly identified as junk. Mail also gives you the option of moving junk email to the junk mailbox or configuring custom actions to identify and handle junk mail. To define custom actions, click the radio button next to **Perform custom actions**. Next, click the **Advanced...** button at the bottom of the preference pane to configure custom actions.

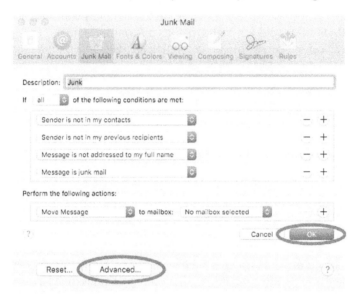

You can exempt email from being considered as junk if the sender is in Contacts, the sender is a Previous Recipient, or the email is addressed to your full name. Use the checkboxes to configure these options, which are all enabled by default.

Trust junk mail header in messages is enabled by default and uses any junk mail detection already present in email you receive to more accurately identify junk email.

You have the option of filtering out junk mail before applying any other mail filtering rules. Doing so, ensures that all email is first evaluated by the junk mail filter before being filtered by any email filtering rules you have created.

A **Reset...** button allows you to restore the default configuration.

Stop Squinting & Make Mail Fonts Bigger

Tired of squinting when trying to read email? There are two methods to increase the font size. You can temporarily increase the font size by using the ⌘+ (command +) keyboard shortcut. Conversely, the ⌘- (command -) decreases the font size.

If you desire a more permanent fix, open **Mail > Preferences...** or enter ⌘, (command+,). Click the **Fonts & Colors** icon at the top of the pane if it is not already selected. You can change the **Message list font**, **Message font**, and the **Fixed-width font**. Click the **Select...** button to change the font and font size.

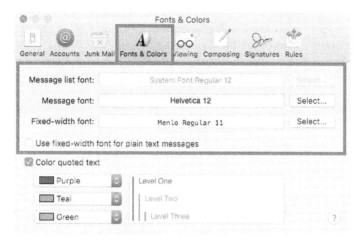

The message list font is used for viewing the list of messages when Mail is in classic layout with the message list above the messages. You can change to classic view by clicking the **Viewing** icon and checking the box next to **Use classic layout**.

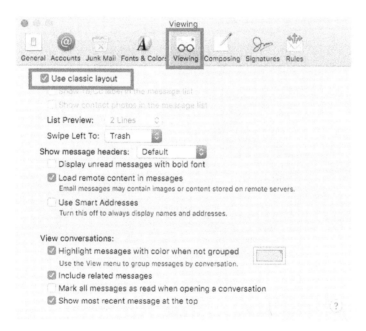

The message font is the font used for viewing and writing email. Emails you receive will use this font unless the sender used a specific font in the message.

The fixed-width font is used for viewing and writing plain text email. Make sure you check the box next to **Use fixed-width font for plain text messages**.

You can also change the color of quoted text when replying to messages.

Switch to Classic View

By default, Mail will list messages in a column with the Mail preview pane to its right. Classic layout puts the message list at the top with the preview pane below. If you want to switch to classic layout, open **Mail > Preferences…** or enter ⌘, (command+,). Click the **Viewing** icon at the top of the pane if it is not already selected.

Check the checkbox next to **Use classic layout** to switch to the classic view. Uncheck to revert back to the default. Note that the 3 options under **Use classic layout** – showing the to/cc lable, contact photos, and list preview – are unavailable in classic view and are grayed out.

Show the To and CC Labels

If you do not use the classic view, you can configure Mail to display the **To** and **CC** labels. This allows you to see which messages were sent directly to you versus ones that you were copied. Check the box next to **Show To/Cc label in the message list** on the Viewing tab of the Mail preference pane to enable this feature.

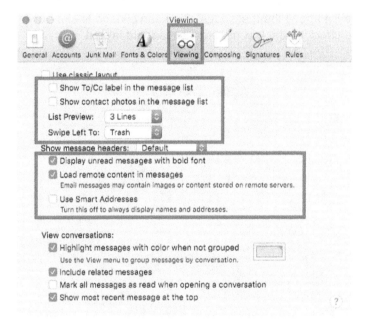

Show Contact Photos in the Message List

If you are not using the classic view, you can configure Mail to display photos of your contacts in the message list. If the sender's photo is available, it will be shown to the left of the message in the message list. Check the box next to **Show contact photos in the message list** on the Viewing tab of the Mail preference pane to enable this feature.

Change the Number of Preview Lines

Mail can preview the first few lines of an email in the message list. This is a handy feature because you often can determine if you want to read or just trash and email message based on the preview. Your options are to show 1, 2, 3, 4, or 5 lines. Select the number of preview lines using the drop-down list next to **List Preview** on the Viewing tab of the Mail preference pane. To disable this feature, select **None** from the drop-down list.

Swipe Left, Swipe Right

A new feature in the El Capitan release of Mail is the ability to swipe left and right with two fingers to take action on an email. Users of iOS will recognize this as a feature on their iPhone or iPad. Swiping right with two fingers will toggle the read/unread status of an email message. The action performed while swiping left is configurable in the **Viewing** tab of Mail preferences. You have the choice of trashing the email or archiving it. Make your choice from the drop-down menu next to **Swipe Left To**. Swipe left with two fingers to execute the command.

Show Smart Addresses

Mail will display the recipient's email address. When the **Smart Addresses** feature is enabled, Mail will only display the name. The recipient must be listed in the Contacts app, Previous Recipients List, or on a network server for the Smart Address to display. To enable this feature check the box next to **Use Smart Addresses Preview** on the **Viewing** tab of the Mail preference pane.

Configure Composing Options

The **Composing** tab of the Mail preference pane is used to configure the options for messages that you create.

You can choose to compose your outgoing messages using **Rich Text** (the default) or **Plain Text** from the drop-down list next to **Message Format**.

Mail checks the spelling of your outgoing email as you type it. You can choose to have Mail check your spelling when you click **Send** or **never** check your spelling from the drop-down list next to **Check spelling**.

You can also choose to have Mail copy or blind copy you by checking the box next to **Automatically** and selecting your choice from the drop-down list.

Select the Sending Email Account

If you have multiple Mail accounts configured, new messages are sent from the account of the selected mailbox by default. If you want your mail to originate from a specific Mail account, open **Mail > Preferences...** or enter ⌘, (command+,). Click the **Composing** icon at the top of the pane if it is not already selected. Choose the account you want to use to send new email from the drop-down list next to **Send new messages from**.

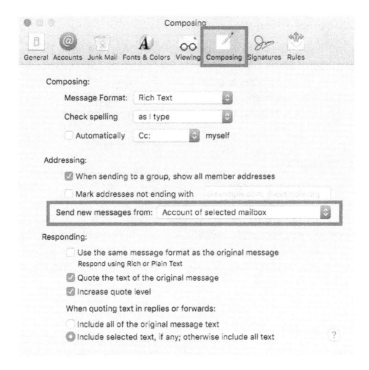

Configure Response Options

The **Responding** section on the **Composing** tab of the Mail preference pane controls the behavior of messages when replying and forwarding email.

You can choose to utilize the same message format as the original email by checking the box next to **Use the same message format as the original message**.

By default, Mail will quote the text of the original message when replying or forwarding an email, indenting all text included from the original email. Uncheck the boxes next to **Quote the text of the original message** and **Increase quote level** to disable these features.

You can choose to include all the text of the original email or selected text when replying or forwarding. Click the appropriate radio button at the bottom of the preference pane to configure your desired style.

Create a Signature

The **Signature** tab of the Mail preference pane allows you to create signatures for each of your Mail accounts. Mail automatically adds the signature configured in the preference pane to messages you send. You can have unique signatures for each mail account. To create, change, or delete a signature, open **Mail > Preferences...** or enter ⌘, (command+,). Click the **Signatures** icon at the top of the pane if it is not already selected.

Select the email account from the left column. To create a new signature click the **+** button at the bottom of the middle column. Enter your desired signature in the right pane. You can use the **Edit** and **Format** menus to change the font, layout, change text into links, or check spelling. If you want to add an image, drag it into the right pane. If you want to use your contact information from the Contacts application, drag your vCard into the right pane

To delete a signature, first select the email account. Highlight the signature you want to delete and click the − button at the bottom of the middle column.

If you want your signature to always use the message font you specified in the **Fonts & Colors** preferences, check the box next to **Always match my default message font**.

Create a VIP List

Not all email messages are created equal. You may want to highlight and prioritize messages received from certain people using Mail's VIP feature.

To add someone to the VIP list, first find an email message from them. Click the empty star next to their name in the email or secondary click on their name and select **Add to VIPs**. Once you have added one person to your VIP list, a new VIP mailbox will appear in the Mail Sidebar and in your Favorites Bar.

To remove someone from the VIP list, find an email message from them and click on the star next to their name or secondary click on their name and select **Remove from VIPs**.

Manage Email Overload

The best way to manage email overload is the create rules so that Mail can automatically process and take action based on various mail attributes. You can use mail rules to organize your mail and highlight mail that is important, separating it from the noise. For example, you could create a mail rule for email from your bank, moving it to a special banking folder, playing a sound, and bouncing the Mail icon in the Dock to notify you. Mail supports 14 different pre-defined actions and 28 conditions, which you can combine to customize how you want your inbound email processed.

To create, modify, or delete mail rules, open **Mail > Preferences...** or enter ⌘, (command+,). Click the **Rules** icon at the top of the pane if it is not already selected. To modify, duplicate, or delete an existing rule, highlight it and click the **Edit**, **Duplicate**, or **Remove** button at the right. Click the **Add Rule** button to create a new mail rule.

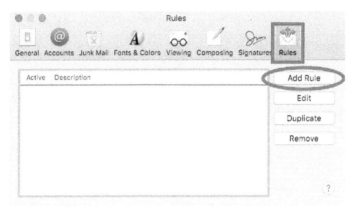

Creating a new mail rule is easy. Rules have 2 components - the **conditions** and the **actions**. After clicking the **Add Rule** button, a configuration sheet will drop down. To create a new rule, first name the rule in the **Description** field.

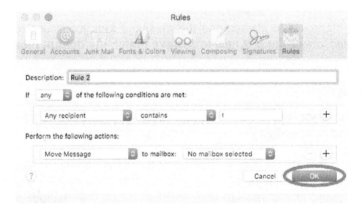

Next, choose whether **any** or **all** of the conditions have to be met to perform the selected actions. If you choose **any** the actions will be performed if only one of the conditions is met. **All**, as the name implies, requires that all conditions be met in order to perform the actions.

Now configure a condition from the more than two dozen conditions from the drop-down list. To add multiple conditions, click the **+** button. Use the **–** button to remove a condition. Under **Perform the following actions**, select the action you want Mail to perform. To add multiple actions, click the **+** button. Use the **–** button to remove an action. Click **OK** when finished.

Let's configure a mail rule to play a sound when a message is received from a particular person.

Create a Rule to Play a Sound

Not all email messages are created equal. You can configure Mail to play a sound and bounce the Mail icon in the Dock to notify you when mail arrives from someone in your VIP list.

First, select **Mail > Preferences...** or enter ⌘, (command+,) to open the Mail preference pane. Select **Rules** if not already selected, and click on the **Add Rule** button. Enter a descriptive name in the **Description** field. In the conditions section, choose **Sender is VIP** from the drop-down menu. In the **Perform the following actions** section, choose **Play Sound** from the drop-down menu and choose whatever sound you like from the next drop-down. Next, click the **+** button to create a new line. Select **Bounce Icon in Dock** from the drop-down menu. Click **OK** to finish and click **Apply** on the next dialog box.

When you receive email from someone in your VIP list, the Hero sound will play and the Mail icon located in the Dock will bounce.

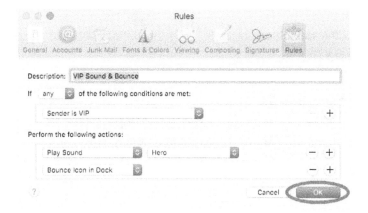

To remove a rule, open the Mail preference pane, select **Rules**, highlight the rule you want to remove, and click the **Remove** button. Rules can also be disabled without deleting them. To do so, uncheck the box in the **Active** column next to the rule in the list to disable it. Check the box to enable the associated rule.

Customize the Toolbar

The **Toolbar**, located at the top of the Mail window, provides a number of tools to make you more productive. Mail allows you to customize the **Toolbar**, adding, removing, and rearranging tools as you see fit. Secondary click in any open area of the Toolbar to reveal a contextual menu with a single option to **Customize Toolbar...**, which reveals a drop-down tools palette with the entire selection of tools available.

The tools palette allows you to add additional tools to the Toolbar by dragging and dropping them onto the Toolbar. Tools can be dragged off the Toolbar and dropped onto the palette to remove them. In addition, any tool can be removed from the Toolbar at any time by holding down the ⌘ (command) key and dragging it off. Tools can be rearranged at any time by holding down the ⌘ (command) key and dragging and dropping them.

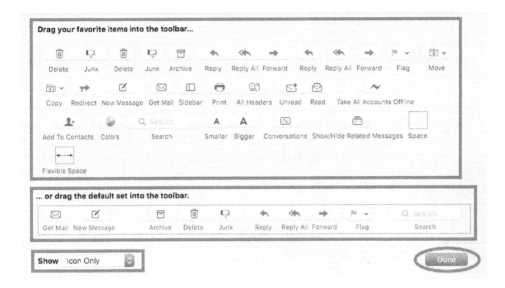

To revert back to the default set of tools, drag the default set onto the Finder toolbar to replace the existing toolset.

Customize the Favorites Bar

Directly below the Toolbar is the **Favorites Bar**, another customizable component of the Mail window. At the extreme left is the **Mailboxes** button, which you can use to toggle the **Sidebar** on and off. The space to the right of the Mailboxes button is completely customizable.

To customize your Mail **Favorites** bar, drag any item from the **Sidebar** on to the Favorites bar. You can drag individual mailboxes, section headings (i.e., **On My Mac**, **VIPs**, **Flagged**), a mail account, or a single flag. Practically anything in the Sidebar can be dragged on to the Favorites bar. Clicking on any item in the Favorites bar will change the Mail window to that view and the button will turn a darker shade of grey to denote that it has been selected.

If an item has sub-items, a small triangular caret will appear to its right. In this case, the button will both toggle the view on and off as well as displaying a drop-down menu. For example, clicking on **VIPs** in the picture above will display all the messages from everyone you have designated as a VIP. If you click the caret to the right of the **VIPs** button, a drop-down list will appear allowing you to select a specific VIP.

Drag and drop any item to rearrange it. To remove an item from your Favorites bar, drag and drop it off.

Embed Links in an Email

An embedded link allows the recipient of an email message to click on a link embedded within an email to go directly to a website, start a chat in Messages, or start a FaceTime call.

To embed a link into an email message, enter ⌘K (command+K). A drop-down dialog box will appear asking you to **Enter the Internet address (URL) for this link**.

To embed a link to a website, enter the following followed immediately by the website's URL or copy the URL from Safari's search and address field.

```
http://
```

To embed a link that will allow the recipient to start a chat session with you in **Messages**, enter the following followed immediately by your ten-digit phone number or email address.

```
imessage://
```

To embed a link that will allow the recipient to start a FaceTime call with you, enter the following followed immediately by your ten-digit phone number or email address.

```
facetime://
```

Links can also be embedded in other types of files, such as Word or Pages documents or Powerpoint or Keynote presentations by using ⌘K (command+K).

Add Emoji

Emoji are those cute (or irritating depending on your point of view) little emoticons that originated in Japan in the late 1990s and have spread around the world since then. You can reveal the OS X emoji set in almost any application by pressing the ^⌘**space** keys (control+command+space).

Not only will you have access to the emoji, but other special character sets are available. Click the icons at the bottom of the window to display the other character sets. Click on an emoji or special character to insert it into your document.

Use Natural Language Search

Like Spotlight, the **Mail** application supports natural language search capability. Therefore, you don't have to remember who sent you an email or the subject. For example, if you are interested in seeing emails that have a photo attached, you can enter "emails with a photo attached" in the Mail search field.

Markup an Email Attachment

A feature from the previous release of OS X is the ability to markup an image or PDF attachment. To markup a PDF attachment, attach an image to your email message by dragging it into the new message window. Hover over the image with your cursor until a small gray icon appears in the upper right corner of the image. Click on this icon and select **Markup**. The image will open in a new Markup window where you can edit the image similar to how you would annotate an image using the Preview application. Click **Done** when finished. The image, with your edits, will appear in the message window. The best part of this feature is that the original image remains untouched as the markups only appear on the attachment in Mail.

Sign a PDF Document

Another feature of Mail is the ability to sign PDF documents. First, attach the PDF requiring your signature to a new email message. Hover your cursor over the PDF in the message window until a small gray icon appears in the upper right corner. Click the icon and select **Markup**.

The PDF will open in a new Markup window. Click the **Signature** tool, click **Trackpad** if not already highlighted, **Click Here to Begin**, and sign your name using the Trackpad. Click **Done** when finished signing.

It is a little difficult to sign your name using your finger and the trackpad, so if you don't like the result, click **Cancel** and try again. Once you are satisfied, click the **Done** button in the upper right.

You can also use the camera to take a picture of your signature and add it to the PDF. Click **Camera** instead of **Trackpad** to use this option.

16

Security & Privacy

Stop Apple & Microsoft from Snooping on your Searches

When you have **Spotlight Suggestions** enabled, your search queries, the Spotlight Suggestions you select, precise geographic location, and usage data will be sent to Apple. According to Apple, this violation of your privacy is a feature that makes your search results more relevant to you by including results from iTunes, the App Store, Internet, and by using your location. If this wasn't bad enough, Apple shares search information with Microsoft!

Apple's snooping is enabled by default, so every time you start typing in Spotlight or in Safari's address and search field, your search terms and location are sent to Apple, Microsoft, and potentially to other third parties.

To stop Apple from receiving your search data, open the **Safari** preference pane by selecting **Safari > Preferences...** or by entering ⌘, (command+,). Once the Safari preference pane appears, make sure **Search** is highlighted from the icons on the toolbar. Uncheck the checkbox next to **Include Spotlight Suggestions**.

Next, turn off **Location Services for Spotlight Suggestions** by opening the **Security & Privacy** preference pane from System Preferences.

Select **Location Services**, then click the **Details** button next to **System Services**. Note that you will have to scroll down to the bottom of the list to see System Services. Click the **Details** button. Uncheck the checkbox next to **Spotlight Suggestions** underneath **Allow system services to determine your location** on the next sheet. Click **Done** when finished.

Apple will still receive the IP address of your Internet connection, which approximates your location to a geographic region, and will send you what it believes to be relevant search results. Note that you do not want to completely disable **Location Services** by unchecking the box next to **Enable Location Services.** Doing so prevents you from locating your Mac with the **Find My iPhone** feature.

Next head over to the **Spotlight** preference pane in the System Preferences application. We'll need to disable **Spotlight Suggestions** and **Bing Web Searches** to keep Apple and Microsoft from snooping on you. Click on **Search Results** if it is not already highlighted. Uncheck the checkbox next to **Bing Web Searches**, which is the second entry from the top. You'll need to scroll to the bottom of the list to find **Spotlight Suggestions** and uncheck the checkbox next to it. Finally, uncheck the checkbox next to **Allow Spotlight Suggestions in Spotlight and Look up**.

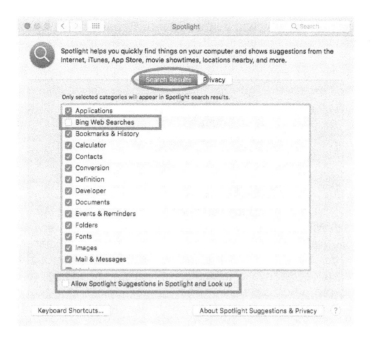

Help Defeat the Evil Empire

You can help defeat the Evil Empire's plans for galactic domination by configuring Safari to not use Google as its search engine. Google gathers a tremendous amount your personal information, more than you realize and most without your knowledge. Two-thirds of all searches in the U.S. and 70% worldwide are done using Google's search engine. The Evil Empire tracks all of your searches, capturing detailed information on your search topics and which search results you clicked. Have you searched for information on a medical condition you'd like to keep private? Too late. The Evil Empire knows. Google states that its mission is "to organize the world's information and make it universally accessible and useful." That includes information that you may prefer to keep private.

If you prefer not to share information with Google, you can configure Safari to use a search engine that does not collect your personal information. Safari offers DuckDuckGo as an alternative search engine. Google's privacy policy, as of the writing of this book, is 8 pages long. DuckDuckGo's privacy policy is a mere 7 words, "We don't collect or share personal information."

To configure Safari to use DuckDuckGo as its search engine, select **Safari > Preferences...** or by entering ⌘, (command+comma). Click on **Search**, if it is not already selected. Using the pull-down menu next to **Search Engine**, select **DuckDuckGo.** Other options are Bing and Yahoo, however, both collect your personal data.

DuckDuckGo even has a handy Extension that will put a tool on Safari's toolbar. To install the DuckDuckGo extension, go to https://extensions.apple.com and search for DuckDuckGo. You can also access the Safari Extensions page by selecting **Safari > Preferences...** or by entering ⌘, (command+comma). Click on **Extensions**, if it is not already selected. Click the **Get Extensions** button at the lower right.

Stay Safe & Secure on Public WiFi

If you have a MacBook, MacBook Pro, or MacBook Air, you probably use public WiFi available at Starbucks, hotels, airports, and other businesses. Public WiFi is horribly insecure. It doesn't matter if the service is free or if you have to pay a fee. When using public WiFi, all of your traffic is sent in the clear, allowing anyone to capture all data you send or receive. Sometimes bad guys will camp out in public places and set up their laptops to mimic a legitimate public WiFi service with a tantalizing name such as FREE Airport WiFi. All they have to do is wait for victims to connect, capture private data, and use it to steal a victim's identity.

A Virtual Private Network (VPN) protects your data by encrypting it while it travels over public WiFi. With identity theft dramatically on the rise, it is just plain reckless to use public WiFi without a personal VPN. There are other reasons why you need a personal VPN account. A VPN makes you anonymous by hiding your Mac's actual IP address, replacing it with the IP address of the VPN service. This makes it more difficult for your Internet Service Provider, employer, or others to track your online activity. If you are traveling in a foreign country, you may lose access to Netflix or to social media sites that the local government censors. A personal VPN will allow you to access services the government considers objectionable or are unavailable in foreign countries. If you want to protect your privacy and security when online, you need to use a personal VPN service.

If your company provides a VPN for business use, you don't want to use it for personal business. Company VPNs are monitored for misuse. Do you really want your employer knowing your personal browsing habits? I think not. That's another reason why you should sign up for a personal VPN service. There are lots of choices available for fees ranging from $3 to $20 a month. Why not choose one of the free VPN services? The free services are more restrictive regarding maximum bandwidth, the ability to stream video, and are sometimes funded by obnoxious advertising. If you can live with these limitations, choose a free VPN service, otherwise better services without these limitations are available for a nominal monthly or yearly fee.

The VPN service I use is **Cloak**, available at http://getcloak.com. The monthly fee for 5 GB of data is $2.99 and the unlimited plan costs $9.99 a month or $99.99 a year. Cloak offers a 30-day free trial, so you have nothing to lose by checking it out. Cloak's VPN performs well using the Ookla speed test available at http://www.speedtest.net/. A nice feature is that I can use the same account on my Mac, iPhone, and iPad. A particularly useful feature is that Cloak can be configured to automatically connect to the VPN when you connect to an untrusted WiFi network so you never forget to enable it.

Disable the Guest User Account

The **Guest User** account is enabled by OS X by default. Selecting the Guest User at login allows someone to get online as a guest, but prevents the guest user from accessing your data. So what's the point of the Guest User account? This account plays a role in the OS X Find My iPhone feature by allowing someone who swiped your Mac to get online so your Mac can be located. Therefore it is recommended that you keep the Guest User account enabled so your Mac can be located if it is stolen.

If you still want to disable the Guest User account, open the **Users & Groups** preference pane in the System Preferences application. Click the lock in the lower left corner to make changes. Enter your password when prompted.

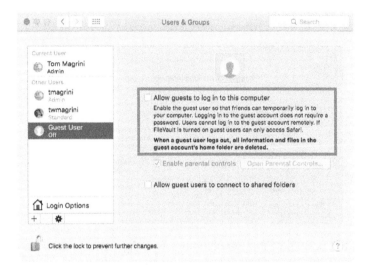

Select the **Guest User** from the left column. Uncheck the box next to **Allow guests to log in to this computer.** Close the Users & Groups preference pane when finished. Checking this checkbox will re-enable the Guest User account.

Switch to a Standard User Account

The account created when you first set up your Mac is an administrator account. Using your Mac for day-to-day work as an administrator poses a security risk. If your Mac becomes infected with malware while you are logged in as an administrator, the elevated privileges allows malware easier access to system resources, applications, and other resources available only to the administrator. Therefore, it is a safe computing best practice to perform day-to-day activities as a standard user and to reserve the administrator account for adjusting system settings and installing applications. If you are using your computer as a standard user and need to make a change that requires administrator access, you will be prompted for the administrator account credentials.

If you have a brand new Mac and have just set it up, creating separate administrator and user accounts is a breeze. By default, Setup Assistant creates the default administrator account. You can use the **Users & Groups** preference pane in System Preferences to create a new standard account for your day-to-day computing activities. However, if you been using your Mac for a while, creating a new standard account won't work for you as all of your settings, applications, and data will only be accessible from your old administrator account. The solution to this dilemma is to first create another administrator account and then to downgrade your existing account to a standard user.

To create a new administrator account, open the **Users & Groups** preference pane in the System Preferences application. Click the lock in the lower left corner to make changes. Enter your password when prompted.

Click on the **+** at the bottom of the left column. A configuration sheet will appear. Choose **Administrator** from the drop-down list next to **New Account**. Enter the **Full Name**, **Account Name**, **Password**, and click **Create User** to finish. Log out and log back in with your new administrator account to see if it works properly and that you did not fat finger the password.

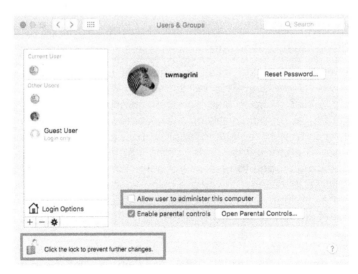

Using your new administrator account, open the **Users & Groups** preference pane from System Preferences. Click the lock in the lower left corner to make changes. Enter your password when prompted. Select your old administrator account, the one you want to downgrade to a standard user, from the left column. Uncheck the checkbox next to **Allow user to administer this computer**. Note the change in the left column to **Standard**. Close the Users & Groups preference pane when finished to save the change. Now log out and log back in with your standard user account.

Create Strong Passwords with Keychain Access

 Keychain Access is the OS X application that handles certificates, stores passwords you create or those created by Safari, and allows you to store other data in an encrypted format. If you're unfamiliar with Keychain Access, it is probably because it is a little hard to find. Keychain Access is tucked away in the **Utilities** folder.

Keychain Access manages all of your login credentials, allowing you to create unique passwords for each website or application you access. This is a security best practice, ensuring that if one of your passwords is compromised, it cannot be used to break into all of the other sites where you have accounts. **Never reuse passwords among websites**. I recommend utilizing strong passwords and changing them every 6 months. Keychain Access in combination with Safari can be used to automate the creation, storage, and retrieval of your passwords.

The advantage of using Keychain Access is that you can configure it to synchronize passwords over iCloud to make them available across all of your Apple devices. Although other third party password managers offer a similar feature. I'll show you a third party password manager later in this chapter that I believe does a better job of synchronizing passwords across Apple devices.

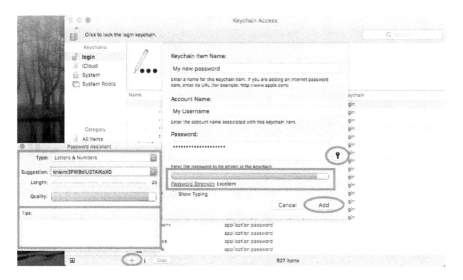

Keychain Access can be found in **Applications > Utilities** or by searching using **Launchpad** or **Spotlight**. To create a new password select **File > New Password Item**, enter **⌘N** (command+N), or click the **+** button at the bottom of the Keychain Access window. Enter the **Keychain Item Name** and **Account Name**. Next, click the **Key** button to the far right of the **Password** field, which will launch **Password Assistant**.

Password Assistant will launch in a separate window. Using the drop-down menu next to **Type**, select the type of password you would like to create. You have several choices: **Memorable, Letters & Numbers, Numbers Only, Random**, or **FIPS-181 compliant**. Password Assistant will suggest a password of 12 characters, which is too short for a strong password. I recommend using the longest password supported by the website or application. Use the **Length** slider to increase the number of characters. As the number of characters increase, you'll notice **Quality** turns to a darker green indicating a stronger password. If your chosen password has any problems, Password Assistant will tell you in the **Tips** box below **Quality**. If your password has a problem, select another password from the drop-down list next to **Suggestion**. When finished, click the red close window control in the upper left corner of the Password Assistant window. Your password is automatically placed in the password field of the new password item you just created. Click the **Add** button to save your new password to your keychain.

When you want to use your password, launch **Keychain Access** and search for the item by name using the search field in the upper right. Secondary click on the item and enter your password when prompted. Your password has been saved to the clipboard and you can paste it into the website or application.

If you are using Safari, you will be asked if you would like to save the username and password. Doing so avoids having to launch Keychain Access and search for your password each time you need it for that particular website.

If you a visiting a site for the first time and are creating a new account, Safari will suggest a strong password. To use the password suggested by Safari, click on **Use Safari suggested password,** which will appear below a website's password input field. Don't worry, you won't have to remember this monster. Passwords are automatically saved to the **Keychain Access** application and are recalled and populated into the password field the next time you log in to the website. And if you use iCloud Keychain, your Safari-generated passwords will be available on all of your Apple devices.

Enable iCloud Keychain

 iCloud Keychain allows you to save usernames and passwords from Keychain Access in iCloud for use on any of your Apple devices. A handy feature is a password generator which suggests strong passwords for you to use, automatically enters them into the password field of a website, and saves them to the **Keychain Access** application.

To enable iCloud Keychain, open the **iCloud** preference pane in the System Preferences application. Scroll down and check the box next to **Keychain** in the list in the right-hand panel of the iCloud preference pane. Enter your Apple ID and password when prompted.

Click the **Options** button to the right of **Keychain**. As an additional security measure, you can configure iCloud Keychain to send a four-digit security code to your iPhone or iPad each time a new device using your iCloud credentials requests access to iCloud Keychain. You will only have to do this once for each device.

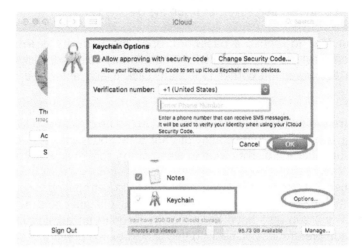

Lock Your Mac Using the Keychain Access Menu Extra

In addition to securely storing your passwords, **Keychain Access** can be used to lock your Mac using its Menu Extra in the Menu Bar.

First, launch **Keychain Access** through Finder by navigating to **Applications > Utilities** or by searching using **Launchpad** or **Spotlight**. Next, select **Keychain Access > Preferences...** or by entering ⌘, (command+,) to launch its preference pane. Click on the **General** tab if not already highlighted. Check the checkbox next to **Show keychain status in menu bar**.

OS X will add the Keychain Access Menu Extra, which looks like a padlock, to the Menu Bar. The drop-down menu offers an option to **Lock Screen**. In addition, you can use the Menu Extra to **Lock Keychain** when it is no longer in use. **Open Security Preferences...** will launch the **Security & Privacy** preference pane. **Open Keychain Access...** does what you'd expect it to do, open the Keychain Access application. The Menu Extra will remain on the Menu Bar even if Keychain Access is not running.

Require a Password to Wake the Display

For security reasons, it is highly recommended that you require a password to wake your computer from sleep, the screen saver, or when the display is asleep.

To configure your Mac to require a password, open the **Security & Privacy** preference pane in the System Preferences application. If not already selected, click the **General** tab. If the padlock in the lower left corner is locked, click it and enter your password when prompted.

Check the **Require password** checkbox as shown in the next picture. OS X offers you the option of requiring a password immediately or after 5 seconds, after 1, 5, or 15 minutes, or after 1, 4, or 8 hours after the display went to sleep or the screen saver began.

Click the **Advanced...** button in the lower right corner to set options to log you out after a period of inactivity. Check the checkbox next to Log out after and set the number of minutes of inactivity. You also have the option to Require an administrator password to access system-wide preferences. Checking this checkbox will prevent users from changing locked system preferences without an administrator's password.

Show a Message When Locked

OS X lets you configure your Mac to show a message when the screen is locked. Open the **Security & Privacy** preference pane in the System Preferences application. If not already selected, click the **General** tab.

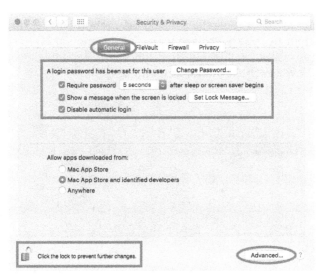

Check the box next to **Show a message when the screen is locked**. If this option is grayed, check the padlock in the lower left corner of the preference pane to ensure it is unlocked. If the padlock is closed, it indicates the preference pane is locked. Click on the padlock and enter your password when prompted.

Check the checkbox and click the **Set Lock Message...** button. Enter your message in the configuration sheet that drops from the top of the pane and click **OK**.

Disable Automatic Login

With automatic login enabled anyone can access your Mac simply by restarting it. They will be automatically logged in as you with access to all of your files, Mail, Messages, etc. I highly recommend that you disable this feature.

To globally disable automatic login, open the **Security & Privacy** preference pane in the System Preferences application. Select the **General** tab if not already selected. If the padlock in the lower left corner is locked, click it and enter your password when prompted. Next, check the box next to **Disable automatic login**. This change takes effect immediately and will also be reflected in the **Users & Groups** preference pane. Your Mac will ask for a user name and password when it starts.

Automatic login can be enabled for a specific user from the **Users & Groups** preference pane by clicking on **Login Options** at the bottom of the left column and turning on **Automatic login** from the drop-down menu. However, I do not recommend using automatic login for security reasons under any circumstances.

Encrypt Time Machine Backups

 Hands down, Apple's **Time Machine** is the easiest backup application I have ever used. Its simple "set it and forget it" interface quietly backs up all of my critical data regularly without any intervention on my part. And the best part of Time Machine is how quickly and easily it can restore one file or your entire Mac.

Time Machine contains a copy of all of your files, including any data you would like to stay private. If you are concerned about unauthorized access, you can encrypt your Time Machine backup. Note that if you are only worried about encrypting your passwords in Keychain, your passwords are already encrypted when stored in the Keychain Access app, so it is not necessary to further encrypt them in Time Machine.

To encrypt your Time Machine backup, open the **Time Machine** preference pane in the System Preferences application. Next, click **Add or Remove Backup Disk...** to reveal a drop-down configuration sheet that will allow you to enable encryption on a new or existing Time Machine backup.

Select the disk drive you would like to encrypt under **Available Disks**. You can select an new drive for your Time Machine backup or select an existing one. Check the checkbox next to **Encrypt backups** to enable encryption. Click the **Use Disk** button. Enter a backup password and hint on the next configuration sheet. Click **Encrypt Disk** when finished.

Make Gatekeeper Less Restrictive

Apple's App Store is the safest and most reliable place to download and install applications because Apple reviews each application before it's accepted into the App Store, checking for malicious or junk software. If an application is later found to be malicious, Apple will remove it. **Gatekeeper** makes your OS X computing experience safer by stopping applications that are not digitally signed with an Apple Developer ID from being installed. Gatekeeper protects your Mac from malicious software by ensuring it is from a trusted source, an Apple Developer, and by verifying the application hasn't been tampered with. Gatekeeper will block the installation of any application that is not signed by a valid Apple Developer ID.

Gatekeeper allows you to download applications from the App Store and from Apple Developers. You also have the option of making Gatekeeper more or less restrictive. Open the **Security & Privacy** preference pane in the System Preferences application. Click **General** if not already highlighted. Ensure the padlock in the lower left corner is unlocked. If not, click it and enter your password when prompted.

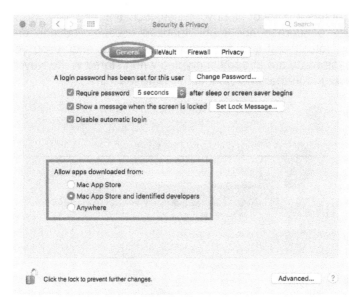

The default setting in OS X El Capitan is **Mac App Store and identified developers**, which ensures that Gatekeeper will check the application you downloaded is signed by a valid Apple Developer ID. You have the option of choosing the most secure setting, **Mac App Store**, which effectively means you cannot install applications unless they have been downloaded from Apple's App Store. The least secure setting is **Anywhere**. I do not recommend this setting as this effectively disables Gatekeeper from checking applications for a digital signature from a valid Apple Developer. Doing so will leave your Mac vulnerable to malicious software.

If you want to install unsigned software, OS X allows you to perform a manual override of Gatekeeper on a case-by-case basis. However, I recommend you only install applications that have been reviewed by a reputable publication. If you try to install an unsigned application, Gatekeeper will block it from being installed and display a warning dialog box. Clicking **OK** only acknowledges the warning.

To install an unsigned application after a Gatekeeper warning, unblock the installation by opening the **Security & Privacy** preference pane in the System Preferences application. Click **General** if it is not already highlighted. You will see a message at the bottom of the pane telling you why Gatekeeper blocked the install. If you want to continue the installation, click the **Open Anyway** button and OS X will install the application.

To revert to the OS X default setting, open the Security & Privacy preference pane and click the radio button next to **Mac App Store and identified developers**.

Encrypt Your Drive

 Encrypting your disk drive protects your data in case your Mac is ever stolen. Encryption combined with the other security customization covered in this chapter makes it more difficult for a thief to access your data. **FileVault 2** can encrypt your entire drive with XTS-AES 128 encryption.

Before enabling File Vault, there are a few things you need to consider. If you are in the habit of forgetting your password (or don't use a password to unlock your Mac) and lose your backup recovery key, your data is unrecoverable. This means your data is gone for good. FileVault's encryption is so strong, it's virtually impossible to break it and access your data. You can set up FileVault to use your iCloud password, so some risk is mitigated, but this will not help you if you forget your iCloud password or are temporarily without Internet access and need to get into your Mac.

FileVault will degrade the performance of some Macs, particularly older Macs with slower hard disk drives. You'll notice the performance degradation when opening large files. If your Mac is new and has a Solid State Drive (SSD), you will see little in the way of performance degradation.

If you want a truly secure system and have a new Mac with an SSD, FileVault is the way to go for the maximum level of security. To encrypt your entire drive with FileVault, open the **Security & Privacy** preference pane in the System Preferences application. If not already highlighted, click **FileVault**. Ensure the padlock in the lower left corner is unlocked. If not, click it and enter your password when prompted.

Click the **Turn On FileVault...** button. You'll be asked if you want to use your iCloud account to unlock your encrypted disk and reset your password if you forget it or use a recovery key instead of your iCloud account. If you choose the recovery code, you'll be presented with your 20-digit recovery code. **Make a copy of this code and store it in a safe place, not on the Mac your are encrypting**. If you lose both your password and the recovery key, you will not be able to access any of the data on your disk drive. It is a very bad idea to keep the copy of your recovery key on your Mac. If you forget your password you will not be able to access any of the data on your Mac including the recovery key. Store your recovery key in a safe, external location.

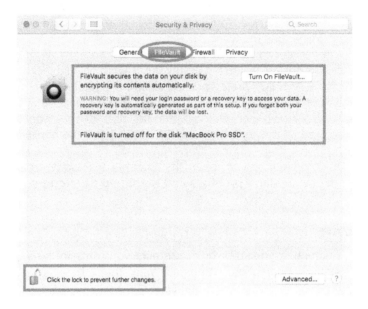

If there is more than one user account configured on your Mac, you'll be asked to identify the users who are allowed to unlock the encrypted drive. Each user is required to enter his or her password in order to have the ability to unlock FileVault. Click the **Continue** button to continue.

Finally, you will be asked to click **Restart** in the next dialog box to begin the encryption process. This is your last opportunity to change your mind. If you've changed your mind, press the **Cancel** button.

Securely Erase an Old Disk Drive

 If you have an old disk drive that you want to get rid of either by trashing it, giving it to charity, or giving it to a friend or relative, I highly recommend you securely erase the drive prior to handing it over. Use the **Disk Utility** application to securely erase your old drive by writing random ones and zeros multiple times over your data.

To securely erase an old disk drive, launch **Disk Utility** by navigating to **Applications > Utilities** or by searching for Disk Utility using Launchpad or Spotlight.

Click on the disk drive you want to erase in the left column. Click the **Erase** tab at the top of the Disk Utility window. Next, click the **Security Options...** button to reveal the **Secure Erase Options** configuration dialog. The large slider in the middle controls the number of passes Disk Utility will make when writing random ones and zeros to the drive.

The fastest option will not securely erase the data on your drive. A disk recovery application may still be able to recover some data if you use this method. Drag the slider to the right to preview each of the other options. The first option writes a single pass of zeros over the entire disk. The next option does two passes of random data followed by another pass of no data. The most secure option meets the US Department of Defense (DOD) 5220-22M standard for securely erasing magnetic media. It erases the disk drive by writing random data over seven passes. Note that It takes a long time to erase a drive using this method, but this is the most secure method and guarantees none of your personal data will be left on the drive. I suggest you let this run overnight.

Once you've selected the method to securely erase your drive, click the **OK** button. Then click the **Erase** button and confirm on the next dialog box. Now sit back and relax because securely erasing a large drive can take many hours, but is well worth it to protect your sensitive data.

Clear Web Browsing History

Safari has always offered the capability to delete your browsing history, cookies, and other website data. **Safari 9.0** makes this task much easier to accomplish. In addition, you have control over the time period that you wish to delete.

To delete your web browsing history, cookies, and other website data, select **Clear History...** from the **Safari** menu. A dialog box will appear allowing you to choose to clear data from four different time periods: **the last hour**, **today**, **today and yesterday**, or **all history**. Click the **Clear History** button to clear your web browsing history.

Enable Find My Mac

If your Mac is ever stolen or lost you can use iCloud to lock or erase it to ensure your private data remains safe. To use this feature, **Find My Mac** has to be enabled in the **iCloud** preference pane before your Mac is lost. Open the **iCloud** preference pane in the System Preferences application. Scroll to the bottom. Ensure the box next to **Find My Mac** is checked.

Remotely Lock or Erase Your Lost Mac

If your Mac is lost or stolen you can use iCloud to lock it to protect your personal data. To lock a stolen Mac, log into your iCloud account at www.icloud.com using your Apple ID and password. Launch the **Find My iPhone** app from iCloud. You can also use the **Find My iPhone** app on your iPhone or iPad. In the **My Devices** list, select your lost Mac. A window will appear offering 3 options: **Play Sound**, **Lock**, or **Erase Mac**. Note that your lost Mac must be found by iCloud before the Lock and Erase options appear.

If you have simply misplaced your Mac, **Play Sound**, will cause your Mac to loudly play a sonar sound. Your Mac will make this sound even if the sound is turned off.

You can lock your Mac by selecting the **Lock** option. A window will appear confirming that you want to lock your Mac. Select **Lock** or **Cancel**. Create a PIN code in the next window and confirm it. Enter a message that you would like to display on your lost Mac. Locking your Mac will stop others from using it. Your lost Mac will reboot and will ask for the PIN to unlock it and will display your message. Note that once you lock your Mac, you are no longer able to erase it. If your Mac is returned to you, enter the PIN and your Mac will reboot and become usable once again.

The last option is **Erase Mac**. A window will appear confirming your desire to erase your Mac and stating that all content and settings will be erased and that it may take a day to complete. Select **Erase** or **Cancel**. Your Mac will be wiped and becomes essentially useless to the thief.

Create Strong Passwords with 1Password

1Password is a third party application that allows you to create unique, strong passwords for every website or application you use. Passwords can be synchronized across all of your Apple devices using iCloud. And 1Password can even log you into a website with a single click. 1Password has won several awards including the Mac App Store Best of 2014, iMore 2014 Hall of Famer, Macworld Eddy Award, Macworld App Hall of Fame, and has a MaclLife Editor's Choice "Awesome!" rating.

Using 1Password you can easily implement a security best practice – creating a unique, strong password for every website or application you use. You'll never forget a password again and your passwords are synchronized across all of your devices, even if they are

Android or Microsoft devices. Your passwords are encrypted with 256-bit AES encryption and secured behind a single Master Password – the only password you have to remember. 1Password creates strong passwords for you with its Password Generator. Using unique, strong passwords ensures that your life won't be turned upside down if a data breach occurs at a website you frequent.

Companion applications for your iPhone and iPad are available and automatically synchronize your passwords and other secure data using iCloud.

1Password supports Safari and can log you into your favorite websites with a single click. A Menu Extra ensures that your passwords are always available, right from the Menu Bar. And 1Password protects more than just passwords. You can store your credit cards, bank account numbers, and create secure notes.

1Password's Security Audit features finds duplicate passwords, weak passwords, and passwords that are too old.

1Password is available for $49.99 in the Mac App Store at:
https://itunes.apple.com/us/app/1password-password-manager/id443987910?mt=12.

Enable Parental Controls

The Internet is a dangerous place and protecting your kids is a parent's full-time job. OS X makes protecting your kids a little easier by letting you control what applications your kids can use, which websites they can visit, and how much time they spend online. To enable **Parental Controls** in OS X, open the **Users & Groups** preference pane in the System Preferences application. Click the lock in the lower left corner to make changes. Enter your password when prompted.

If your child doesn't already have an account on your Mac, click the **+** sign in the lower left to open the **New Account** configuration sheet. Select **Managed with Parental Controls** in the drop-down menu next to **New Account**. Select the **Age** from the drop-down list. You have a choice of **4+**, **9+**, **12+**, or **17+**. Create entries for the **Full Name**, **Account**

Name, and choose a **Password**. Click the **Create User** button when finished. Enter your adminstrator password when prompted.

To configure parental controls, click on the child's account in the left-hand column in the **Users & Groups** preference pane. The checkbox next to **Enable parental controls** will be checked. Click the **Open Parental Controls...** button and enter your administrator password when prompted.

The **Parental Controls** preference pane will open. This preference pane contains a number of tabs to configure **Apps**, **Web**, **Stores**, **Time**, **Privacy**, and **Other**. The first tab we will open is the **Apps** tab. This tab allows you to configure options such as whether your child can use your Mac's camera and which applications your child is allowed to launch. You can set limits on **Game Center** activities and limit **Mail** to only allowed contacts that you have approved.

Clicking **Manage...** next to **Limit Mail to allowed contacts** lets you add allowed email addresses. The allowed contacts list prevents your child from sending or receiving mail from someone who is not on the allowed list. Check the box next to **Send requests to** and enter your email address. You will receive email whenever your child attempts to send or receive mail from anyone who is not in the allowed contacts list.

In the **Web** tab, you can implement **Browser Restrictions** so your child accesses only websites with content appropriate for his or her age. You can **Allow unrestricted access to websites**, **Try to limit access to adult websites**, or **Allow access to only these websites**. The last option allows you to whitelist websites and restrict your child's web browsing to only the sites on your allowed list. Click the **+** to add a website to the allowed list or the **–** to remove a website.

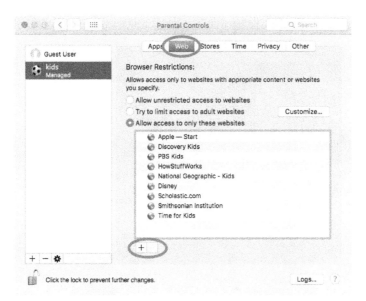

The **Stores** tab lets you disable access to the iTunes Store, iTunes U, and the iBooks store. You can also restrict music with explicit content, movies and TV shows to a particular rating, age appropriate apps, and books with explicit sexual content.

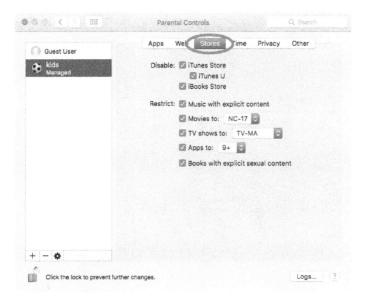

In the **Time** tab, you can set both weekday and weekend time limits, limiting the number of hours each day that your child can access your Mac. The **Bedtime** options ensure that your child cannot access your Mac during his or her bedtime on both school nights and on the weekend.

The **Privacy** tab limits requests to location data, photos, contacts and other applications. From Privacy, you can control whether you will let new apps make changes to the Contacts, Calendars, Reminders, Twitter, Facebook, and Diagnostic apps. Unchecking the checkbox next to any app locks the current settings and prevents new apps from gaining access to them.

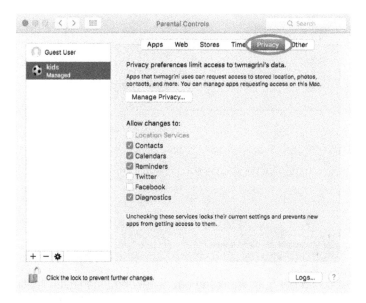

The **Other** tab enables or disables various OS X features including the ability to use Dictation, editing printers and scanners, burning CDs and DVDs, looking up explicit language in the Dictionary app, and modifying the Dock. For younger children, OS X provides a simplified view of Finder. Check or uncheck the desired options.

A **Logs...** button on each page allows you to review your child's activity.

17

Bunch of Tricks, Tweaks & Hacks

Create a Bootable El Capitan USB Flash Drive Installer

 If you own multiple Macs that you want to upgrade to El Capitan, you are facing a lot of downloading from the App Store. A better option is to create a bootable USB flash drive installer. You'll need a copy of the OS X El Capitan installer on your Mac and a USB flash drive with at least 8 GB capacity. Be sure there is nothing important on the USB drive as it will be erased as part of the creation of the installer.

Creating a bootable USB flash drive installer is a multi-step process.
1. Download OS X El Capitan from the **Mac App Store**.
2. While El Capitan is downloading, connect your USB flash drive to your Mac and launch **Disk Utility**.
3. Select your USB drive in the left-hand pane. Erase the USB drive. Don't bother naming it. It will be renamed as part of the command in #5 below. Disk Utility will pick the name **Untitled**.
4. When El Capitan finishes downloading, you will see a window asking you to click continue to set up the installation of OS X El Capitan. **STOP HERE!** Exit the installation by quitting.
5. Open Terminal and enter the following command. All four lines are a single command. **Do not** press the **return** key until you have entered the entire command. Because this command uses **sudo**, you will need to enter your admin password when prompted. Don't worry if nothing appears in Terminal as you type your password. This is a security feature.

```
sudo /Applications/Install\ OS\ X\ El\
Capitan.app/Contents/Resources/createinstallmedia --volume
/Volumes/Untitled --applicationpath /Applications/Install\
OS\ X\ El\ Capitan.app —nointeraction
```

6. Terminal will warn you that it needs to erase your USB drive. Enter **Y** to continue.

```
Ready to start.
To continue we need to erase the disk at /Volumes/Untitled.
If you wish to continue type (Y) then press return:
```

7. You can quit Terminal when it is done creating the installer disk. Open Finder and check the Devices in the Sidebar. You should see a device called **Install OS X El Capitan**.

```
Copy complete.
Making disk bootable...
Copying boot files...
Copy complete.
Done.
```

8. You are now finished with the creation of your OS X El Capitan USB flash drive installer.

To use your flash drive to install El Capitan, insert your USB drive into your Mac and hold down the ⌥ (option) key while restarting to display the startup disk menu. Select your USB installer drive to continue booting your Mac directly into the El Capitan installer. Follow the on-screen instructions. It should take about 45 minutes to an hour to complete the installation.

Tweak Background Updates

 By default, El Capitan will automatically download and install updates in the background. If you would like to manually review the updates OS X plans to make to your Mac before they are installed, OS X offers a number of configuration options. To configure background updates, open the **App Store** preference pane in the System Preferences application.

When the checkbox next to **Automatically check for updates** is checked, your Mac will automatically check the App Store for updates. If you uncheck this box, OS X will no longer check or notify you of the availability of updates. You will have to manually check the App Store for updates.

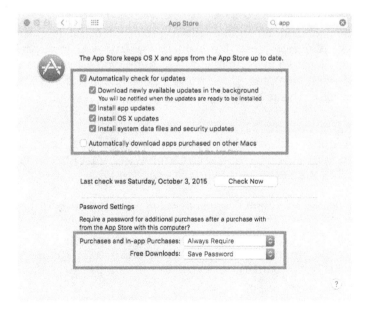

When automatic updates are enabled, you can control how updates are downloaded and installed using the next 4 checkboxes. If you check the box next to **Download newly available updates in the background**, OS X will automatically download updates without asking your permission, however, you will be notified when updates are ready to be installed. Installation of updates is controlled via the next 3 checkboxes.

If the checkbox next to **Install app updates** is checked, OS X will automatically update applications without asking for permission. Uncheck it to disable automated application updates.

When the box next to **Install OS X updates** is checked, your Mac will install OS X updates automatically. Uncheck the checkbox to disable this feature.

If the box next to **Install system data files and security updates** is checked, OS X will automatically install system files and security updates without asking for permission. Uncheck the box to disable this feature.

Disabling any of the automatic installation options will require you to open the App Store app and review the list of updates and manually choose which ones to update.

The **Password Settings** section controls whether a password is required to make **Purchases and In-app Purchases**. You have two choices in the drop-down menu: **Always require** or **Require After 15 minutes**. For **Free Downloads**, you can always require a password or your password can be saved so you do not have to enter it to download a free app from the Mac App Store.

Precisely Adjust the Volume

Sometimes it seems you never can get the volume adjusted to your liking. One segment more is too much. One less is too little. Wouldn't it be awsome if you could adjust the volume in smaller increments? OS X has a solution for you!

Hold down the ⇧⌥ (shift+option) keys to adjust the volume in quarter-segment increments, allowing you to precisely adjust the volume exactly to your liking. This trick also works when adjusting the display brightness and the keyboard backlight.

Temporarily Quiet the Volume Adjustment

OS X makes an annoying popping sound each time you press the **F11** or **F12** key to decrease or increase the volume. If you're working in a quiet office environment the popping can disturb your concentration or the concentration of others. It is also annoying and loud when listening to music using earbuds.

To temporarily quiet the popping sound when adjusting the volume, hold down the ⇧ (shift) key while pressing **F11** or **F12**. Unfortunately, this trick doesn't work when adjusting the volume in quarter segment increments. To turn off this annoying, loud popping sound, check out the next tweak.

Permanently Quiet the Volume Adjustment

OS X allows you to permanently turn off the annoying and loud popping sound it makes when adjusting the volume. This is a blessing to anyone who routinely uses earbuds or headphones because this popping is so loud it is ear shattering. Also, your office mates will appreciate not being interrupted by your Mac's popping.

To permanently turn off the annoying popping sound, open the **Sound** preference pane in the System Preferences application. Next, click **Sound Effects** if it is not already highlighted. Uncheck the checkbox next to **Play feedback when volume is changed**.

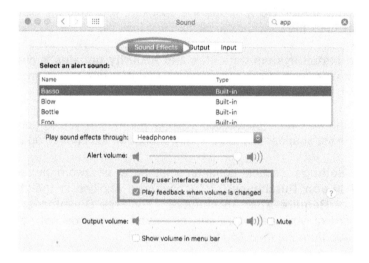

Disable User Interface Sounds

Your Mac will play various sound effects for certain actions like dragging and dropping an item into the trash. If you want to disable these sound effects, open the **Sounds** preference pane in System Preferences. Uncheck the checkbox next to **Play user interface sound effects**.

Make Help Center Behave

The OS X **Help Center** has a rather obnoxious habit. It refuses to act like other windows by stubbornly refusing to go to the background when it is not the active window. Help Center stays on top of all other windows whether it is active or not. This tweak changes this rather obnoxious behavior and forces Help Center to act like all other OS X windows.

First, close the Help Center window if open. Enter the following command in Terminal. This change takes effect immediately.

```
defaults write com.apple.helpviewer DevMode -bool TRUE
```

The next time you open Help Center you'll notice its more polite behavior. It no longer blocks other windows when it is not the active window.

To revert back to the Help Center's default obnoxious behavior, enter the following command in Terminal.

```
defaults delete com.apple.helpviewer DevMode
```

Save Changes Automatically When Closing Documents

By default, OS X will ask you if you want to save any unsaved changes when you close a document. You can turn off this behavior and have OS X automatically save unsaved changes to documents when you close them.

To enable automatic save of documents when closing them, open the **General** preference pane in System Preferences. Uncheck the checkbox next to **Ask to keep changes when closing documents**.

Stop Closed Windows from Reopening

Some more obnoxious behavior you may have noticed is that OS X will reopen files that were open the last time you quit an app. While this is occasionally useful if you're working on a single document over a long period of time, it is annoying most of the time because you have to close the old document to continue your new work. Those switching from a Windows PC may find this behavior particularly annoying since Windows does not exhibit this odd quirk.

This behavior is easy to correct. Open the **General** preference pane in the System Preferences application. Check the box next to **Close windows when quitting an application** and OS X will stop opening old documents when you launch an application.

Change the Highlight Color

The default highlight color when highlighting text in a document is blue. If you prefer another color, you can change the highlight color in the **General** preference pane in System Preferences. You have the choice of red, orange, yellow, green, blue, purple, pink, brown, or graphite. Choosing **Other...** displays a color wheel where you can select your own custom highlight color.

Enable Key Repeat

Another odd behavior you may wish to correct is how key repeat behaves. By default, holding down a key in OS X does not activate key repeat as expected. Instead, a contextual menu appears, which allows you to choose to insert diacritic characters (i.e., accented and other non-English characters). Unless you often write in a foreign language, you may find this feature to be an annoyance. OS X allows you to make key repeat operate as you expect it to when holding down a key.

To enable key repeat, open Terminal and enter the following command. You'll have to log out and log back in for this change to take effect.

```
defaults write -g ApplePressAndHoldEnabled -bool FALSE
```

To revert back to the OS X default, enter the following command. You will have to log out and log back in for the change to take effect.

```
defaults delete -g ApplePressAndHoldEnabled
```

Enable QuickTime Autoplay

QuickTime will not start playing a movie until you click the **Play** button. Use this tweak if you would like to turn on the **QuickTime Autoplay** feature, which will start playing a movie immediately after you open it.

First quit QuickTime and then launch Terminal. Enter the following command. Note that both lines are a single command. Do not press **return** until you have entered the complete command.

```
defaults write com.apple.QuickTimePlayerX MGPlayMovieOnOpen -bool
TRUE
```

To revert back to the OS X default of having to press the **Play** button to start a QuickTime movie, enter the following command.

```
defaults delete com.apple.QuickTimePlayerX MGPlayMovieOnOpen
```

Take a Screenshot

With OS X, you can take a screenshot of your entire desktop, an area of your desktop, or a window using keyboard shortcuts. To take a screenshot of your desktop, use ⇧⌘3 (shift+command+3). To capture a specific area of the desktop or a window, enter ⇧⌘4 (shift+command+4) to bring up a set of crosshairs. Drag the crosshairs across the area and release your hold when done. To capture a window, enter ⇧⌘4, move the crosshairs over the window you want to take a screenshot of, press the **spacebar** to change the crosshairs to a camera, then click your mouse or trackpad. The window does not have to be the active window to take a screenshot of it.

Change Screenshot Keyboard Shortcuts

To review, the following table lists the six keyboard shortcuts to take a screenshot.

⇧⌘3	Takes a screenshot of the desktop and saves it to the Desktop or designated folder.
^⇧⌘3	Takes a screenshot of the desktop and saves it to the Clipboard.
⇧⌘4	Takes a screenshot of a user-defined area and saves it to the Desktop or designated folder.
^⇧⌘4	Takes a screenshot of a user-defined area and saves it to the Clipboard.
⇧⌘4 + space	Takes a screenshot of a window and saves it to the Desktop or designated folder.

^⇧⌘4 + space	Takes a screenshot of a window and saves it to the Clipboard.

If you want to change the default keyboard shortcuts to take screenshots, you can redefine or disable them using the **Keyboard** preference pane.

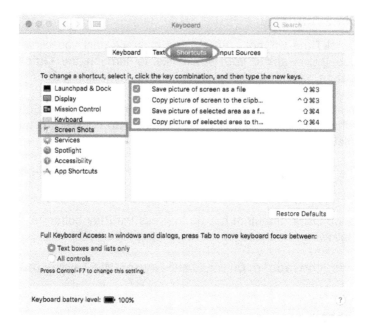

Change the Screenshot Destination Folder

OS X saves screenshots to the **Desktop** folder. If you are taking a lot of screenshots, your Desktop can quickly fill up with clutter. OS X lets you change the default destination folder to something other than the Desktop.

First, determine where you want to save your screenshots. For this example, I'll create a folder called **Screenshots** in my **Documents** folder. The path I'll need to enter in the command to change the destination folder is:

```
~/Documents/Screenshots/
```

To change the default destination for screenshots, launch Terminal and enter the following commands. Note that the first two lines are one command. Do not press the **return** key until you have entered the entire command. There is a space after location. Replace **~/Documents/Screenshots/** with the path to your desired folder.

```
defaults write com.apple.screencapture location
~/Documents/Screenshots/

killall SystemUIServer
```

To revert back to the OS X default of saving screenshots to the Desktop folder, enter the following commands.

```
defaults write com.apple.screencapture location ~/Desktop/

killall SystemUIServer
```

Save Screenshots to the Clipboard

Saving screenshots to a file is handy if you need to annotate the screenshot, however, sometimes you just need to copy the screenshot directly into a document. In this case, it is much easier to save a screenshot to the **Clipboard**. Add the ^ (control) key to the screenshot keyboard shortcuts and OS X will save your screenshot to its Clipboard. All you have to do is to paste the screenshot into your document using **Edit > Paste** or ⌘V (command+V).

Remove Shadows from Screenshots

OS X inserts a gray shadow around an image captured by a screenshot. If you would like to remove the shadow, launch Terminal and enter the following commands.

```
defaults write com.apple.screencapture disable-shadow -bool TRUE

killall SystemUIServer
```

To revert back to the OS X default, enter the following commands in Terminal.

```
defaults write com.apple.screencapture disable-shadow -bool FALSE

killall SystemUIServer
```

Change the Screenshot File Format

OS X saves screenshots and Portable Network Graphics (PNG) format, an open extensible image format supporting lossless data compression. PNG was created as an improved, non-patented replacement for Graphic Interchange Format (GIF). OS X supports the ability to save screenshots in other graphics formats.

If you would prefer to save your screenshots in **jpg** format, launch Terminal and enter the following commands.

```
defaults write com.apple.screencapture type jpg

killall SystemUIServer
```

OS X also supports **tiff**, **PDF**, **bmp**, and **pict** formats.

To change the default file save format for screenshots, replace **jpg** in the above command with your desired format.

To revert back to the OS X default, enter the following commands in Terminal.

```
defaults write com.apple.screencapture type png
```

```
killall SystemUIServer
```

Open the **Keyboard** preference pane from System Preferences. Select **Shortcuts** if not already highlighted. Choose **Screenshots** from the left column. Uncheck any shortcut you wish to disable. To change the keyboard shortcut to a combination other than the default, double-click on the shortcut and enter your desired key combination in the field at the right.

Enable the Expanded Save Dialog

OS X offers a small list of folders in its default save dialog. If you prefer to navigate the folder hierarchy to find the exact location where you want to save, you can enable the expanded save dialog as the default. The expanded save dialog displays the Finder Sidebar and allows you to navigate to your chosen destination folder. To switch between the minimalist and expanded views, click the little triangle at the end of the **Save As** field.

To enable the expanded save dialog, quit all open applications. Launch Terminal and enter the following command.

```
defaults write -g NSNavPanelExpandedStateForSaveMode -bool TRUE
```

To revert to the OS X default, quit all open applications and enter the following command.

```
defaults write -g NSNavPanelExpandedStateForSaveMode -bool FALSE
```

Use Multiple Libraries in Photos & iTunes

Photos stores all of your photos in a single photo library. If you have a large volume of photos, management of them becomes increasingly difficult as the photo library grows in size over the years. Creating photo libraries offers an option for better management than utilizing a single, gigantic Photos library.

To create a new photo library, quit Photos if it is currently open. Hold down the ⌥ (option) key while launching Photos. A dialog box will appear asking which photo library you want Photos to use.

Click the **Create New...** button and enter a name for the new photo library when prompted. If you want to save your new photo library in a location other than the **Pictures** folder, select a new location from the drop-down list next to **Where**. Click the **Save** button when finished and Photos will open your new library. To create additional Photos libraries, simply lather, rinse, and repeat.

Note that once you have multiple photo libraries, Photos will consider the last one you opened as the default. That means the library you last used will open automatically when you launch Photos. If you want to open another photo library, you will need to hold down the ⌥ (option) key while launching Photos. A dialog box will appear asking you which photo library you want Photos to use. Select the appropriate library and click **Choose**.

This trick also works for **iTunes**, allowing you to create multiple music libraries.

Add ½ Star Ratings to iTunes

iTunes allows you to rate songs from 1 to 5 stars. If you need more precise ratings, you can enable ½ star ratings. I find this feature very useful when a song is not quite 5 stars, but it's better than 4 stars. 4½ perfect! To enable ½ star ratings in iTunes, first quit iTunes if it is open and then enter the following commands in Terminal.

```
defaults write com.apple.iTunes allow-half-stars -bool TRUE
```

To use the ½ star rating, simply drag your cursor left or right to change the rating in ½ star increments.

To revert back to the default of full star ratings, into the following command into Terminal. Be sure to quit iTunes first if it is open.

```
defaults delete com.apple.iTunes allow-half-stars
```

Any ½ star ratings will be lost upon disabling this feature as any existing ½ star ratings will be rounded down to the nearest full star. For example, if you rated a song or album with 4½ stars, it will be rated as 4 stars when ½ star ratings are disabled.

Synchronize External Calendar Sources

The **Calendar** application is able to synchronize calendars between a number of email services and Facebook. It only takes a couple of steps to configure Calendar to synchronize with an external source. Launch the Calendar application. Select **Calendar > Add Account...** to reveal a drop-down. Click the radio button next to the desired source and enter your login credentials when prompted.

To change how often Calendar synchronizes with external sources, select **Calendar > Preferences...** or enter ⌘, (command+,) to launch the Calendar preference pane. Select **Accounts** at the top of the pane if not already highlighted. Select the account in the left-hand pane. You have the choice of synchronizing every 1, 5, 15, or 30 minutes, every hour, or manually. For iCloud, you have the additional choice of Push, which updates the account any time you make a change. Close the Calendar preference pane when finished.

Subscribe to a Calendar Feed

iCalendar, often referred to simply as iCal, is a standard Internet calendar format that allows you to share calendars. Apple's **Calendar** application utilizes the iCal format. By default, Calendar does not have holidays preloaded. You have to subscribe to an iCal feed to add holidays to your calendar. If you are in the U.S., you can subscribe to Apple's U.S. Holidays calendar available at:
http://www.apple.com/downloads/macosx/calendars/usholidaycalendar.html

If you are not in the U.S., you are not out of luck. Calendars are available on the Internet for holidays for many countries. Additionally, you can subscribe to sports schedules, religious holidays, and academic schedules, to name a few examples. All you need is a direct calendar download link. You can subscribe to almost any iCal calendars you stumble upon on the Internet. Two good sources of calendars in iCal format are Mozilla and iCalShare at the following URLs:
https://www.mozilla.org/en-US/projects/calendar/holidays/
http://icalshare.com/

There are two methods to add an iCal file to the Calendar, subscribing or importing. To subscribe, the website must allow you to directly access the iCal file. The URL will begin with **webcal://** for you to subscribe. Some websites have a **Subscribe** button. After clicking subscribe, a dialog box will appear with the URL of the calendar feed populated in the **Calendar URL** field. Click **Subscribe** to subscribe to the calendar feed.

If the website doesn't provide a subscribe button and only allows downloading of the .ics file, secondary click on the download link and select **Copy Link**. Next, launch the Calendar application if it is not already open. Choose **File > New Calendar Subscription** or enter ⌥⌘S (option+ command+S). Paste the URL to the calendar file you just copied into the dialog box and click **Subscribe**. Next, you'll be presented with a dialog box to configure options such as event color, alerts, attachments, and how often to automatically refresh the calendar. If you plan to synchronize this calendar with your iPhone, iPad, or other Macs, select **iCloud** as the location.

Another method is to import a calendar by downloading the .ics file. I do not recommend this method. Subscribing is the preferable option as calendars to which you are subscribed are automatically updated and can be easily removed.

To change subscription settings, color, or to remove a calendar to which you are subscribed, click the **Calendar** button at the top of the Calendar window to reveal the sidebar. All calendars to which you are subscribed will be listed. A subscription will have an icon that looks something like a WiFi icon. Secondary click on a calendar. You can access the subscription settings, change the color, or **Delete** the subscription using this contextual menu.

Add Favorite Locations to the PDF Drop-Down Menu

When you select the PDF drop-down menu from the lower left corner of the Print dialog box, did you notice **Add PDF to iBooks**, **Mail PDF**, **Save PDF to Web Receipts Folder**, or **Send PDF via Messages**? These are pre-configured printing workflows that allow you to send or save your PDF.

OS X allows you to add your own favorite locations to this drop-down menu as a printing workflow. To add your own favorite locations to the **Save as PDF** drop-down menu, select **Edit Menu...**, located at the bottom of the menu, to reveal the **Printing Workflows** dialog box. Click on the **+** and navigate to the location you wish to add. Continue clicking the **+** until you have added all of your favorite locations. Your favorite locations will appear on the Save as PDF drop-down menu below **Send PDF via Messages**.

To remove a favorite location, first highlight the location and then click the **–** button.

A Better Way to Add Favorite Locations

While the **Edit Menu...** feature works well, the limitation is that your favorite locations appear at the end of the menu regardless of where they should appear alphabetically. Additionally, you may have absolutely no need for one or more of the existing printing workflows and want to delete them.

A better way to customize the printing workflows shown in the Save as PDF drop-down menu is to add or remove them from the **PDF Services** folder in the **Library**. To open the PDF Services folder, launch **Finder** and enter ⇧⌘G (shift+command+G) to open the **Go to the folder** dialog box. Enter the following path and click **Go**.

`/Library/PDF Services/`

You will find the four printing workflows listed on the Save as PDF drop-down menu in the **PDF Services** folder. If you have no need for one or more of the workflows, drag them to the Trash. If you think you may need them later, drag them to another folder in your Home directory. Any change to the PDF Services folder requires you to authenticate using your administrator password. Enter your password when prompted.

To add a favorite location, enter ⌘T (command+T) to open another Finder tab. Navigate to the folder containing the folder you wish to add. Create an alias of the folder you want to add as a favorite by secondary clicking on it and selecting **Make Alias**. Rename the alias by adding "**Save PDF to**" or "**Send PDF to**" at the beginning of the alias name. Drag your alias into the PDF Services folder and enter your administrator password when prompted. OS X will order the contents of the PDF Service folder alphabetically, which is the reason why I suggested prepending the alias with "**Save PDF to**" or "**Send PDF to.**"

To remove a printing workflow from the PDF Services folder, simply drag it to the Trash. Enter your administrator password when prompted.

Disable the Caps Lock

Why should you disable the caps lock? Because things like thIS HAPPEN WHEN YOU ACCIDENTLY HIT THE CAPS LOCK. If your Mac's caps lock is driving you nuts, OS X allows you to disable it.

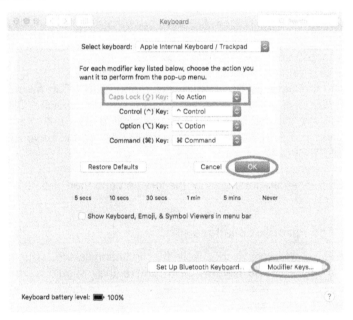

To disable the caps lock key, open the **Keyboard** preference pane in System Preferences. Select **Keyboard** if not already highlighted. Next, click the **Modifier Keys...** button to reveal the Modifier Keys configuration sheet. Choose **No Action** from the drop-down list next to **Caps Lock**. You can re-enable the caps lock key by choosing **Caps Lock** from the drop-down list.

Precisely Adjust the Keyboard Backlight

Sometimes it seems you never can get the keyboard backlight adjusted to your liking. One segment more is too much. One less is too little. Wouldn't it be awesome if you could adjust the keyboard backlight in smaller increments? OS X has a solution for you!

Hold down the ⇧⌥ (shift+option) keys while adjusting the keyboard backlight to adjust it in quarter-segment increments. This feature allows you to precisely adjust the brightness exactly to your liking. This trick also works when adjusting the display brightness and volume.

Turn Keyboard Backlight Off When Idle

One of the great features of a MacBook, MacBook Pro, and MacBook Air is that keyboard backlighting is standard on all models. Anyone who has fumbled around in dim light on a cheap PC keyboard knows the value of keyboard backlighting. Keyboard backlight is on by default and does not turn off even if your Mac is idle.

If you would like to dim your keyboard lighting when your Mac has been idle for a period of time, open the **Keyboard** preference pane in the System Preferences application. Click the **Keyboard** tab if not selected already.

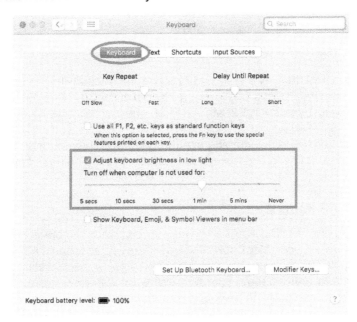

Check the box next to **Adjust keyboard brightness in low light**. Use the slider to adjust the amount of time you want your Mac to be idle before the keyboard backlight is dimmed.

Make the F Keys Act Like F Keys

When you press an **F** key, it will execute the function associated with it (i.e., Mission Control, Launchpad, Play/Pause, Volume, etc.). If you want to press **F12** and have it execute the keyboard shortcut configured in the **Keyboard** preference pane instead of increasing the volume, you have to hold down the **fn** (function) key. This is particularly confusing for former Windows PC users switching to a Mac. OS X allows you to configure the **F** keys so that they act like standard function keys.

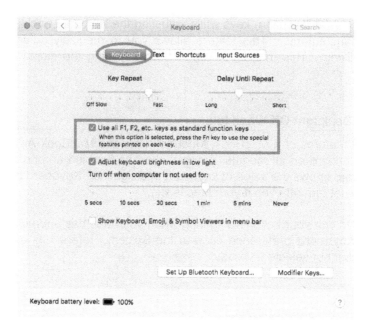

To make the **F** keys perform like standard function keys, open the **Keyboard** preference pane in the System Preferences application. Click **Keyboard** if it is not already selected. Check the box next to **Use all F1, F2, etc. keys as standard function keys**.

But how do you increase the volume and use the other special features? Hold down the **fn** key while pressing an **F** key to use the special features printed on each function key.

Pair an AppleTV Remote

Do you own an AppleTV? Did you know you can pair your remote so that it can control your Mac? If you had your MacBook, MacBook Pro, or MacBook Air in your lap while watching your AppleTV, you may have experienced your Mac interacting with the remote. This feature is buried pretty deep. Your Mac will work with any Apple infrared remote by default, however, you can pair it to a specific remote or disable this feature altogether.

To pair your Mac to an AppleTV remote, open the **Security & Privacy** preference pane in the System Preferences application. Select the **General** tab if not already selected. Click on the **Advanced** button at the lower right to reveal a drop-down sheet.

Click the **Pair...** button to pair your Mac to an AppleTV remote. Hold your remote a few inches away from your Mac and press and hold the remote's **Menu** and **Next** buttons until the paired-remote graphic appears on your display. Click **OK** when done.

To disable your Mac's remote control infrared receiver, check the box next to **Disable remote control infrared receiver**. Click **OK** when finished.

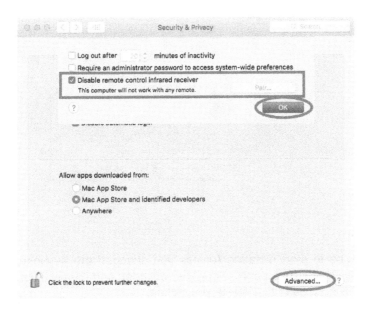

Talk to Your Mac

Done

Dictation is my favorite feature of OS X. Dictation is extremely useful, allowing you to quickly turn your thoughts into large blocks of text whether you're writing a term paper, a report, an email, posting to Facebook, or tweeting your followers.

Dictation is system-wide. You can dictate in any application anywhere text can be entered. This includes not only the usual suspects like Microsoft Office, Apple's iWork productivity suite, or Mail, but other time savers like the address bar in Safari, the search box in Google or Amazon, or in a web form. You can dictate text practically anywhere you're able to type it! Dictation is perfect for when you need to pull an all nighter to finish a term paper or project for work while avoiding getting grease from your extra pepperoni pizza on your keyboard.

To turn Dictation on, open the **Dictation & Speech** preference pane in the System Preferences application. Click on the **Dictation** tab if not already highlighted.

Click the **On** radio button next to **Dictation** to enable. The default shortcut to start dictation is to press the **fn** key twice. Press the **fn** key once to finish. You can change this using the drop-down menu next to **Shortcut**.

Check the box next to **Use Enhanced Dictation** so that you are not dependent upon an Internet connection for Dictation to work. When Enhanced Dictation is enabled, text will appear while you are speaking. When first selected, you will be prompted to select and download a language. Without Enhanced Dictation, your text will appear after you have finished dictating. This is due to the fact your speech has to be sent to Apple to be analyzed.

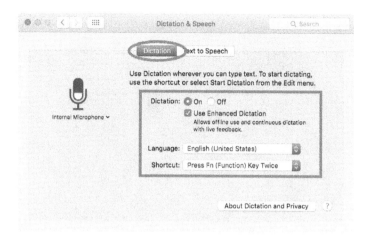

Hit the **fn** key twice to start dictating (unless you changed the keyboard shortcut in the Dictation & Speech preference pane). Your Mac will beep and the Dictation icon will appear to let you know OS X is ready to listen to you dictate.

It's cool to see your text appear immediately. You can also edit your text live without having to stop dictating. Move your cursor or highlight the text you want to correct and dictate your corrections or use the keyboard. Press the **fn** key again to finish dictating.

Tell Your Mac to Talk to You

OS X includes a number of voices for text to speech applications, such as reading an iBook. The default voice is a male voice named Alex. OS X allows you to change the voice, download new voices, and change the rate of speech in the **Dictation & Speech** preference pane.

To change the voice OS X uses in text to speech applications, open the **Dictation & Speech** preference pane in the System Preferences application. Click on **Text to Speech** if it is not already highlighted.

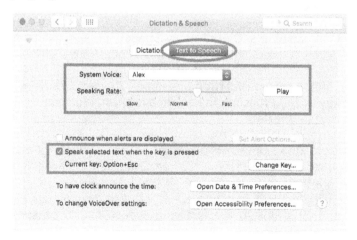

Use the drop down menu next to **System Voice** to change the voice or select **Customize...** to download other voices. For iPhone and iPad users who like Siri's voice, choose **Customize...** from the drop-down menu and download Samantha's voice. Change the **Speaking Rate** using the slider.

The voice you selected will be utilized when your Mac reads to you. If you check the box next to **Speak selected text when the key is pressed**, you will be able to highlight any text and have it read to you by pressing ⌥**esc** (option+escape). You can change this keyboard shortcut by clicking the **Change Key...** button in the Dictation & Speech preference pane.

Change the Behavior of Print & Save Dialogs

When printing or saving a document, a print or save dialog box will slowly slide downwards from the window's Title Bar. If you would prefer to see print and save dialog boxes appear immediately, launch Terminal and enter the following command. You will have to log out and log back in for the change to take effect.

```
defaults write -g NSWindowResizeTime -float 0.01
```

To revert back to the OS X default, enter the following command. You will have to log out and log back in for the change to take effect.

```
defaults delete -g NSWindowResizeTime
```

Change Your Profile Picture

It's easy to change your profile picture. You can use any picture for your profile. Apple provides a number of default pictures you can utilize, but if you don't like the defaults you can choose a picture from iCloud, Photos, a folder on your Mac, or you can take a picture using your Mac's camera.

To change your profile picture, open the **Users & Groups** preference pane in the System Preferences application. Click the **Password** tab if it is not already highlighted. Click on your user name in the left-hand column. You'll see your current profile picture at the top of the right-hand pane.

To use a picture located in a folder on your Mac, open Finder, find the picture, and drag it onto your current profile picture in the **Users & Groups** preference pane.

Put Disk Drives to Sleep Faster

If you own an older MacBook Pro with a hard disk drive, you can conserve battery power by putting your hard drive to sleep when not in use. For example, if you are simply browsing the Internet with your Mac, your hard drive is wasting precious battery power while spinning. OS X allows you to put your hard drive to sleep when it has been idle for a period of time.

To put your hard drive to sleep to save power, open the **Energy Saver** preference pane in the System Preferences application. Check the checkbox next to **Put hard disks to sleep when possible**. OS X will put your disk drive to sleep if it has been idle for 10 minutes.

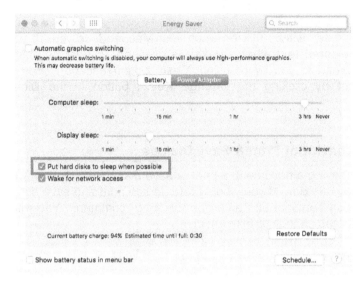

The idle time can be adjusted to be more aggressive in order to save more battery power. To shorten the idle time, open Terminal and enter the following command. Enter your admin password when prompted. This command will put your disk drives to sleep if they have been idle for 5 minutes.

```
sudo systemsetup -setharddisksleep 5
```

To revert back to the OS X default, enter the following command. Enter your admin password when prompted.

```
sudo systemsetup -setharddisksleep 10
```

Enable Sticky Keys

If you have trouble holding down two or more modifier keys simultaneously, the **Sticky Keys** feature allows modifier keys to be set without having to press all of them simultaneously. The following modifier keys can be enabled as sticky: ⇧ ^ ⌥ ⌘ **fn** (shift, control, option, command, function). When the Sticky Keys feature is enabled, pressing a modifier key will stick it. The "stuck" key will display in the upper right of the screen to let you know it was pressed. To "unstick" the key, press it again.

To enable Sticky Keys, open the **Accessibility** preference pane in the System Preferences application. Select **Keyboard** in the left column and check the box next to **Enable Sticky Keys**. Click the **Options...** button to configure sound and display options. By default, OS X will beep and display the key in the top right of the screen when a modifier key is stuck. You can select where you want the sticky keys to display with choices of the upper right (the default), upper left, bottom right, or bottom left of the display.

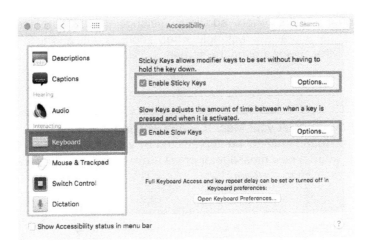

OS X allows you to configure the amount of time you have to hold down a sticky key, called the **Acceptance Delay**, before it is accepted. To enable this feature, click the checkbox next to **Enable Slow Keys** in the Accessibility preference pane. Click **Options** to reveal a slider that will allow you to adjust the Acceptance Delay.

Zoom the Entire Display

OS X allows you to zoom the display using a keyboard shortcut or scroll gesture. To enable the display zoom feature, open the **Accessibility** preference pane in the System Preferences application.

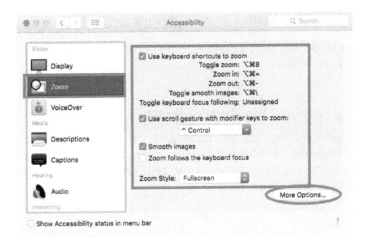

Select **Zoom** in the left column and check the boxes next to **Use keyboard shortcuts to zoom** and/or **Use scroll gesture with modifier keys to zoom**. The scroll gesture is a two finger drag up to zoom while holding down the chosen modifier key, ^ ⌥ ⌘ (control, option, or command). Two finger drag down while holding down the chosen modifier key to zoom back out. Be sure to check the checkbox next to **Smooth images** so the images won't pixelate as they become larger.

The **More Options...** button offers additional settings to configure the maximum and minimum zoom, show a preview rectangle when zoomed out, and to control the screen image as you move the cursor around the screen.

Set Visual Alerts

Sometimes you have to quiet your Mac. If you're working in a quiet office environment the cool alert sound you found may not be appreciated by your office mates. However, you still want to be alerted when a new message or email arrives. Instead of using an audible alert, OS X can flash the screen to alert you.

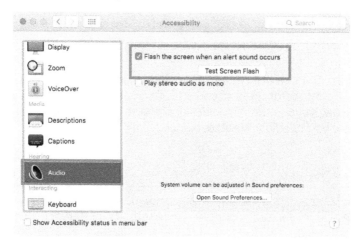

To turn on visual alerts, open the **Accessibility** preference pane in the System Preferences application. Select **Audio** in the left column and check the checkbox next to **Flash the screen when an alert sound occurs**. You can click the **Test Screen Flash** button to preview a visual alert.

Kill the Spinning Rainbow Pinwheel of Death

Occasionally Finder will crash or get hung and you will experience Apple's spinning rainbow pinwheel of death. Finder will become completely unresponsive as the rainbow pinwheel defiantly spins and mocks you as you twiddle your thumbs hoping it disappears. Sometimes you just have to kill the darn thing.

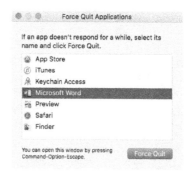

To kill the pinwheel, relaunch Finder by holding down the ⌥ (option) key and secondary clicking on the Finder icon in the Dock. A contextual menu will appear with the option to **Relaunch** Finder. Sometimes Finder becomes so hosed that you will have to switch to another desktop space to make this command work.

An alternate method is to select > **Force Quit...** and choose Finder from the list of applications. Click the **Relaunch** button to kill the spinning pinwheel. You can also display the Force Quit dialog by entering ⌥⌘esc (option+command+escape).

Die rainbow pinwheel, die!

Thoroughly Uninstall Unwanted Apps

 In OS X you can uninstall an application by dragging it from the **Applications** folder to the Trash. You also can uninstall apps in Launchpad by clicking and holding until the apps begin to shake and an **X** appears in the upper left corner of the app's icon. Clicking the **X** deletes the app. Compared the process to uninstall an application on a Windows PC, this almost sounds too good to be true. And it is. Applications distribute many files throughout your system. Often applications will leave their detritus scattered across your hard drive or SSD after they are deleted using the above two methods.

AppCleaner is a small application that will thoroughly uninstall unwanted apps, hunting down their associated files and safely deleting the detritus. To delete an app with AppCleaner, launch AppCleaner and then drag the unwanted app from the Applications folder and drop it into the AppCleaner window. AppCleaner will find all files associated with the unwanted app. Delete the app by clicking AppCleaner's **Delete** button.

AppCleaner is free to download from the following website:
http://www.freemacsoft.net/appcleaner/

Restore a Previous Version of a Document

In OS X many applications will automatically save versions of documents as you are working on them. This safety feature lets you restore a previous version of a document if needed. OS X allows you to browse through various document versions and restore and older version. Versions are typically saved every hour, when you open, save, duplicate, rename, or revert to an earlier version of the document. If you are actively making changes to your document, OS X will save it more frequently.

To restore a previous version of a document, open the document if it is not already open. Select **File > Revert To > Browse All Versions...** to see which versions are available. Browse through the available versions and click the **Restore** button to restore the previous version you selected. You also have the option to revert back to the last saved version, which is timestamped by OS X, by selecting **File > Revert To > Previous Save**.

This feature may not be available in third party applications, most notably the Microsoft Office 2016 productivity suite.

Enable the Hidden OS X Power Chime

When you connect your iPhone or iPad to their chargers, they emit a chime to let you know they are charging. By default, your Mac does not sound a power chime when you connect it to its power connector. This hidden tweak will configure OS X to sound a chime when you connect your Mac to AC power.

To enable the hidden power chime, first disconnect your Mac's power connector. Launch Terminal and enter the following commands.

```
defaults write com.apple.PowerChime ChimeOnAllHardware -bool TRUE

open /System/Library/CoreServices/PowerChime.app
```

Now reattach the power connector and your Mac will emit an iOS-like chime to indicate it is charging. Be sure the sound is not muted and is turned up so you can hear the chime.

To disable the hidden power chime, enter the following commands in Terminal.

```
defaults write com.apple.PowerChime ChimeOnAllHardware -bool FALSE

killall PowerChime
```

Disable Power Button Sleep

You can put your Mac to sleep immediately by pressing and releasing its power button. OS X allows you to disable this feature if you have no need for it.

To disable power button sleep, launch Terminal and enter the following command. Do not press the **return** key until you have entered the entire command. Log out and log in for this change to take effect.

```
defaults write com.apple.loginwindow PowerButtonSleepsSystem -bool
FALSE
```

With power button sleep disabled, pressing and releasing the power button will cause OS X to verify that you want to shut down.

Shut Down Immediately without Confirmation

When shutting down, OS X will confirm whether you really want to shut down. A dialog box will ask, "**Are you sure you want to shut down your computer now?**" You are presented with a choice of **Shut Down** or **Cancel** or you can wait until the timer expires.

If you want to shut down immediately without OS X confirming your intention, hold down the ⌥ (option) key while selecting > **Shut Down**.

Another method is the hold down the ^⌥⌘ keys (control+option+command) while pressing the **eject** button to force your Mac to shutdown immediately.

18

TinkerTool

 TinkerTool is a slick application created by Dr. Marcel Bresink of Software-Systeme that allows you to quickly and easily customize OS X. TinkerTool lets you access additional preference settings including a few of the customizations shown in this book that are only available using the Terminal application. You do not need administrator privileges to use TinkerTool, making it perfect for users who want to customize their OS X user experience but do not have administrative privileges. Preference changes made with TinkerTool only affect the current user and can be reset back to the OS X defaults. At the time of this writing, TinkerTool was available at no cost at: http://www.bresink.com/osx/TinkerTool.html.

When you launch TinkerTool, you will be presented with its preference pane. Along the top of the Toolbar are tools for **Finder**, **Dock**, **General**, **Desktop**, **Applications**, **Fonts**, **Safari**, **iTunes**, **QuickTime X**, and **Reset**. Any of the tools can be accessed from the **View** menu. You can hide the toolbar at the top of TinkerTool by selecting **View > Hide Toolbar** or by entering ⌥⌘T (shift+command+T). Enter ⌥⌘T again to unhide the Toolbar or select **View > Show Toolbar**.

Customize Finder

TinkerTool allows you to customize various preference settings within Finder. Select **Finder** from the TinkerTool toolbar if not already selected.

The first set of preference settings is labeled **Finder options**. In this section you can configure Finder to **Show hidden and system files**, which are normally hidden from view to prevent accidental deletion or movement to another folder which would make OS X unstable. Sometimes an advanced user of OS X will need to view and modify these files.

Disable sound effects quiets OS X sound effects like emptying the trash. Normally, you would need to use Terminal to disable the trash sound effect. For more information, see "Quiet the Trash" in the Finder chapter.

If you like a desktop free of the clutter of icons and external drives, **Disable Desktop features** will clean up your desktop. No files are moved or deleted. Files can be found in the **Desktop** folder in your **Home** directory and disks can be accessed in the **Finder Sidebar** under **Devices**. This setting will speed up your Mac because all of those unsightly icons littering your desktop make your Mac slower by stealing CPU and memory resources to render each icon and preview its contents. For more information see the section "Create a Pristine Desktop" in the Desktop chapter.

You can add a quit command to the Finder menu by checking **Add a "Quit" Item to Finder menu**. To see why you may want to add this handy feature, see "Add a Quit Command" in the chapter on Finder.

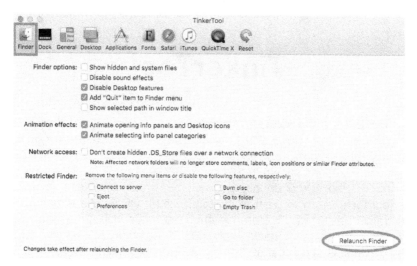

Checking **Show selected path in window title** shows the path to the current folder in Finder's title bar. See "Show the Path in the Title Bar" in the Finder chapter for more information.

If you share a network drive between your Mac and PC, you may notice small **.DS_Store** files littered across the directory structure on your PC. You don't see them when using your Mac because they are hidden files which contain data about the directory. However, they are not essential and you can configure OS X to stop saving .DS Store files by checking the box next to **Don't create hidden .DS_Store files over a network connection** in the **Network access** section. Log out and log back in for this change to take effect.

In the **Restricted Finder** section you can disable various Finder features such as connecting to a server, ejecting a drive or media, burning data to an optical disk, and Finder's Go to the folder feature.

Be sure to click the **Relaunch Finder** button to execute the changes to the Finder preference settings.

Customize the Dock, Stacks, & Launchpad

TinkerTool allows you to customize various preference settings for the **Dock**. Select **Dock** from the TinkerTool toolbar if not already highlighted.

The **Dock** preferences includes both **Dock** and **Launchpad** preference settings. You can also configure preferences for **Stacks** and window minimization animation. Under **Dock Options**, you can configure the Dock to dim application icons when hidden by checking the box next to **Use transparent icons for hidden applications**. This feature is described in "Dim Hidden Apps" in the Dock chapter.

Disable animation when hiding or showing Dock completely disables the animation when the Dock is hidden or unhidden. When disabled, the Dock will disappear and reappear immediately when you hide or unhide it. OS X allows you to tweak the animation timer in addition to completely turning it off. See "Change the Hide/Show Animation Speed" in the Dock chapter to learn how to tweak this timer.

The **Restricted Dock** section locks and unlocks 2 of the 5 attributes that can be locked or unlocked. Checking the box next to **Don't allow to change size manually**, locks the Dock's size. And checking the check box next to **Don't allow modify content** locks the Dock's contents so they cannot be deleted or added to. Unchecking either of these check boxes unlocks these attributes so you can make changes. To see how to lock and unlock the Dock position, magnification, and autohide attributes, see "Lock the Dock" and "Unlock the Dock" in the Dock customization chapter.

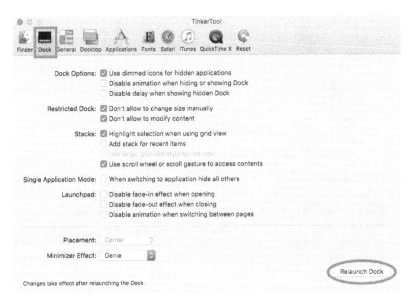

In the **Stacks** section, you can configure highlighting in grid view by checking **Highlight selection when using grid view**. See "Highlight Stack Items" in the chapter on Stacks for more information. To learn how to temporarily highlight stack items, see "Temporarily Highlight Stack Items" in the Stacks chapter.

TinkerTool provides a quick and easy method to add a recent items stack, which normally requires entering a lengthy command into Terminal. Check **Add stack for recent items** to add a recent items stack. For more information on the recent items stack, see "Add a Recent Items Stack" in the chapter on customizing Stacks.

You can configure the Dock to activate stacks with a two-finger upward scroll gesture by checking the box next to **Use scroll wheel or scroll gesture to access contents**. For more detailed information, see "Activate Stacks with a Scroll Gesture" in the Stacks chapter.

Single Application Mode, when checked, will switch the Dock into single application mode. See "Single Application Mode" in the Dock chapter for more information on how this feature operates.

The next 3 preferences change various animation effects in Launchpad. When opening **Launchpad**, you'll notice an ever-so-slight delay before it appears. The same slight delay in the animation also occurs when you exit Launchpad. If you would like Launchpad to appear and disappear immediately, check the two check boxes next to **Disable fade-in effect when opening** and **Disable fade-out effect when closing**. See "Remove the Launchpad Show & Hide Delays" in the chapter on Launchpad for more customization information. OS X introduces a delay when scrolling between pages in Launchpad. Check the box next to **Disable animation when switching between pages** to remove the delay. This tweak is also described in "Remove the Page Scrolling Delay" in the chapter on the Launchpad.

OS X features 3 animation effects when windows are minimized or maximized. The default is **Genie Effect**. The second option is the **Scale Effect**. The third option, the **Suck Effect**, is hidden and not available from the Dock preference pane. TinkerTool allows you to select any of the 3 window minimization effects. See "Change How Windows Minimize" in the chapter on the Dock.

Be sure to click the **Relaunch Dock** button to execute the changes to the Dock preference settings.

Change General Preference Settings

TinkerTool's **General** preference settings seem to be a catch all category for a number of different customizations for the keyboard, scrolling, power button, screenshots, configuration sheets, windows, application features, and recent items.

Holding down a key in OS X does not activate key repeat as you might expect. Instead, a contextual menu appears, which allows you to choose to insert accented and other non-English characters. A radio button allows you to toggle between **Support key repeat** and **Hold key to select diacritic characters** (the OS X default). See "Enable Key Repeat" in the Bunch of Tricks, Tweaks & Hacks chapter for more information.

You can remove the scrolling inertia, which is enabled by default, by checking the box next to **Without inertia** under the **All scrolling devices category**. See "Disable Scrolling Inertia" in the Finder chapter for more information.

Pressing and releasing the power button on your MacBook Pro or MacBook Air will put it to sleep immediately. TinkerTool allows you to disable this feature by unchecking the check box next to **Press and release to switch to sleep mode**. To see how to do this in Terminal, see "Disable Power Button Sleep" in the Bunch of Tricks, Tweaks & Hacks chapter for more information.

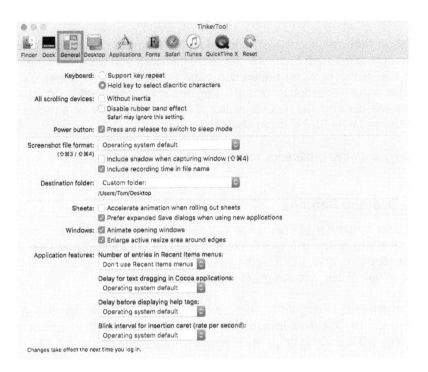

TinkerTool provides 4 customizations for screenshots. You can change the default file format from Portable Network Graphic (PNG) to any of 8 other options including PDF, TIFF, JPEG, BMP, GIF, PSD, or TGA. Select your desired format from the drop-down list next to **Screenshot file format**. The check box next to **Include shadow when capturing window** allows you to include or remove shadows from your screenshots.

OS X includes the date and time in the screenshot's file name. To remove this, uncheck the box next to **Include recording time in file name**. OS X saves screenshots to the **Desktop** folder. Tinkertool lets you change the default destination folder to something other than the Desktop. Select **Custom folder** from the drop-down list next to **Destination folder** to save to a location other than the Desktop. See the section "Take a Screenshot" in the Bunch of Tricks, Tweaks & Hacks chapter for more customizations for the OS X screenshot feature.

In the **Sheets** and **Windows** section, TinkerTool lets you accelerate the animation of drop-down configuration sheets. OS X offers more granular control over the drop-down sheet animation, which I detail in "Change the Behavior of Print & Save Dialogs" in the Bunch of Tricks, Tweaks & Hacks chapter.

If you prefer an expanded dialog box that allows you to save files to any folder over the minimalist version OS X provides, you can change the save dialogs to let you navigate to and choose the destination folder. For more information on the expanded save dialog, see "Enable the Expanded Save Dialog" in the Bunch of Tricks, Tweaks & Hacks chapter.

Window animation can be toggled on or off with the check box next to **Animate opening windows**. If you find the resize area a little small, you can increase it by checking the box next to **Enlarge active resize area around edges**. If you want more granular control over the resize area, see "Increase the Window Resize Area" in the Finder chapter.

The **Application features** section lets you select the **Number of entries in Recent Items menus**. You can select from 5, 10, 15, 20, or 30 items. If you want 50 entries, you'll need to configure this in the **General** preference pane in the System Preferences application. TinkerTool also offers the option of not using a recent items list. Choose **Don't use Recent Items menus** from the drop-down list. To learn how to create a recent items stack, see "Add a Recent Items Stack" in the chapter on Stacks.

All of the changes on this preference page take effect after you log out and log in.

Customize Desktop Settings

TinkerTool offers a number of preference settings on the **Desktop** pane. You can enable the hidden keyboard shortcut ^⌥ ⌘T (control+option+command+T) for Dark Mode which toggles **Dark Mode** on and off. This keyboard shortcut is disabled by default. For more information on Dark Mode, see the chapter on the Menu Bar.

If you want to show the file path of your current wallpaper image, check the box next to **Show Unix path of Desktop image file**. Once configured, the path of your current wallpaper image will display in large white letters across your Desktop.

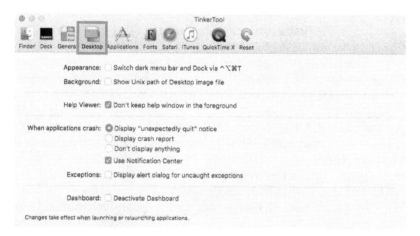

The check box next to **Help Viewer** corrects the rather obnoxious behavior of Help Center where it refuses to act like other windows by stubbornly refusing to go to the background when it is not the active window. I describe this tweak in "Make Help Center Behave" in the Bunch of Tricks, Tweaks & Hacks chapter.

TinkerTool allows you to change how OS X reacts when applications crash. You have 3 different alerting options available under **When applications crash**. In addition, the check box next to **Use Notification Center** ensures the notification of an application crash is displayed in Notification Center.

The **Dashboard** option lets you disable the Dashboard. See the chapter on customizing the Dashboard for more information.

Customize Mission Control & Quick Look

 Click **Applications** in the TinkerTool toolbar to access Mission Control and Quick Look preferences. Under **Mission Control**, you can set the **Delay when dragging window to adjacent space** to **no delay**, **short** delay, or the OS X **Default**.

You have far more granular control over the workspace edge delay when configuring it using Terminal. Additionally, if you are using BetterSnapTool, you will need to adjust the drag delay. Too small a delay will interfere with BetterSnapTool's ability to snap to the left or right edge. For this reason, I highly recommend that you use Terminal to adjust the workspace edge delay and not TinkerTool. To learn how to adjust the workspace edge delay, see "Remove the Drag Delay When Moving Windows between Spaces" in the chapter on Mission Control. To learn more on how to adjust the workspace edge delay when using BetterSnapTool, see the discussion in the Window Snapping chapter.

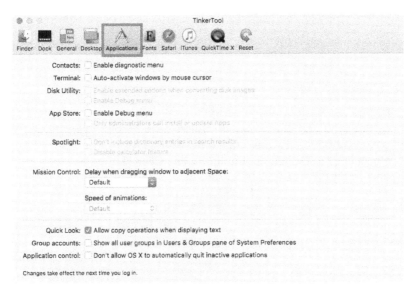

Check the box next to **Allow copy operations when displaying text** under **Quick Look**. This feature will allow you to copy and paste text from documents you are viewing in Quick Look without having to open them.

The **Applications** pane also allows you to customize preferences for **Contacts**, **Terminal**, **Disk Utility**, and the **App Store**.

The preference settings on this pane require you to log out and log in to take effect.

Customize Fonts

TinkerTool allows you to customize various OS X systems fonts in **Fonts** in the toolbar.

Click the **Show preview** button to see a preview of your font selections. To return to the OS X default fonts, click the **Set to default** button.

Customize Safari

TinkerTool offers 2 customization options for Safari. You can configure Safari to allow you to use the **backspace** key to navigate to the previous web page. Click **Safari** in the TinkerTool toolbar and check the box next to **Backspace key can be used to navigate back** to enable. The other available option is to change Safari's default fonts.

Add ½ Star Ratings to iTunes

iTunes allows you to rate songs from 1 to 5 stars. If you need more precise ratings, you can enable ½ star ratings. I find this feature very useful when a song is not quite 5 stars, but it's better than 4 stars. 4½ perfect! To enable ½ star ratings in iTunes, first quit iTunes. Click **iTunes** in the TinkerTool toolbar and check the box next to **Allow ratings with half stars**.

To use the ½ star rating, simply drag your pointer left or right to change the rating in ½ star increments. For more information, see "Add ½ Star Ratings to iTunes" in the Bunch of Tricks, Tweaks & Hacks chapter.

Enable QuickTime AutoPlay

By default, **QuickTime** will not start playing a movie until you click the **Play** button. To enable autoplay, click **QuickTime** X in the TinkerTool toolbar and check the box next to **Automatically play movies when opened**. When enabled, movies will start playing immediately after you open them.

Be sure to quit QuickTime before enabling or disabling this feature. The change will take effect the next time you launch QuickTime. For more information, see "Enable QuickTime AutoPlay" in the Bunch of Tricks, Tweaks & Hacks chapter.

Export TinkerTool Preference Settings

If you want to export your TinkerTool preference settings to another Mac, select **File > Export** or enter ⇧⌘E (shift+command+E). Choose the destination location to save your settings. Click **Export** and TinkerTool will create a .ttps file that can be imported.

Import TinkerTool Preference Settings

Select **File > Import** or enter ⌘O (command+O) and locate the TinkerTool preference settings .ttps file that you want to import into TinkerTool. Click **Import**.

Reset Preference Settings

TinkerTool's **Reset** tab allows you to reset your preferences back to their pre-TinkerTool state or back to Apple's defaults.

Reset to pre-TinkerTool state resets customizations that you accomplished using TinkerTool, leaving previous preference settings intact. **Reset to defaults** will reset all preference settings back to their Apple defaults. You can also access these two reset options from the **TinkerTool** menu. Log out and log in for the changes to take effect.

TinkerTool is a great application that I use often to quickly change OS X preference settings that are not available in the Systems Preferences application. I highly recommend that you download this free application.

19

Boosting Performance

Has El Capitan got your older Mac feeling a bit sluggish? While El Capitan runs super fast on new Macs with their beefy CPUs and Solid State Drives (SSD), the performance of older Macs suffer due to some El Capitan features. If you have an older iMac, MacBook Pro, or MacBook Air, these 23 tips will help you squeeze every last drop of performance out of your older Mac.

Disable Eye Candy Animations

OS X El Capitan has a lot of eye candy, which looks spectacular on a brand new top-of-the-line MacBook Pro Retina, but all this eye candy tends to bog down your older Mac. Disabling unnecessary animations, those that really have no value other than eye candy, can add a little boost to the performance of your older Mac.

To disable unnecessary animations, open the **Dock** preference pane in the System Preferences application. Uncheck the checkboxes next to **Magnification**, **Animate opening applications**, and **Automatically hide and show the Dock**. These changes take effect immediately.

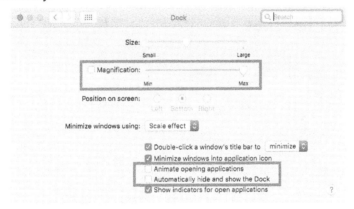

Disable More Eye Candy

Transparent windows, menus, and Menu Bar all require CPU and memory to render. If you own a newer MacBook Pro, particularly one with a retina display, this eye candy looks amazing. If your MacBook Pro or MacBook Air is older, you may notice a considerable drop in responsiveness and performance. The one single change you can make to El Capitan to increase performance on an older Mac is to disable transparency.

Open the **Accessibility** preference pane from the System Preferences application. Select **Display** from the left-hand column if it is not already highlighted. Check the box next to **Reduce transparency**. This change takes effect immediately.

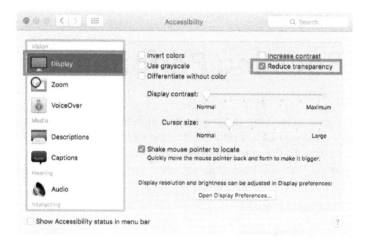

Disable All My Files

All My Files is a **Smart Folder** that searches for, displays, and categorizes every single file owned by the current user. I'm pretty certain your older Mac has tons of files on it. Attempting to display thousands of image, movie, document, spreadsheet, PDF, and presentation files in a single Finder window takes quite a bit of system resources. If you are noticing sluggishness when opening a new Finder window, this is the reason. That's because El Capitan opens new Finder windows with the All My Files Smart Folder as the default. You can speed up the opening of new Finder windows by choosing another folder such as your **Home** directory, which typically contains only 8 to 10 folders.

Launch Finder and open its preferences by selecting **Finder > Preferences...** or by entering ⌘, (command+comma). Select the **General** tab if it is not already highlighted. Use the drop-down menu under **New Finder windows show** to select your **Home** directory.

If you want to occassionally display the All My Files Smart Folder, add it to the Finder Sidebar. From Finder, select **Preferences...** from the **Finder** menu or enter ⌘, (command+comma). Select **Sidebar** from the set of four icons at the top of the pane. Check the box next to **All My Files**. This Smart Folder will now be available in the Sidebar when needed.

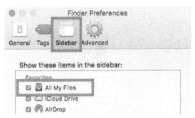

Close All My Files Windows When Not In Use

Be sure to close a **All My Files** Finder window when you are finished with it. All My Files isn't your generic run-of-the-mill static folder, it's a Smart Folder that is continually updated in real time each time a file is created, modified, deleted, downloaded, or copied. This activity steals CPU cycles to refresh this Smart Folder in the background.

Clean Up Your Messy Desktop

If your desktop is littered with file and drive icons, you are hurting your Mac's performance. Not only does this mess make your desktop look unsightly, it steals CPU and memory resources because each icon must be rendered and its contents previewed. If your desktop has more icons than wallpaper, you have made your Mac slower by forcing OS X to dedicate resources to render all this clutter. Keeping your desktop clear of icon clutter will boost your Mac's performance.

Enter the following commands in Terminal.

```
defaults write com.apple.finder CreateDesktop -bool FALSE
```

```
killall Finder
```

The icons that would have appeared on your desktop are tucked away in the **Desktop** folder in your **Home** directory, where they belong. External drives can be accessed through the **Finder Sidebar** under **Devices** or by creating a **Volumes Stack** in the **Dock**.

Disable Unused Extensions

Unused **Notification Center** extensions slow down your Mac when it is restarting, making the login process longer as they update. Your Notification Center also takes a performance hit because each extension has to update its data.

Open the **Extensions** preference pane in the System Preferences application. Click on **Today** and uncheck the box next to any extension you do not use.

Disable Icon Preview

By default, OS X displays a preview of the contents of a file in the Finder window. The icon previews take CPU and memory resources to render. Disabling **Icon Preview** can help restore a little system performance. OS X will no longer render the contents of a file in the icon's thumbnail, instead it will use default icons for the file type.

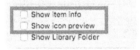

Launch Finder, browse to your Home Directory and enter **⌘J** (command+J). Uncheck the check box next to **Show icon preview**. Click the **Use as Defaults** button to make this the default for all Finder windows.

Disable Item Info

Item info provides handy data like file size, image dimensions, and the number of items contained within a folder. However, it requires CPU resources and degrades the performance of older Macs.

Launch Finder, browse to your Home Directory and enter **⌘J** (command+J). Uncheck the check box next to **Show item info**. Click the **Use as Defaults** button to make this the default for all Finder windows.

Disable Size Calculation

When you are viewing the contents of a folder in Finder's List view, OS X lists the size of all files, but not folders. If you have **Calculate Sizes** enabled for folders, it takes time and

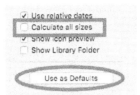

CPU resources to calculate folder size especially if the folder is large and contains a huge number of files.

Launch Finder, browse to your Home Directory, switch to **List** view, and enter ⌘**J** (command+J). Uncheck the check box next to **Calculate all sizes**. Click the **Use as Defaults** button to make this the default for all Finder windows.

Switch to the Scale Effect

OS X El Capitan's **Genie** effect to minimize windows is another piece of eye candy that can degrade the performance of your older Mac. The **Scale** effect has slightly less impact on performance when minimizing or maximizing windows.

To change how windows minimize, position your pointer over the Dock divider. When the pointer turns into a two-headed white arrow, use a secondary click to open the Dock contextual menu. Select **Minimize Using** and choose **Scale Effect**.

You can also change how windows minimize from the **Dock** preference pane in System Preferences. Choose **Scale effect** from the menu next to **Minimize windows using**.

Disable Unneeded Login Items

Disabling unnecessary login items will speed up the boot process by reducing the number of applications launched when booting. These login items also steal CPU and memory resources when running. If you don't need them, disable them.

Open the **Users & Groups** preference pane in System Preferences. Click **Login Items** if it is not already highlighted. Click the padlock in the lower left corner and enter your password when prompted. Select your user account in the left column. Select the item you no longer want to open when you log in to your Mac and press the − button.

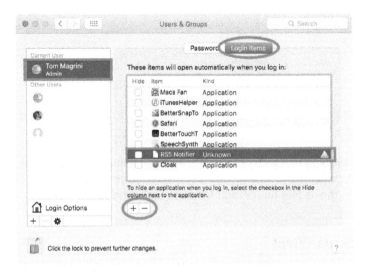

Quit Applications When Done

This sort of sounds like a no brainer. But we are all guilty of leaving applications open instead of quitting them when done with them. If your Mac has a limited amount of RAM, leaving apps open when you are not using them leaves less memory for the apps you are actually using. This slows down the performance of all applications running on your Mac.

Use Single Application Mode

If you have multiple applications open, their windows must be rendered. This steals some CPU cycles. In Single Application Mode, launching a new app causes all other apps and their windows to hide. You can make Single Application Mode permanent by entering the following commands in Terminal.

```
defaults write com.apple.dock single-app -bool TRUE

killall Dock
```

Close Unused Browser Tabs

If you are in the habit of opening a lot of tabs in Safari, Firefox, or Chrome, close them when you are done with them or limit the number of tabs you open. Each tab requires resources especially if the webpage uses plug-ins and extensions.

Hunt Down Misbehaving Apps

 Sometimes an app misbehaves, hogging CPU and memory. You can use **Activity Monitor** to hunt down the culprit and kill it (by quitting or force quitting). Activity Monitor is in the **Utilities** folder in your **Applications** folder. Launch it from Launchpad or Spotlight. To see if an app is hogging CPU,

Click the **CPU** tab. For memory, click the **Memory** tab.

Verify Your Disk Drive

Hard disk drive problems are the silent killer of Mac performance. It pays to do a routine hard drive check up by verifying your disk drive. To verify your hard drive, launch **Disk Utility** and select your disk drive in the left-hand column. Click the **First Aid** button and then click **Run** from the drop-down sheet. If a problem is detected, Disk Utility will repair it or provide instructions on how to repair your hard drive.

Clean Up Your Disk Drive

If your Mac is low on disk space, it will slow down dramatically. As you use your Mac, apps create temporary cache files and items are swapped to and from RAM to the disk. If your disk drive is full, these processes will take much longer to accomplish because old cache and swap files have to be deleted before new ones can be written. Lack of disk drive space is a real performance killer. You should always have a minimum of 10% of your disk free.

 You can use an app like **Disk Diag**, which is available in the App Store for $5.99 at the time of this writing, to reclaim disk space. Disk Diag will free disk space by deleting unneeded caches and logs, clearing browser data, and removing empty downloads. Disk Diag is available in the Mac App Store at: https://itunes.apple.com/us/app/disk-diag/id672206759?mt=12

 Or you can purchase Intego's **Washing Machine**, which in addition to reclaiming disk space by deleting uneeded caches, logs, and downloads, will hunt down and delete duplicate files wasting precious drive space. Washing Machine is available for $29.99 at: http://www.intego.com/mac-cleaner.

Keep Your Apps & OS X Updated

Old versions of apps and OS X often do not run as well as the latest versions. OS X El Capitan can automatically keep OS X and the apps on your Mac up to date. Verify that OS X is configured to automatically download and install app and OS X updates in the **App**

Store preference pane in System Preferences. Ensure the checkbox next to **Automatically check for updates** and the four checkboxes below it are checked.

Uninstall Unwanted Apps

 If your older Mac has a hard disk drive and you are running low on space, you should delete any unwanted apps to free up space. Not only do unwanted apps take up precious drive space, they can increase the load time of other apps and documents. The best way to uninstall unwanted apps is to use **AppCleaner**, which will do a thorough uninstall.

AppCleaner is a small application that will thoroughly uninstall unwanted apps, hunting down their associated files and safely deleting the detritus. To delete an app with AppCleaner, launch AppCleaner and then drag the unwanted app from the Applications folder and drop it into the AppCleaner window. AppCleaner will find all files associated with the unwanted app. Delete the app by clicking AppCleaner's **Delete** button.

AppCleaner is free to download at: http://www.freemacsoft.net/appcleaner/

Disable the Dashboard

The **Dashboard** is disabled by default in OS X El Capitan. If you upgraded from an earlier version of OS X and the Dashboard was enabled, it will be enabled in El Capitan. Some widgets run silently in the background, stealing valuable system resources. You are better off disabling the Dashboard entirely. To disable the Dashboard, open the **Mission Control** preference pane in the System Preferences application and select **Off** in the drop-down menu next to **Dashboard**.

Do a Clean Install of OS X

This is the nuclear option. Sometimes it's just best to start over. If you updated your Mac from a previous version of OS X to El Capitan and are having performance issues, completely formatting and reinstalling Yosemite can do wonders. Unfortunately, this is a time consuming task. However, you will feel like you have a brand new Mac. First, you must ensure you have a current Time Machine backup. Next, you'll have to create a bootable El Capitan USB flash drive installer.

Hardware Solutions

When all else fails, it is time to consider hardware solutions. Both of these upgrades can be done for a few hundred dollars especially if you do them yourself. If you are not comfortable tinkering with the innards of your Mac, these upgrades can be done at an Apple Store or by a computer repair professional, but at a higher cost.

Add More RAM

The single best upgrade you can make to an older Mac is to add more RAM. Applications, files, processes, and OS X all require memory to run. If your Mac has only 4 GB of memory, you can increase performance by upgrading to 8 GB or even 16 GB. Note that not all MacBook Air and MacBook Pro models can be upgraded. You can see if your Mac's RAM can be upgraded by heading over to www.crucial.com and using their Crucial Advisor Tool.

Replace your Hard Drive with an SSD

Replacing an old hard disk drive with an SSD can breathe new life into an older Mac. You will be shocked at how fast your Mac boots, launches applications, and opens files with an SSD. Once you have used an SSD, you will never go back to using a hard drive again. Prices for SSDs have come down dramatically over the past few years and although they are more expensive than a hard disk drive, SSDs are very affordable.

About the Author

Tom Magrini is the author of 4 books in the Customizing OS X series, which teach Mac users to completely customize their OS X experience with hundreds of tweaks, hacks, secret commands, and hidden features. Tom's books teach Mac users how to customize OS X to give their Macs their own unique and personal look and feel.

Tom is an information technology professional with over 30 years experience as an engineer and senior manager. He has worked with Macs since 1984 and still fondly remembers his first Apple Macintosh computer with its 8 MHz Motorola 68000 processor, 9-inch 512 x 342 pixel black-and-white screen, 128 kB of RAM, and built-in 400 kB 3½ inch floppy drive. Tom also worked with NeXT computers and the NeXTStep operating system, the forerunner to Apple's OS X. And yes, Tom has crossed over to the dark side and has worked extensively with Windows-based PCs.

During the work week, Tom is a busy IT director, leading a team of IT professionals who maintain two data centers and the network, telephony, server, storage, operating systems, and security infrastructure for a large city. Tom has taught programming, operating systems, Cisco Networking Academy, and wireless technology courses as a Computer Information Systems professor at two colleges. He has worked for numerous technology companies including SynOptics Communications, Bay Networks, FORE Systems, 3Com, and Cisco Systems, Inc.

When Tom isn't working on his MacBook Pro or hanging out with his family and dogs, he enjoys reading, movies, writing, and the beautiful Arizona weather with its 300 days of sunshine.

Please subscribe to Tom's Flipboard magazine, *Apple OS X + iOS*, where he keeps you up-to-date on the latest OS X, iOS, and Apple news, features, tips, and tricks.

Books by Tom Magrini

Customizing OS X – El Capitan Edition – *Fantastic Tricks, Tweaks, Hacks, Secret Commands, & Hidden Features to Customize Your OS X User Experience*

Customizing OS X – Yosemite Edition – *Fantastic Tricks, Tweaks, Hacks, Secret Commands, & Hidden Features to Customize Your OS X User Experience*

Catch the Wave: Customizing OS X Mavericks – *Fantastic Tricks, Tweaks, Hacks, Secret Commands, & Hidden Features to Customize Your OS X User Experience*

Taming the Pride: Customizing OS X Mountain Lion – *Fantastic Tricks, Tweaks, Hacks, Secret Commands, & Hidden Features to Customize Your OS X User Experience*

www.ingramcontent.com/pod-product-compliance
Lightning Source LLC
Chambersburg PA
CBHW080352060326
40689CB00019B/3982